MONTANA JUSTICE

MONTANA JUSTICE

Power, Punishment, & the Penitentiary

KEITH EDGERTON

UNIVERSITY OF WASHINGTON PRESS

Seattle and London

University of Washington Press, P.O. Box 50096, Seattle, WA 98145
www.washington.edu/uwpress

Library of Congress Cataloging-in-Publication Data
Edgerton, Keith.
Montana justice : power, punishment,
& the penitentiary / Keith Edgerton.
p.   cm.
Includes bibliographical references and index.
ISBN 0-295-98443-0 (alk. paper)
1. Montana State Prison—History.   2. Montana State
Prison—Finance—History.   3. Montana State Prison—
Corrupt practices—History.   I. Title.
HV9475.M92M664 2004   365'.978687—dc22   2004049600

Contents

Acknowledgments *ix*

Introduction *xi*

1 / The Majesty of the Law: Vigilantism and Western Prisons *3*

2 / Penitentiary on a Shoestring *19*

3 / "The Accursed Thing": The Territorial Penitentiary *35*

4 / No Warden More Efficient: Frank Conley *69*

5 / Getting Tough on Crime: 1921 to the Present *97*

Notes *113*

Bibliography *153*

Index *175*

Charts and Tables

CHART 1

Average Number of Inmates Incarcerated
Monthly Per Year, 1871–1889   *36*

CHART 2

Monthly Average Inmate Population (Annual Figures), 1871–1921   *38*

CHART 3

Per Capita Incarceration Per 100,000: U.S., Montana,
and West, 1880–1923   *39*

CHART 4

Average Number of Inmates Incarcerated Monthly, 1890–1920   *71*

CHART 5

Average Yearly Inmate Population, 1921–1959   *98*

TABLE 1

Daily Bill of Fare for the State Prison, 1891   *46*

TABLE 2

Crimes for Which Males Were Incarcerated, 1871–1885   *48*

TABLE 3

Crimes for Which Females Were Incarcerated, 1878–1910   *49*

TABLE 4

Stated Occupations, Males, 1871–1885   *50*

TABLE 5

Stated Occupations, Females, 1878–1910   *53*

TABLE 6

Ages of Male Inmates, 1871–1885   *54*

TABLE 7

Ages of Female Inmates, 1878–1910   *55*

TABLE 8

Race and Ethnicity of Male Inmates, 1871–1885   *59*

TABLE 9

Race and Ethnicity of Female Inmates, 1878–1910   *60*

Acknowledgments

AFTER SO MANY YEARS of on-again, off-again research and writing on this project, I owe a great deal of gratitude to many people who have helped me along the way. Susan Armitage, Harry Fritz, Robert Swartout, Michael Allen, Orlan Svingen, Anne Butler, LeRoy Ashby, T. V. Reed, Matt Redinger, Julidta Tarver, Mary McDuffie, Rene DeAragon, Norton Moses, Kathy Otto, Jodie Foley, Robert Clark, Jean Christoph-Agnew, Ted Nitz, Rick Hines, Carla Homstad, Crystal Cambron, Xinyang Wang, Dave Emmons, Bob Lindsay, Jim Flightner, Paul Lauren, Julie McVay, Melinda Antoni, Barbara Radziemski, Pat Amundsen, Sandy Haley, Rita Rabe-Meduna, Joni Moody, Pat Hawkins, Ann Berry, Jo Wilson, Dorothea Simonson, Elaine Way, Ellie Arguimbau, Brian Shovers, Sue Jackson, Christian Frazza, and Bill Lang have all contributed in large and small ways to making this manuscript better. Most of all, I appreciate my family, who stuck this thing out for so many years—Charlie, Bonnie, Wilda, Ethan, Colin, and Marina, especially. To my many mentors, colleagues, friends, and family, thank you very much!

I also benefited greatly from the James H. Bradley Fellowship, generously bestowed by the Montana Historical Society, and from the Pettyjohn Fellowship of Washington State University and the Littleton-Griswold Fellowship of the American Historical Association. Montana State University–Billings provided research funds and a sabbatical to allow me to complete the bulk of this project. Without all of this assistance, this work would never have become a reality.

Introduction

THIS BOOK IS, in part, a history of the evolution of the power to punish individuals by incarcerating them in bleak prison cells. Its venue is one of the most remote and chronically impoverished corners of the American West. This same evolution has occurred in many places at many times in American history, as this power to punish has the knack of replicating itself over vast expanses of time and space. Although that power manifests itself in a specific place—in this case in a collection of imposing iron and granite buildings in one of the nation's most picturesque spots, the Deer Lodge Valley in western Montana—it also has efficiently penetrated the distant regions of America's fourth largest state, and it shapes contemporary public policy.

Certainly prisons, more than any other modern societal institution, make the abstractions of power visible, tangible, and real for individuals. As sociologists and penologists tell us, their simple presence broadcasts a variety of messages both from and to the society that built them, funds them, guards them, and inhabits them, or, most important, potentially *could* inhabit them. What follows is, in sum, a history of how those abstractions become concrete.

Montanans, like most Americans, have always had an uneasy relationship with their prisons. And like all troubled relationships, this one had its roots deep in the past. Originally, Montana's prison consisted of a single building partially constructed in 1871 in the tiny mining and ranching com-

Map showing location of Deer Lodge in west central Montana

munity of Deer Lodge City; it operated on a shoestring annual budget of less than $25,000.[1] Since that modest beginning, a more modern and complex penal system has emerged, complete with regional facilities that incarcerate thousands and cost millions annually to run. It is spread across a state that encompasses some 147,000 square miles, is home to a population of less than a million, and whose income per capita ranks between forty-seventh and fiftieth nationally.

Throughout Montana's nearly 140-year storied history there has always existed the will to punish criminals forcefully, even severely. Montanans like to think that they have never been soft on crime as they have tenaciously sought to protect themselves from themselves. The history of punishment has evolved from infamous vigilante hangings of the 1860s to imposing concertina-wired correctional institutions that now dot the contemporary landscape. Like many Americans, Montanans have always wanted their prisons to be tough places, even places where acceptable, measured violence is meted out, places of no return.[2] Consequently, Montana and its people, like many states and many people, have remained perennially shackled to their prisons and the evolving, expanding, uneven system of punishment, state-condoned violence, rehabilitation, supervision, and surveillance.

Yet hardly ever has the government—territorial and then state—had sufficient resources to back this public resolve. More often than not, legal and penological philosophies about the prison's primary function collide with penurious and put-upon legislatures faced with the demands of funding an ever-expanding infrastructure. Public opinion has vacillated over the years about just how draconian the prison system should be, especially relative to the financial costs and questionable benefits of rehabilitation. Indeed, much of Montanans' uneasiness is similar to that of Americans in general, and it rests somewhere within the competing, often incompatible philosophies of the role and function of this uniquely American invention: the penitentiary. Should penitentiaries be places to punish, vengefully, criminals or places to reform wayward, disadvantaged individuals to turn them into productive, law-abiding citizens? Or some combination of the two?

No matter which historic attitude momentarily prevails, it has always cost a lot of money to keep criminals incarcerated, and the penitentiary in Montana has always strained grim and perennially austere territorial and state budgets. Every Montana state institution—from the prison to the universities—has always had to operate in an atmosphere of near perpetual poverty and an accompanying immutable tradition of strict, nearly stifling fiscal austerity in all of its day-to-day dealings. But the prison (along with its close institutional cousin, the mental asylum)—swinging persistently between its two dichotomous philosophies of rehabilitation versus long-term punishment and housing society's most reprehensible, most racially and ethnically marginalized members, those most easily disposed of—has been exceptionally vulnerable to the damage caused by poverty and neglect.

All states, of course, have experienced, and continue to experience, the tensions of these dueling ideologies and the stress that long-term incarceration of criminals places on cash-strapped budgets. Some states have addressed them more satisfactorily, more imaginatively, or more brutally at various moments in time than others. Montana is no exception. The state's penitentiary is an institution that, despite its infrequent pretensions toward humanity—a humanity that reflects an enlightened and civilized people—is, at its foundation, and has always been, primarily a monument to personal failure, or as one observer called it in 1871, a "monument to folly."[3]

It remains a matter of intense public debate just how successful the American prison has been historically, particularly in the rural American West.

This is not a study that attempts to analyze or measure in any objective or rigorous way the overall success of a prison, however that highly charged term might be defined. That task is best left to policy makers and criminologists.[4] Nor does this study offer any palliatives, alternatives, or solutions (however broadly those terms can be defined) to crime, punishment, and imprisonment. And though relativism has lately fallen out of fashion and though the public clamors for moral absolutes and looks to its traditional institutions to provide them, success, particularly in regard to prisons, is highly relative. The fact that Montana has periodically expanded or, more recently, replicated its prison system across the state does not indicate successful implementation of society's overall objectives with respect to punishing criminals. No matter how many cells the state has built, the presence of those cells has *never* prevented additional crime from occurring. There has always been a seemingly inexhaustible supply of fresh inmates to occupy those cells. There is little hope of that changing in the foreseeable future.

The genesis of this study for me was a Sunday morning in April 1988, in Helena. I was in Montana's capital city to interview a former chief supervisor of the Montana Highway Patrol for an oral history project. We were discussing Montana law enforcement in the 1950s, and he mentioned in passing that the governor once dispatched both the patrol and the Montana National Guard to Deer Lodge (in the southwestern part of the state) during a two-day prison riot in 1959. The uprising ultimately claimed three lives and caused tens of thousands of dollars in damages. Even though I had been a Montana resident for some time, I had never been aware that the state had suffered from bloody calamities such as prison revolts, incidents that I vaguely and naively believed happened only in far-off, urban locales. Montanans often take false comfort in their isolation.

I became increasingly interested in the event and eventually interviewed many of the principals involved. As I dug deeper into the history of the prison, I discovered an institution that had suffered for much of its history from chronic overcrowding, antiquated and spartan facilities (even for a prison), mismanagement, and periodic political scandal—all of this despite the crucial functions the penitentiary plays in the criminal justice system. In September of 1991 another dramatic and tragic incident rocked the men's prison: inmates broke into a security station and forced the guards to flee in panic.[5] While in control, the prisoners opened cells, then tortured and killed five other inmates held, ironically, in the protective custody wing. Eventually, as in 1959, the Montana National Guard, law enforcement agencies, and the prison staff stormed the prison and reestablished control. Myriad lawsuits, investigations, public outrage, and bureaucratic hand-wringing followed.

Thus it seemed clear that despite its geographic remoteness Montana's prison has experienced all the afflictions (and then some) that urban and less-isolated institutions have suffered, even though the federal government originally conceived of a penitentiary, at least partially, as a means for the territory in the 1870s to bring legal order to an unruly place and to assist with the development of a stable capitalist economy and society. In many ways the institution's haphazard history has both supported and defied the rigid and rational theories that the influential and imaginative French philosopher Michel Foucault posed in *Discipline and Punish* (1975), his seminal but problematic study of the origins and evolution of western society's modern prisons and penological philosophies. Early-day Montana (and other western areas) punished criminals publicly and brutally (much like *ancien* France, Foucault's primary focus); in nascent Montana, society's power to punish was very graphic, very visual, and very public. But with the establishment of a federally funded prison, punishment became less public, more secretive, more coercive, even more efficient, as Montanans attempted to rein in both criminality and one brutal response to it: vigilantism.

In 1889 Montana achieved statehood, and the United States relinquished control of its prison to the newly minted state. The Montana government consequently delegated the daily administration of the prison to two private contractors, who then modified the previous custodial approaches explicitly in order to turn a profit, following the earlier lead of lessees at the territorial mental asylum (or "insane asylum" as early westerners commonly referred to it). These lessees attempted to make the institution even more cost effective for themselves and the state than it had been during the federal government's administration. Ultimately, they succeeded well beyond their wildest expectations, so much so that running the Montana prison became, for a time, their personal economic bonanza. Eventually, however, the resulting excesses and abuses provoked a full-scale, statewide scandal in the 1920s that, in a moment of high political drama, pitted a reform-minded, progressive governor against a trust-backed, boss-style warden, leading ultimately to the demise of each man's career.

In the early 1920s, while the rest of the nation prospered, the Montana economy stagnated because of drought and depressed wheat prices. State revenues declined during the early years of the Great Depression as the price of copper plummeted (copper mining was the chief extractive resource industry and linchpin of Montana's economy). Advancing decrepitude and fiscal neglect marked the Deer Lodge facility as the modern government shifted its limited funds to other agencies. By the 1950s the prison experienced substantial personnel turnover and inept administrative leadership. Two riots erupted late in the decade, a bloodless one in 1957, followed by the violent 1959 outbreak. Incredibly, it would be twenty more years before the state abandoned its aging institution in favor of a new facility outside of town, though it, too, has been fraught with controversy, violence, and occasional scandal.

During the 1990s and into the new century, the Montana state government, responding ostensibly to a public that has been willing to pay nearly *any* cost to ensure that the state remains tough on crime, has substantially expanded its penal system. In less than a decade the state has committed resources that have fostered an unprecedented growth of the prison system: it has increased the prison's administrative bureaucracy, added new cells to the main institution for men outside of Deer Lodge, built a new facility for women in Billings, constructed three new regional correctional centers in Great Falls, Missoula, and Glendive, and contracted with private prisons both within and outside of Montana to hold still more of the state's inmates. Montana, like a growing number of other states, even incarcerates inmates from other states as governments shuffle criminals from region to region and as private correctional enterprises have become a boom industry.

But for Montana, that expansion has failed miserably to deter crime while it has strained the state's limited resources. The state and its people face the same problems today in the twenty-first century that the young territory faced in 1871: overcrowding, underfunding, and political indecision or indifference regarding the prison, or, more aptly now, the prisons.

Although I deal with the more recent history of this expansion in my last chapter, this study focuses on the formative years between the 1860s and 1920s. I examine primarily the territory's and later the state's prison at Deer Lodge, and not the many county and local jails. Although I devote passing attention to the establishment of the mental asylum at Warm Springs (which occurred within just a few years of the construction of the first prison), the study centers on the Deer Lodge prison. Clearly, there is sufficient material—with more generated every day—for another full-length study of the burdens placed on local communities to incarcerate an ever-increasing number of individuals, the result of the nationwide crackdown on crime. The United States, ignominiously, now leads the industrialized world by a substantial margin in the number of individuals it incarcerates per capita. And yet it is local, cash-strapped communities that often must bear the financial costs of expedient political decisions made by distant and disconnected legislatures run by opportunistic, shortsighted politicians. This dogged, though extraordinarily expensive, assault on crime through incarceration has not succeeded in lowering the crime rate significantly anywhere. Ironically, though we Americans tout ourselves as the freest people on earth, that freedom is partly an illusion as we continue with a defiant "lock 'em up and throw away the key" mentality. But that mentality, as this study in part attempts to demonstrate, has come at a considerable cost. By 2002 over two million Americans were incarcerated in a federal or state prison or local jail.[6] Unfortunately, as discussed throughout this study and accentuated in my conclusion, in impoverished states like Montana getting *really* tough on crime has served only to deplete state coffers and has contributed to a steady erosion of state funding in other critical areas, particularly in education, human services, and environmental protection, to name just a few.

Over the course of our history we Montanans have remained, in many ways, prisoners of our prison. As a result, the only way we can begin to unshackle ourselves is to begin to make long-term sense of this institution, to understand its cultural, political, and economic functions, the twists and turns in its history. Perhaps this institution's lengthy, storied, and often painful history can provide some guidance to longstanding policy issues— issues that, as I mentioned at the outset, have deep historic roots. Hence, I offer this study.

MONTANA JUSTICE

1 / The Majesty of the Law

Vigilantism and Western Prisons

So as I have learned more I have had to give up the illusion of a romantic gun-toting past.—WALLACE STEGNER, *Wolf Willow*

J. A. Slade and George Dixon came to the northern Rockies within three years of each other in the mid-1860s, though they may as well have arrived centuries apart. Although their individual motives for migrating into the region are unclear, they undoubtedly, like most young men at the time, wanted to gain a fresh start in one of the least populated regions of the American West and possibly strike it rich in the area's rapidly expanding gold and silver mines. Regardless of what motivated them to make the journey, both of them would have their dreams and futures shattered after they collided headlong with what passed for criminal justice in Montana. Their collective, though wildly disparate, experiences within just a few short years of each other reveal how dramatically the power to punish changed in territorial Montana—and all over the American West, for that matter.

J. A. Slade ("Captain Slade" to his friends and cohorts) was, by most accounts, a nuisance and a town drunk.[1] After stints as a soldier, freighter, and stage driver (when he had once met a young Mark Twain), he had come to the crude mining camp of Virginia City in south-central Montana, then part of the vast, thinly populated Idaho Territory, in 1863 from Illinois.[2] Within just a few short months he managed to alienate most of the citizenry through his alcoholic belligerence; one of his favorite pastimes was

3

wanton destruction of property. According to one observer, he would, on all-too-frequent occasion, "ride his horse into stores; break up bars . . . and use most insulting language to parties present." The local sheriff arrested him several times; after sobering up, Slade willingly and contritely paid the court-imposed fines.[3]

On the evening of March 9, 1864, after Slade and friends had spent the day drinking and making the town "a perfect hell," the sheriff attempted to arrest him again. Slade derisively tore up the warrant, spat on it, and crushed it into the dirt. As the journalist Thomas Dimsdale observed, Slade's action "was a declaration of war." A number of miners had already taken steps to form a local vigilance committee patterned after those that dispensed rough and putatively expedient justice in the California goldfields. Virginia City's vigilance committee convened, and a representative informed Slade directly that he should leave town.[4] Instead, Slade, still drunk, sought out the local magistrate who had issued the warrant and proceeded to take him hostage. A messenger then rode to the mining areas, several miles from town, and informed the miners there of the scene back in Virginia City. Dimsdale described what subsequently occurred:

> The miners turned out almost en masse, leaving their work and forming in solid column, about six hundred strong, armed to the teeth they marched up to Virginia. . . . Halting in front of the store, the executive officer of the Committee stepped forward and arrested Slade, who was at once informed of his doom. . . . Scarcely a leading man in Virginia could be found, though numbers of the citizens joined the ranks of the guard when the arrest was made. All lamented the stern necessity which dictated the execution. Everything being ready, the command was given, "Men do your duty," and the box being instantly slipped from beneath his feet, he died almost instantaneously.[5]

Slade's hanging was one of a number of vigilante executions that occurred in the region that two months later would officially become Montana Territory and a formal political unit of the United States. The vigilance committee worked especially hard that winter as it hanged some twenty-three other suspected criminals, many of whom were road agents, malefactors who preyed upon miners in the mountains and goldfields around Virginia City and its sister camp, Bannack, seventy-five miles to the west. Vigilantism, as practiced in Montana and elsewhere, was swift, retributive, expedient, and cheap, though—and increasingly—not always entirely sure, and it had a long tradition in American frontier culture.[6]

Yet even in these raw mining districts, the local citizenry was growing increasingly uneasy over such extreme measures. Many people neither liked nor endorsed lynching but felt that the community, such as it was, had little choice under the immediate circumstances. Dimsdale again attempted to justify the extralegal incident:

> The execution of Slade had a most wonderful effect upon society. Henceforth, all knew that no one man could domineer or rule over the community. Reason and civilization then drove brute force from Montana. The Vigilantes deplored the sad but imperative necessity for the making of one example. Necessity was the arbiter of these men's fate. They acted for the public good, and when examples were made, it was because the safety of the community demanded a warning to the lawless and desperate, that might neither be despised nor soon forgotten. The death of Slade was the protest of society on behalf of social order and the rights of man.[7]

By the winter of 1870, George Dixon would unwittingly discover that definitions of "social order" and "the rights of man" had shifted in the northern Rockies. As a consequence of that shift, he would become another kind of example in Montana.

Dixon was born a slave in Missouri in 1851.[8] After obtaining his freedom during the Civil War, he moved west. He lived for a time in Leavenworth, Kansas, and drifted through Colorado before finally arriving at Virginia City some time in 1866 or 1867. He worked in a restaurant there briefly and, for a short period, was even in the employ of the then-territorial governor, Green Clay Smith. In the winter of 1870/71, Dixon, penniless, migrated a hundred some miles north to the raw mining town of Helena. In January he found himself trapped in what became a ten-year nightmare.

Upon his initial arrival in Montana he had befriended a woman in Virginia City, Nellie Montgomery, a prostitute, who, like Dixon, eventually moved to Helena. During the afternoon and evening of January 19, 1871, one of Montgomery's patrons, John Hanson, visited her and Dixon at Montgomery's dwelling (it is unclear whether Dixon was lodging there). Hanson drank a bottle of whiskey and then Dixon agreed to go to a nearby saloon to purchase another.

After returning with the liquor, Dixon discovered Hanson and Montgomery quarrelling loudly over money Hanson alleged that Montgomery had stolen from him. Dixon then left the pair for a few hours. When he returned, around 3:00 A.M., Hanson had gone, but Dixon found Montgomery in her bed either dying or already dead from stab wounds to the head.[9] Dixon quickly ran into the street, told an acquaintance of Montgomery's condition, and then proceeded to rouse three of the town's doctors, to whom he then related the events of the evening. He identified Hanson as the individual whom he had last seen with Montgomery.

The constable arrested Hanson later in the day and discovered a bloodstained knife in his possession. Soon, however, three of Hanson's friends provided him an alibi by swearing, falsely, that Hanson had been with them at his home in Prickly Pear Gulch—adjacent to downtown Helena—at the time of the murder. After a hurried coroner's investigation, the sheriff, who admitted that he had received "conflicting testimony," exonerated Hanson, conceding that the blood on the knife had really been rust. He then arrested Dixon and locked him in the local jail.[10] Later that night, eight or nine "prominent citizens," as Dixon later described them, visited the jail, hauled him upstairs, and threatened lynching unless he confessed. "You black son-of-a-bitch," one of them declared, "if you don't confess you will be strung up right here." A terrified Dixon confessed:

> I was coming over the woodpile, and when I was approaching the house she [Montgomery] was standing in the back door and said I had been after Nellie Howard. I told her no. She said I was a damned liar, and fired at me with a derringer; after which she went back into the middle room and grabbed the ax which was standing at the foot of the bed, and struck at me, but missed. She attempted to strike me again, and I grabbed the ax with my right hand and drew my knife with my left, and threw the knife at her, and struck her about the temple, and the knife stuck into her head. I drew the knife out and

stuck her with it again a little below the first wound. . . . After I stuck the knife into her a second time, I drew it out and threw both the knife and pistol away. . . . I then went after the doctor.[11]

The next evening, after the local newspaper printed the confession and during the course of a preliminary examination at the courthouse, a few in the restive crowd that had formed goaded the court to "Hang him! Hang him!" Only through the efforts of Judge George Symes, who stood on a table and appealed to "the reason and better nature" of the mob by exhorting it "to let the law take its course," did the crowd not lynch Dixon immediately. As the local reporter proudly noted the next day:

> Suffice to say, that if this prisoner is securely kept until the next session of
> the court, is fairly tried, and if found guilty, [and] executed, it will stand a
> precedent to the fact that any man, be he white, black, or copper colored,
> suspected of or confessing a great crime, can be assured at the hands of the
> people of Montana, that inalienable privilege which all men have under our
> laws, the right of a fair trial.[12]

Later in the evening, at the jail, another crowd formed, but the sheriff was "prepared to assert the majesty of the law," and he "compelled the crowd to disperse."[13]

Several days later, at his arraignment, Dixon pleaded not guilty, but an all-white jury quickly convicted him of second-degree murder and sentenced him to twenty years in the unfinished territorial prison, despite the lack of a murder weapon and the coercive circumstances surrounding his confession (not admitted during the trial).[14]

For three and a half months Dixon waited in the cramped and primitive confines of the Helena jail until the U.S. marshal took possession of the half-completed federal penitentiary at Deer Lodge City, forty miles to the west. Finally, on July 2, 1871, Dixon became part of the inaugural group of territorial prisoners received at the penitentiary. Eight others—including two Chinese immigrants, a painter, a shoemaker, and several miners— joined him in the stark six-by-eight-foot brick-and-mortar–lined cells. Several of the men were illiterate; all were indigent.[15]

Dixon spent nine years at the penitentiary in Deer Lodge, and by the account of the warden he behaved himself well. Though the Montana territorial governor, Benjamin Franklin Potts, had been aware of the details of Dixon's coerced confession and the nature of the crime for at least six years, for reasons unknown he did not act until 1880. This was surprising because he pardoned many inmates indiscriminately during the same time because of the lack of cell space. Potts eventually ordered Dixon released, nearly ten years into his sentence, due to, in Potts's mind, "serious doubts of his being guilty of the crime of which he was convicted."[16] After his discharge, Dixon drifted out the front door of the prison, past the makeshift wooden fence that encircled the institution, and vanished from the historical record.

The events surrounding the administration of justice and the subsequent punishments of J. A. Slade and George Dixon are a study in contrasts. The exploits of people like Slade and of the vigilantes who hanged them have provided fodder for countless pulp fiction works and a good deal of western mythology. Vigilantism, while undeniably spectacular and dramatic, was relatively short-lived during the early history of the northern Rockies. Imprisonment—and the transformation and consequent diffusion of state power that the institutions of confinement represented—has had a far longer, much more important history. The experiences of George Dixon and the other many thousands who followed him into the cells at Deer Lodge, or Laramie, or Boise, or the other western penitentiaries built in the nineteenth century, were much more commonplace than those suffered by J. A. Slade.

Between 1864 and 1870, Montana changed how it dispensed criminal justice. That change illustrates how much societal attitudes toward crime and the punishment of criminals had altered in a relatively short period. A few years earlier, perhaps even a few months earlier, Dixon, because of his confession, would have been lynched in Helena. Two men had, in fact, been lynched within sight of the courthouse less than a year previously.[17] Both J. A. Slade, a wrongfully hanged man, and George Dixon, a wrongfully convicted man, sat on the cusp of this transformation.

Reports back to the federal government of incidents like those that occurred with Slade helped put vigilantism on the road to extinction in Montana and other isolated areas of the northern West. Vigilantism was an embarrassment, and politicians and local boosters increasingly viewed it as a barbaric relic, not the stuff of an advanced, civilized people. By the late 1860s and early 1870s, the United States Congress, concerned about vigilantism, appropriated money and authorized construction of a series of penitentiaries in the western territories. By the spring of 1871, prisons had been built or were under construction in Montana, Idaho, Wyoming, Colorado, Nebraska, and Dakota; federal judges and U.S. marshals had been appointed; and "the rule of *law*" and not "the rule of *men*," as one historian has characterized the transformation, now ostensibly governed judicial proceedings in Montana and other western localities.[18] George Dixon's life was spared, and he received a trial, though obviously not a fair one. The jury found him guilty and sentenced him to prison, where he remained virtually anonymous and invisible, removed from the community, for nearly ten years.

Yet neither by lynching nor through a trial and subsequent imprisonment was justice truly served in these cases. With these two examples, the results at best were illogical and prejudiced, at worst, cruel and criminal: society punished both men wrongly and unjustly. The difference now was that society administered and measured out George Dixon's anguish for ten long years; J. A. Slade had to suffer only the quick snap of the noose.

The men and women imprisoned by territories and early western states have left behind practically no written records or narratives and have been long forgotten, if they were ever even considered beyond serving as nuisances to their local communities. They exist now only as statistics in legal records and prison registers. Their experiences have remained mostly hidden and neglected, as they and their crimes have been overlooked in favor of the more sensational and romantic episodes of a heavily mythologized western past. Criminals, along with the thousands upon thousands incarcerated in the mental asylums in the nineteenth century, have been traditionally consigned to the very bottom rungs of society. The institutions that society has designed and built to warehouse, monitor, and rehabilitate them have been equally neglected in the historical record, even though the institutions have existed throughout American history and have played critical social, legal, and economic roles that have consequently affected political and policy decisions at nearly every turn.

In the annals of western history, the reasons for the neglect of the people who inhabited society's lowest rung are clear. Prison or asylum inmates were not town builders, or pathfinders, or railroad or mining magnates, or officers in the United States cavalry. Instead, they have always been considered society's excrescence, its "warts and pustules," in the words of one scholar, easily dismissed or ignored.[19] Clearly, any history that involves criminals and prison inmates is a history undertaken "from the bottom up" in the phrase's truest sense.[20]

Mostly nineteenth-century western criminals' offenses were, as far as crimes go, typical and mundane. Chronic public drunkenness, narcotic addiction, prostitution, assault, and especially crimes associated with theft or destruction of property (larceny, burglary, arson, robbery) and not gunning down sheriffs (or murder or even *attempted* murder) were the predominant crimes for which western judges and juries historically sentenced and continue to sentence people to jails and prisons.[21]

The George Dixons of western history have remained invisible in the historical record partially because they wanted to be. As mentioned earlier, they have left behind few written documents of their own. Consequently, they are nearly impossible to trace, often by their own design. They existed on the shadowy fringes of western society in an era long before prerelease centers, innovative community-corrections programs, or probation and parole officer monitoring.[22] Most of them were illiterate or barely literate, incapable of preparing written accounts of their exploits, their experiences, and their lives.

Yet prisons and their closely related cousins, mental asylums, are veritable treasure troves of information, as historians in other regions of the United States and other countries have known for some time.[23] The prison administrators and political officials—and Montana's are no exception—generated and continue to generate and preserve an enormous amount of detailed written documentation about their institutionalized residents; that documentation reveals much about the nature of power in a discrete location and it reveals a great deal about the values those in power hold at any given historical moment. What society fears, how it reacts to deviancy—indeed, how it defines deviance and its obverse, normality—and its level of humaneness in treating the lowest of the low in the economy and society are all present in high relief. Dostoevsky's classic, multilayered observation of the nineteenth-century Russian gulag rings across the ages: "The standards of a nation's civilization can be judged by opening the doors of its prisons."[24]

But surely the chief reason for the scholarly neglect of western prisons is the myth of western criminal justice that has shaped our historical perceptions.[25] Western territorial, state, and federal prisons were and are as much part of the American West as cowboys, but cowboys and gunslingers have received nearly all of the attention.[26]

Popular misperceptions about the nature of western crime and punishment abound. In many forms, from the dime novels of the late nineteenth century to the twentieth-century westerns of Owen Wister, Zane Grey, Louis L'Amour, and others, to especially the countless Hollywood movies and television shows, the mythologized exploits of any number of western desperadoes like Billy the Kid, Jesse James, Deadwood Dick, and Butch Cassidy are familiar to most. George Dixon, Mary Drouillard, William Smith, Lee Yim, Axe Handle, George Jessrang, and the thousands upon thousands of others incarcerated in the American West remain virtually anonymous.

Recently some scholars have undertaken focused regional and local studies that have begun to reveal a much different, more nuanced and complicated history of western crime and justice and the role of the prison in western American history.[27] A handful of prisoners, though not an overwhelmingly large number, were brown-skinned like Dixon, punished by a white-run legal system. Almost all western prison inmates were poorly educated; some, like George Dixon, were former slaves, many were immigrants, and a handful were women, incarcerated in facilities built exclusively for males. Most were unskilled laborers who had come West and were unable (or unwilling) to locate gainful employment in the mining camps or embryonic urban areas; the majority were young and, despite their youth, in poor health. Nearly to a person they did *not* fit the description of the pistol-packing misfits of popular romance, other than being young. "'Go West young man' . . . and do time," has not been part of America's grand story. But for a strikingly large number of individuals, that was the case.

Western prisons themselves evolved into imposing edifices constructed of stone and steel. They incorporated strict disciplinary regimes, lockstep marching, "silent systems" and other punishment and reformative techniques developed and perfected in the early nineteenth century in the eastern United States. They were places where calculated physical torture, hard labor, chronic overcrowding, and infectious disease were normal occurrences. Not surprisingly, the picture that has emerged shows that the reality of crime and especially punishment, then, like now, was not very glamorous.

Myth, of course, also controls the way historians fashion their interpretations and selection of past events.[28] In the most recent and comprehensive scholarly overview of Montana's history, for example, the authors include few references—anecdotal or otherwise—to crime and punishment in the region after the 1860s, the heyday of vigilantism.[29] Missing are the historical roots of the prison even though it remains one of the state's most important institutions. Certainly it is the one with the longest history, longer than the state capitol, longer than the main state universities in Missoula and Bozeman, longer than the famous and fabulously wealthy copper mines in Butte. When one reads any number of histories about Montana, scholarly or popular, the impression one gains is that Montanans virtually solved the conundrum of crime and punishment by the mid-1860s through the efforts of just-minded and righteous vigilantes; crime and its consequent punishment would never plague Montanans thereafter. The prison is invisible. However, Montana incarcerated its population at the third highest rate in the nation during its territorial years (1864–1889), and the prison consumed an extraordinarily large amount of official federal and territorial attention and resources. The contemporary prison remains one of the most expensive and highly politicized of all state institutions.[30]

Territorial Montana also was home to significant numbers of Native Americans, first-generation working-class European immigrants, and, for a brief twenty-year window, one of the largest bodies of Chinese immigrants outside of California. Studying incarceration patterns and demography allows one to determine with some degree of certainty how the judicial system sentenced and then released from custody whites, Chinese, Native Americans, and other members of minority cultures, ethnicities, and races. One can determine if punishment was as racially based historically as many feel it is today. Was George Dixon's plight unique? Typical? Was punishment more draconian than now, especially for racial minorities? Less?

The scholarly inattention extends into the twentieth century as well. A major political scandal, with the prison at the center, rocked the state in the early 1920s and culminated in a political showdown between a corrupt warden, backed by one of the West's most powerful trusts, the Anaconda Copper Mining Company, and a progressive, reform-minded governor, Joseph M. Dixon.[31] Over the course of the middle decades of the twentieth century, the prison suffered from neglect, mismanagement, and a long series of penurious legislatures. Spectacular and bloody riots occurred in 1959 and 1991, each costing the state dearly in precious and limited resources that it could ill afford to lose. Moreover, there are ongoing issues of vital importance linked to the prison that continue to affect contemporary public policy in the state. These issues range from the state's shameful incarceration of Native Americans in numbers drastically disproportionate to their presence in the general population to the dramatic increase in state funding for prison construction during the 1990s, which has been to the detriment of other state-funded institutions and programs. Crime, punishment, and the social control of deviants in an isolated, geographically vast, mostly rural, and relatively impoverished area are all important historical issues that can inform continuing public policy debate about the nature, purpose, function, and future of prisons in the rural West. The problems that plagued public officials a century ago still plague them today. They are neither new nor unique. Yet all of this has remained virtually invisible in the historical record of a state whose people rightfully pride themselves on their rich history.[32]

The prison, any prison, is also an ideal place in which to study power. Cut away a cross-section of a prison in any given society at any given moment, and you will see multiple layers of social control. Cultural and sociological theorists of many stripes have long known this, but historians have been slow to recognize the possibilities of placing power of this sort at the center of their analyses. While one should not overstate the historic importance of the prison, it was, arguably, a place in the American West where societal and "normative" power, at least, bore most directly on an individual.[33]

The emergence of prisons and penitentiaries was also part of a larger and complex economic transformation of the American West. The 1870s through 1890s marked a period when, throughout the West, entrepreneurs, promoters, railroad boosters, and those simply motivated by a desire to acquire capital and supported by the federal government attempted to consolidate the authority of law and jurisprudence in ostensibly lawless areas. Ultimately, this consolidation aided these mostly middle- and upper-class individuals in their quest to stabilize society and to provide order in the perceived chaos by imposing their own set of bourgeois values and morality upon others. Capitalism, thus, would flourish. At the heart of this transformation, according to the western historian Richard Maxwell Brown, "was the conservative, consolidating authority of capital," which often carried out its "campaigns for the economic and cultural conquest of the West in legislative halls and judicial chambers." And, it can be argued, in its prisons.[34]

Over the course of the late nineteenth century, the lure of mineral wealth drew the federal government into an increasingly closer relationship with its western territories. In the wake of the Civil War, the problems posed by rampant crime and vigilantism were significant enough for the federal government to commit precious financial resources to the region. The construction of the first United States penitentiary in Montana was a means for the government to bring order to a disorderly place and to help stabilize an inchoate society. Investment and the consolidation of capital in a market economy would follow accordingly. Consequent social control through incarceration, and particularly reformation of those who committed crimes—especially those who violated the sanctity of property— was part of this struggle to establish and reproduce familiar institutions and social order during the colonization of the northern West by the United States.[35] As an intended result, free-wheeling, exploitative, laissez-faire capitalism, wholly supported and endorsed by the United States government, rooted itself firmly in the western territories very quickly.

Once out of the wreckage of the Civil War, the federal government began its decades-long process of creating a nationalistic, centralized, modern, bureaucratized, and ultimately impersonal but extremely powerful and invasive American state. This was a broad process that the cultural historian Alan Trachtenberg once identified as "the incorporation of America."[36] Trachtenberg felt that in the last three decades of the nineteenth century, America witnessed "the emergence of a changed, more tightly structured society, with new hierarchies of control."[37] The prison was an obvious and visible part of this new hierarchy of control in the West.

Capitalistic development would not have been possible without a concurrent and supporting judicial framework to identify, discipline, and punish miscreants, deviants, and those who generally resisted capitalistic values. Democracy, capitalism, power, and punishment were, in short, distinctly intertwined threads in the American West as they were, and still remain, elsewhere.[38]

It is no coincidence, thus, that the prison, Indian reservations, railroads, and large-scale industrialization appeared in fairly rapid-fire historical sequence between 1870 and 1890 in Montana. Serendipitously, too, the fabulously wealthy Butte copper mines were a mere forty miles from Deer Lodge; closer still, at the head of the Deer Lodge Valley, was the great Anaconda copper smelter, for a time, the world's largest. Indeed, by the 1890s the Butte and Anaconda region in the west-central part of the state was home to one of the most lucrative copper-producing complexes in the world. Again, implementing the values associated with industrialization required discipline, and the prison would contribute to that discipline.[39]

Construction of territorial penal institutions came after Americans had spent decades obsessing about how to respond to crime. Jackson-era reformers perfected the penitentiary and defined its role in American society in the first decades of the nineteenth century. By the 1820s and 1830s, sweeping social and demographic changes prompted reformers to devise new strategies to combat crime and deviance. Penitentiaries appeared in many eastern states, designed for the express purpose of reforming and reshaping criminal characters (as opposed merely to exacting retribution for an individual's crimes). Such an ideological shift, reflected by the establishment of these institutions, prompted even European politicians and observers, most notably Alexis de Tocqueville, to take notice of the importance of these new institutions.[40] The establishment of the Montana prison—in fact of all the federal prisons in the western territories—was an attempt to remold individuals. It reflected both a continuing attack on deviance and the role incarceration played in the evolution of American bourgeois cultural values, even in the Far West.[41] The appearance of the prison marked the hand of this new American middle class in an area where it had not been hitherto. The penitentiary was a *socializing* institution and a definite by-product, an integral by-product, of this incorporation of western America.

The creation of prisons was also a form of institutional conquest, a means of marking boundaries and subjugating chaos while creating order out of disorder.[42] Deviance, crime, pauperism, and the increasingly visible itinerants, especially in the fluid and mobile populations of the mining and timber camps and communities, were viewed as potential threats to rational, orderly capitalistic development and the creation of a relatively safe environment in which to produce and maintain communities and to acquire capital. Prisons, while relatively recent socializing institutions, were familiar enough cultural landmarks for westerners to use to replicate eastern American society. By the mid-nineteenth century the traditional institutions in society, the church and the family particularly, faced new strains and pressures because of rapid urbanization and social relationships—forged in the crucible of Jacksonian America—and because of the movement into the new western lands after the Civil War. New institutions—often based on therapeutic and reformative ideologies best achieved in pastoral, rural settings—maintained social order. The picturesque Deer Lodge Valley would prove an ideal venue.[43]

By the 1870s and 1880s, deviance appeared to be on the rise nearly everywhere within America's borders. Hitherto unfamiliar cultures were increasingly visible as the first wave of late nineteenth-century central and eastern European immigrants began pouring into the East and Chinese sojourners continued migrating into the West. Meanwhile, former slaves from the South had begun moving to the North, displacing lower-class urban workers. Political radicalism had begun to surface among labor groups and in industrializing areas, East and West. These "dangerous classes," as the urban reformer Charles Loring Brace first categorized them in an 1872 study of New York, "the product of accident, ignorance, and vice, formed great masses of destitute, miserable, and criminal persons, . . . hidden below the surface" but ready and willing followers of revolutionary and incendiary philosophies. Penitentiaries helped insulate the emerging American middle class; its members could literally wall themselves off from these perils.[44]

Americans, westerners especially, looked to the government for assistance. The creation of the Department of Justice in 1870 to address civil rights issues in the South, disputed land claims in the West, the Mormon polygamy issue in Utah, and federal criminal and civil cases throughout America's growing empire was an early federal response to criminal deviance.[45]

In 1870 the newly formed National Prison Association lobbied Congress for an increased federal role in prison building. Congress responded by boosting the status of the Department of Justice and by such legislative fiat as instructing the Census Bureau to gather and organize detailed statistics on the increase of crime in the country. State governments responded, too, through reform efforts, mainly the expansion and upgrading of police forces and state prisons between the 1870s and 1890s. Enoch Wines, a powerful advocate for national prison reform during this period and the person chiefly responsible for creating the National Prison Association in 1870, lamented that the federal government "has no control, no voice, no influence over the discipline of the prisons to which they have been committed."[46]

Bureaucrats and politicians listened and took heed. By the late 1880s and early 1890s, Congress had begun creating a federal prison system by financing and constructing federal prisons in Fort Leavenworth, Kansas, Atlanta, Georgia, and McNeil Island, Washington. By early in the next century, the system would expand to include several dozen institutions across the United States.[47] According to the director of the Bureau of the Census in 1880, no portion of his lengthy investigation into "the defective, dependent, and delinquent classes [was] more important than that which relates to crime and punishment." And "to deal with crime is the primary purpose of government, and its efficiency may be said to be measured by the degree of its success in preventing and repressing it."[48]

The building and staffing of federal penitentiaries in the farthest reaches of the American West was similar in some respects to the establishment of a vast network of Indian reservations (and supporting bureaucracy) during approximately the same period. It was similar, as well, to the spatial bounding and segmenting that the Northern Pacific Railroad undertook in building cookie-cutter towns along its railway line, which sliced through the heart of the region by the 1880s. As the historian Kate Brown writes, "The gridded spaces that first organized on a huge scale the settling of . . .

the Great Plains made a lasting stamp on the nature of the lives that took up residence there," and "at some point the abstract survey lines turned into boundaries." As Brown notes, "Boundaries fix labels in space, defining who is inside and who is outside . . . and gradually . . . [they] transformed into walls, laws, and social customs, which worked to define who was alien and who was native, who was a prisoner and who was a guard."[49]

Equality itself could even be defined more sharply when the powerful in society could determine more precisely than hitherto who was *not* equal. Creating prisons allowed the United States and its far-flung colonial holdings to facilitate this differentiation. Punishment now became more logically and uniformly dispensed within institutions that were more humane than in previous ages, and reformation of individuals replaced the need of society to exact public vengeance upon criminals. Private pain, meted out invisibly behind granite walls, came to replace the public pain experienced by the likes of J. A. Slade.

The appearance of the prison reflected the federal government's effort to designate cultural and political boundaries, to segment space in order to make sense of what people perceived as vast, chaotic, and unmanageable; it was one way, among several, to conquer the extremities of sprawling, open country. As Michel Foucault noted, prisons made it "possible to bring the effects of power to the most minute and distant elements." Imprisonment, as a result, eventually became seen as "the most immediate and civilized form of all penalties" by nineteenth-century society.[50]

In the American West, and especially in Montana, state-sanctioned, ostensibly rational punishment, carried forth in a central penal institution, quickly supplanted irrational, illogically administered and localized vigilantism. It happened in nearly a historic eye-blink, and it swept up George Dixon. Thousands more would follow.

2 / Penitentiary on a Shoestring

The founders of a new colony, whatever Utopia of human virtue and
happiness they might originally project, have invariably recognized it
among their earliest practical necessities to allot a portion of the virgin soil as a cemetery, and another portion as the site of a prison.

—NATHANIEL HAWTHORNE, *The Scarlet Letter*

By virtue of its expanding mining industry, Montana achieved territorial
status in May of 1864. The United States then sent to the new territory a
governor and three judges who were to govern and preside over large judicial districts.[1] The general political turmoil and acrimony they initially
encountered was at a fever pitch, due mainly to the rapid influx of both
northerners and southerners into the mining districts. The prevailing culture of vigilance and the pusillanimity of local juries were of immediate
and special concern.

From nearly the moment miners discovered gold in the mountain valleys
of what was then the sprawling central region of Idaho Territory, controlling crime was an immediate and vexing problem.[2] The closest semblance
to organized territorial government was in Lewiston, 250 miles to the west
over the rugged Bitterroot Mountains. Even those few charged with maintaining law and order could not always be trusted. For several months in
1863, the sheriff of Virginia City (on the east side of the mountains), Henry
Plummer, led the region's and one of the West's more notorious outlaw

gangs. Out of self-protection, individuals joined vigilance committees and began actively seeking out criminals and miscreants who brazenly flouted what little social order existed. Law and order was a major political issue in the region between 1864 and 1866 and was of serious concern both to members of Congress charged with overseeing territorial affairs and to governmental officials appointed within the executive department who wished to stabilize what they perceived as near-anarchy. A federal prison would be a cornerstone of the solution.[3]

Vigilante justice, though temporarily convenient, was neither entirely sure nor uniform. The unfortunate town drunk J. A. Slade, ignobly lynched in 1864, was undoubtedly an annoyance and a menace, even in the relative lawlessness of a two-year-old mining camp. There had been rumors that he fled west because of a murderous past. But drunkenness has never been a capital crime in America, and innuendo, even in the 1860s, was not sufficient evidence to condemn anyone. With Slade (and several others subsequently), vigilance had passed the point of sanctioned expediency to a form of criminality itself.

Compounding these law and order problems, hastily convened juries, fearing reprisal from accomplices of the accused (or the accused himself), had proved undependable in convicting. Furthermore, suspected criminals often vanished into the wilderness before trial. Incarceration in the very few isolated and improvised jails was expensive and unreliable. By 1866, the maintenance of prisoners in Virginia City, to give one example, cost upward of $6 per day, pricey even by gold camp standards.[4] Vigilance had provided temporary deterrence to the commission of more heinous acts in the northern Rockies gold camps. At the very least, the mere thought of lynching had to have circulated in the minds of most potential wrongdoers in the immediate vicinity of the hangings.[5]

The brute force of lynching, in the words of the historian David Johnson, dramatically pitted "the lone criminal against the overwhelming crowd." In Montana this was the case in many lynchings, but this powerful display was acutely present in Helena in 1870 during that community's last lynching, when vigilantes dispatched two suspected rogues in full view of the recently constructed courthouse. The crowd that turned out, estimated at "several thousand" (probably most of Helena's population), was even larger than that that had attended Slade's execution.[6] During this period of open vigilantism, criminals who committed their crimes against the community faced that same community squarely during their hastily convened trials (usually an ad hoc collection of miners called together on a moment's notice) and met their demise just as publicly. The ritual in its entirety was a swift community affair. Regardless of the nature of their crimes, their characters, or their reputations, the condemned maintained their humanity and were even allowed to address the citizenry—in the form of last words—just prior to their executions. Both they and the community that they had wronged maintained a visible, public relationship up to the moment of execution. The community felt avenged.

Lynchings were displays of naked might, the will of the community stripped to its essence. They were political and social ceremonies, bringing accused and society face to face, symbolizing the retributive power of society over the body of an individual in these regions far removed from constituted power and its loosely interlaced, supporting network of police, sheriffs, courts, and prisons. Johnson argues:

> In one sense, the legitimacy enjoyed by these popular tribunals stemmed from the moral authority that . . . [westerners], like other Americans of their era, gave to the "people" over the coercive power of the state. But the intricate practice of vigilantism encompassed as well a set of interrelated and reinforcing ideas about the nature of popular action, the character of the criminal, and the meeting of crowd and criminal in a public ritual of punishment, atonement, and example.[7]

In the American West, these public rituals and "spectacles of suffering" served, in Johnson's view, "as tangible manifestations of the people's power, and affirmations of the vast gulf between their moral authority and the morally alienated individual. With the punishment of the accused, the affirmation was complete—the war between criminal and the community came to a close."[8]

But with the imposition of imprisonment as the natural and legitimate means of enforcing society's will—a change that occurred within a year of the Helena spectacle—that "war" between convicted and community never ended or at least did not end very quickly, the relationship never completely severed, and criminal punishment took on entirely new forms.

By 1871 punishment had been dramatically transformed in the territory, after the federal government involved itself, at the behest of individuals within the territory, more directly in the administration of justice. It was a relatively abrupt movement from vigilance to societally sanctioned incarceration, from what Johnson called "the rule of men" to "the rule of law." With it came the imposition of new forms of discipline and punishment, which included some limited attempts at reforming wayward individuals. The events in Montana mirrored larger patterns occurring in the late nineteenth century in relation to crime, deviance, and society's need to cope with serious threats to good order and social harmony.[9] Instead of brutal hangings that left corpses twisting at the end of hastily tied nooses, Montanans would now use prisons to administer retribution and vengeance and enforce the collective will. But prisons would cost money.

For the upper classes and humanitarian reformers, lynching and even capital punishment itself had become an increasingly anachronistic and unacceptable practice. It recalled a feudal and barbaric past instead of reflecting a modernizing, optimistic, rational, and more humane present.[10] As Montana's population swelled in the late 1860s, it quickly became apparent that in order to encourage settlement—which would bring women, families, capital investment, lucrative railroad contracts, and other fruits of "progress"—territorial officials *had* to demonstrate to the eastern centers of political and economic power that they had the ability to protect society from both criminals *and* vigilantes. In an increasingly rational, order-seeking world, what had to be dispensed was justice, unwavering and ceaseless, through the long and dispassionate arm of the law.

After Congress intervened to nullify acts of the second and third territorial legislatures of 1865 and 1866 (because the legislatures had been called unconstitutionally by the acting governor), Congressman Benjamin Wade lamented, Montana "is in a state of anarchy."[11] In a progress report to President Andrew Johnson, Acting Territorial Governor Thomas Francis Meagher noted in early 1866 that

brave and persistent adventurers were extending the out-posts of our civilization at a desperate hazard, and in many instances, at a fearful cost. [Yet]
within the more settled portion of the Territory, the civil magistracy and
lawfully constituted tribunals were powerless to suppress the devilish outrages perpetrated by an organized conspiracy. . . . Robberies and murder,
of the most desperate character, were committed by these miscreants with
impunity, the civil authorities, Federal as well as local, having no power to
curb and paralyze them; and juries, where the ruffians were brought into
Courts of justice, (being afraid to convict) serv[ed] rather to embolden than
deter them.

Though, as Meagher admitted, the "Vigilance Committee rendered emi-
nent and vital good service to the community," its continued presence "cannot be sanctioned, but, to the contrary, it must be completely overcome
and set aside, the legitimate magistracy and tribunals reinstated . . . and the
community placed . . . in a condition of reliable safety and strength."[12] A
few years later, another governor, Benjamin Franklin Potts, lamented that
despite the passage of time and the assistance of the federal government
in Montana, "law is a failure and insufficient for the protection of our
people."[13] As Potts explained to President Ulysses Grant in 1870, "an able
Judge has more power for good here than all the Federal officers put
together." Potts told Grant that he would be wise to "send us a Civilizer."[14]

The "Civilizers" (U.S. marshals and judges) sent to Montana by the
United States government expressed similar indignation at the contempt
for the process of the provincial courts and the near-mockery displayed
by much of the citizenry. They also deplored the fact that they "have no
secure jails in which to confine criminals."[15] One jurist noted "the utter
contempt in which the United States laws are held in this territory," and
he "felt chagrin almost amounting to humiliation at the facility with which
criminals escape."[16] Montana's U.S. marshal, William Wheeler, reported
in January 1870 that ten inmates were confined in territorial county jails
for felony convictions, but "as many more have escaped during the past
year owing to their insecurity." Wheeler noted that "if we had had a secure
prison during the past two years we would have had at this time 40 prisoners in it." Governor Potts confirmed to the U.S. attorney general that

"escapes are of frequent occurrence," and "the best interests of the territory will be advanced by the early completion of the penitentiary."[17]

In his initial comments to the grand jury in his first judicial district courthouse in Virginia City, Judge Lyman Munson deplored the erection of "impromptu scaffolds" and warned that "however satisfactory an excuse might hitherto have been for secret trials, and midnight executions, no such necessity longer existed, and that all such proceedings must now be left to the Courts."[18] Hezekiah L. Hosmer, chief justice of the territorial supreme court (which comprised the three appointed judges), cautioned, "Much as we may approve the means of self-protection thus employed, and the promptitude with which they were applied, our admiration ceases, when .they assert an authority defiant of law, and usurp office[s] which belong only to Government itself." He advised that "to go farther is to commit crime, and undo what has been so well done." Furthermore, "Courts of law and equity . . . recognize[d] as authority . . . [were] clothed with ample power to investigate and punish all offenses against . . . the good order of society," because crime in Montana was no different from crime anywhere else. "Shall we wonder less," Hosmer asked, "amid the pure atmosphere of the Rocky Mountains, at the improprieties which meet our observation . . . than we should to find the same, in the streets of New York or Philadelphia?" Montanans must "correct these gross immoralities" as "much—very much[—]of our future character as a people, depends upon the manner in which crime is met at the commencement." Only "a steady and uniform application of law to every offence, in such an exigency, is the surest resource."[19]

Territorial Governor Green Clay Smith concurred with Hosmer. In his 1867 address to the legislature, Smith noted that with the arrival of judicial officers and other government officials from the East the region had undergone a transformation. "It is true," Smith argued, "that difficulties, outrages and violations of law and good order exist in the incipiency of government," making it "necessary to resort, occasionally, . . . to harsh and exemplary means." But the governor was confident that "Montana has passed through her ordeal of troubles and outlawry; has assumed a shape in which she is recognized as a great part of the Government, and her people demand laws, rules and usages, conformable to the Constitution and statutes of the United States." Most important, these rules would "elevate man and society in the scale of *rational* and moral existence." Montanans, after all, had made "rapid strides" in just a short while "in all that refines, elevates and ennobles a people." This progress was especially remarkable considering that "but two or three years since, the wildest disorder pervaded the whole Territory; every one carried his life in his hands; highway robbery, murder, arson, and theft were rife everywhere; but 'tis not so today," Smith reported. "Men are safe in their lives, their liberty and their property" because United States officials, such as himself, had "produced order out of confusion."[20] But to continue the progression, the governor warned the legislature, "it is altogether important that you should take immediate action" on selecting a penitentiary site in order "to have a portion of the building put up, to save expense to the counties, the Territory and the government, and secure punishment to the criminals."[21]

The local Virginia City newspaper editor agreed with Smith and endorsed the need for a penitentiary. "The expenses of keeping the Territorial prisons are enormous . . . while in many of the States, with several hundred convicts, they are not only self-sustaining, but produce a revenue to the State." Thus, "buildings sufficiently large for present purposes, in which to confine all the Territorial convicts, where they could be kept at labor, and their escape rendered impossible could be erected for less than the first year's appropriation" (which he estimated at roughly $13,000).[22] By 1867 anyway, punishment as a means to raise revenue and offset the costs of incarceration to a frugal territory had already become an alluring possibility.[23]

The lack of an adequate central penitentiary bedeviled these early judicial officers and confounded their plans for the rational and uniform application of law. Compromised sentencing and improvised confinement were the result. In the 1860s territorial district courts sentenced individuals to the local jails in Virginia City, Helena, and Deer Lodge. These were often little more than log structures, "unsafe and unfit for the safekeeping or comfort of prisoners," as Meagher, Hosmer, and others complained to the secretary of the interior.[24] In 1866 any individual convicted under federal jurisdiction of a murder committed in one of the many parcels of

"Indian Country" in Montana (as both locals and federal officials characterized them) was sentenced to imprisonment in the nearest federal facility, as required by recently enacted federal law. In Montana's case, the closest
federal house of correction was in Detroit, some 2,000 miles away.[25] En
route several individuals sentenced under these provisions escaped and were
never recaptured. Even when the fortunate marshal managed to deliver a
prisoner, the cost of the undertaking was prohibitive.[26] Indeed, cost of
confinement became of paramount concern immediately and was an issue
that persisted throughout the territorial period in Montana. Acting Governor Meagher informed the legislature in 1866 of an individual awaiting
trial in Helena who had to be chained to the U.S. marshal's bed each night
during his trial because of the lack of a secure prison within the territory.[27]
If this situation was not difficult enough, Meagher released an individual
previously convicted of assault with intent to kill because his confinement
would have created an unnecessarily heavy burden on the local taxpayers.[28]
As territorial governor Green Clay Smith informed the secretary of the interior, during 1867 the annual "cost of maintaining prisoners [was] over
$36,000," a figure he charitably believed "could be reduced fully by one half
by the building of a Penitentiary."[29]

Individual citizens, such as the venture capitalist and eventual territorial governor Samuel T. Hauser—undoubtedly one of the wealthiest and
most politically powerful citizens in territorial Montana—very quickly saw
the benefits a territorial penitentiary might provide. For Hauser and his
associates there was enormous personal incentive to attract increased
investment and the political and economic advantages of additional settlement (which would lead to statehood and less federal intervention in
Montana's affairs).[30] Hauser—through his operatives—publicly distanced
himself from vigilante justice and lobbied the United States for both legislation and funds to construct a federal prison to house the more egregious lawbreakers within the territory. Hauser realized the reward cheap
convict labor could provide to his own enterprises, to local communities
in the form of government contracts, and generally to the territory. He also
had business ties with territorial Chief Justice Hosmer, with the Deer Lodge
banker and, later, mining magnate William A. Clark, and with numerous
eastern financial contacts. In 1866 Hauser purchased property near the min-

ing camp of Argenta (conveniently located between the two major mining camps of Bannack and Virginia City) and began lobbying for the prison.[31]

Argenta seemed a perfect locale for the proposed penitentiary. There was sufficient water power for machinery, ample farm and ranch land, and a smattering of silver mines—complete with the territory's first silver smelter, courtesy of St. Louis capital. There, "the labor of convicts" could, Hauser's agents reported, "be made profitable."[32]

One of the chief problems in Argenta was not lack of capital but a shortage of suitable labor. Friends of Hauser's, including his business partner, W. B. Dance, a former vigilante and future Deer Lodge merchant, recommended to the Montana legislature that the site be selected and the Interior Department (the agency that oversaw institution financing and building within the trans-Mississippi territories) notified. Within a few months, however, Hauser and his associates, primarily due to insufficient labor to work their holdings and the smelter, relocated to the Deer Lodge Valley, some seventy miles to the north and one of the first valleys where whites established farms and ranches. They brought their plans for prison building with them. The entrepreneurs convinced the territorial legislature to situate the prospective penitentiary in Deer Lodge, which had more mines and agricultural activity than Argenta. Further, by 1870 the area had become a burgeoning population center.[33]

The clamor in Washington for western penitentiaries had begun several years earlier, and the Department of the Interior, Congress, and the United States attorney general were aware of the problems posed by the lack of facilities within the territories. Other intermountain and southwestern territories, hoping to both solve their confounding crime problems as well as minimize the increasing expense of confinement, lobbied Congress and the Interior Department for prisons during and immediately after the Civil War.[34]

As early as 1864 Congress had begun debate on the necessity of penal institutions in the West. Later that year, it formally charged the Interior Department with developing plans that addressed the lack of prison space in the western territories. As a stopgap measure, the secretary of the interior made contracts with the House of Correction at Detroit and the Iowa

State Penitentiary to house territorial prisoners with sentences of two or more years.[35]

Though prisons were mainly a matter of concern for the respective states, since the 1820s the federal government had dabbled in the penitentiary business by distributing money (after lobbying by territorial citizenry) to several midwestern territories in the 1840s and the southwestern territories of New Mexico and Utah in the 1850s.[36] The United States had also financed and constructed a "national prison" outside of Washington, D.C., in the 1820s—an early and relatively feckless attempt at federal penology.[37]

Eventually Congress placed this national prison under the direction of the Department of the Interior. The agency had been created after the Mexican War to oversee and administer the expanding territorial empire, to regulate Indian affairs, and to manage the enormous western public lands conquered from Mexico. But increasingly the more mundane duties of Capitol building maintenance and coordination of the few charitable institutions within the territories and the District of Columbia devolved to the department. Ultimately, by the early 1860s, the department had assumed many of the responsibilities for the governing and administration of institutions within the western territories.[38] During this time, however, and much to the frustration of individuals in the trans-Mississippi West who sought its assistance, the department also shared responsibilities for judicial affairs with an informal Territorial Bureau within the Department of State and with the United States attorney general's office.

After the Civil War, mainly due to the increased sentiment within the territories for secure confinement facilities, Congress passed a modest— as judged by the skimpy appropriation—Territorial Penitentiaries Act in January 1867. Because of the Interior Department's experience with the earlier national prison and its contracting with state facilities during the war for the maintenance of territorial inmates, Congress delegated to it the burden of overseeing the administration of the act.[39] The financing—$40,000 per facility—would come directly from territorial coffers by way of internal revenue collected for that specific purpose (from the period of June 30, 1865, to June 30, 1868). The respective territorial legislatures would select sites and building contractors. After the secretary approved those decisions, he would authorize release of the funds.[40]

It is unclear who determined or derived the figure of $40,000. This seemed to be the amount Congress had traditionally appropriated for the construction of prisons in previous requests from the territories; Wisconsin and Iowa in the late 1830s and Oregon in 1855 had each received this amount. But it became clear from the outset that this figure— considerably devalued by the high inflation caused by the Civil War—had been grossly underestimated, and it would be nearly impossible to construct even a barely habitable, albeit small, facility, with that amount.

One early and ominous portent that problems loomed came from the Treasury Department. In mid-1868 the secretary of the interior employed an architect from the department to prepare plans for both Colorado and Montana after their respective legislatures each had acted quickly in their site selections and had raised and budgeted the necessary funds. The architect's report back to the secretary was gloomy.

> These plans contemplate penitentiaries that will accommodate 40 convicts, and are a[s] cheap a class of buildings as can be erected for penitentiary purposes. The estimate cost, at prices here, is $44,395.54, exclusive of the iron cells, the estimate cost of which is $800 each. I do not, however, believe that the buildings can be erected in the localities indicated for less than $100,000 each and unless the management of the superintendent is extremely economical, they will probably exceed that sum. . . . I do not think your department would be justified in attempting the erection of any cheaper class of buildings for the purposes for which they are designed.[41]

There is no indication that the secretary of the interior heeded the report or made any attempt to secure an increased appropriation. Prisons, and Montana's isolated one would be no exception, would have to make do until they could pay for themselves.[42]

From the outset, the long delays in communication between Washington and Montana plagued the project. Executive departments disbursed funds haphazardly and sporadically at best. Payments to the contractors and subcontractors were calculated through a very complicated formula and were paid out of the judiciary fund in the attorney general's office after the Treasury Department had received the funds from the territory's internal revenues. The process took months. If this were not difficult enough, the Interior Department went through a change of administration in early 1869, and for many weeks letters and telegrams simply went unanswered or were misplaced. At times the department appears, not surprisingly, to have forgotten about the western penitentiaries. It helped little, too, that out in Montana the contractor initially hired by the territorial legislature in 1868 to supervise the building of the prison (as required by terms of the congressional act and directives of the secretary of the interior) had a serious drinking problem and was an "inveterate enemy" of the Grant administration. Two years passed before building commenced in earnest.[43]

By early 1871, the Interior Department—finally having tired of the persistent and increasingly anxious tone of the correspondence from the territories concerning the nonpayment of the building contracts and myriad petty subcontractual squabbles—wished to rid itself of this growing administrative headache. It suggested to Congress that the newly created Department of Justice (under the attorney general's purview) administer the territorial penitentiaries. Congress agreed, and in early 1871 it transferred authority to the new department. Justice would supply the federal marshals to supervise the new penitentiaries, create the rules and regulations to administer the institutions, and appoint wardens.[44]

At Deer Lodge, construction finally began in the early spring of 1870 with appropriate fanfare: the laying of a cornerstone on June 7, 1870, and a 200-gun salute.[45] When the contractor and subcontractors finally completed construction in October of 1870, the construction superintendent, A. H. Mitchell, a Deer Lodge physician and businessman, quizzed the Department of Interior, "What should I do with the building?" Neither the marshal nor any other government official was on the scene to assume custody of the prison nor had Mitchell heard from the Department of the Interior in months about the disposition of the facility.[46] Indeed, there was no record of response to Mitchell's query until early the next spring, nearly six months later. Meanwhile, the structure sat empty and unused. The editor of the town's newspaper, the *New North-West,* observed that the prison "is an excellent building, and stands in solemn grandeur at one end of the town, a reminder to evil doers." Nevertheless, despite the fact that the entirety of the appropriation was already spent, the penitentiary still required at the very least "temporary buildings for furnaces, cooking, and accommodation of the jailors," as well as "additional security window gratings and lining [for] the cells" before it was usable.[47] Unless these tasks were completed, the editor warned, "it will require about as many active and vigilant guards as it would to herd the same number of prisoners on the prairie."[48] There was also, he noted, "no Warden to take charge of it." As a result, the prison "is as useless yet as a fifth wheel to a coach." In January of 1871, Governor Potts toured the site personally and noted that it would "require an expenditure of at least four thousand dollars to put the building in a condition to receive convicts."[49]

Members of a U.S. grand jury empanelled at Deer Lodge, after having visited the facility themselves in May of 1871, concurred. They reported that "the brick cells . . . are not safe and should be removed" and replaced with something more secure, preferably granite cells. Furthermore, they recommended that iron bars cover *all* the windows (not just those on the lower level, which were all that heretofore could be afforded) and that "as an additional safeguard, a stout board fence not less than twelve feet in height should be built around the penitentiary."[50] Yet surprisingly—and despite the delay in payments, the myriad construction problems, and the general ambivalence of the United States government surrounding the project— Montana's United States Penitentiary at Deer Lodge City, as it was officially termed, became the second western territorial penitentiary to open under the 1867 congressional act (Colorado's debuted a month earlier).[51]

Even after its inauguration in July of 1871, the completed penitentiary was but a shell and little better than a warehouse. The territorial prisons had been designed by a government architect working from plans designed for the Wisconsin territorial penitentiary built three decades previously. They were modeled, and philosophically patterned, loosely, upon what was then known as the Auburn-style plan of prison architecture. The architectural design—a product of a penal philosophy instituted during the 1820s in the Auburn prison in New York and the most popular and economically feasible style among several competing ones in nineteenth-century America—called for two wings of forty-two cells attached to a central administration building. Each wing supported three stories of individual cells, fourteen to a story. Ideally, in an Auburn-style prison, individual inmates occupied the cells only at night and worked in various prison-based industries during the day. They might interact with other prisoners— minimally—while they worked, but during other activities—meals, bath times, and religious services—they were to maintain scrupulous silence in order to meditate upon their predicament and complete their penitence through the doses of moral, primarily Christian-oriented, suasion they periodically received.[52]

Yet the budget-pinched penitentiary could hardly implement such idealistic philosophies. In July of 1871, when those first nine inmates arrived (some nine months after the prison's "completion"), they faced only thirteen six-by-eight-foot cells on the bottom floor of the contemplated three stories; not enough money remained to complete the remaining twenty-eight cells on the other two stories.[53] For several months, only grates covered the lower window openings. There was no money to build anything resembling "the panopticon," the internal surveillance tower occupied by omniscient guards, that the English liberal and early penologist Jeremy Bentham first conceived in the previous century as ideal for any reformative institution.[54] Indeed, the new prison had no offices, no guards' or warden's quarters, no steel reinforcement in the cells, no surrounding wall, no kitchen or outhouses, no hospital, and, most significant, no industries for the employment of the inmates. Workers hastily added a temporary cookhouse prior to the opening in July, but offices, guards' and warden's quarters— all employees were required to live on the premises during the duration of their appointments—as well as the additional twenty-eight cells, did not come until later in the decade.[55] A few days after the prison's opening, a Deer Lodge observer commented that "the penitentiary . . . is about as useless a piece of property as Uncle Sam has had since the war. . . . As it now stands it is a monument to folly."[56]

The Justice Department placed the care and custody of the territory's prison and prisoners under the regional U.S. marshals. They, in turn, selected wardens and reported to the territorial governors, who authorized them to hire local unskilled, usually unemployed laborers or political hacks as guards.[57] Two months prior to the opening of the prison, Territorial Governor Benjamin Franklin Potts urged William Wheeler, the regional U.S. marshal, to "find employment for some machinists, blacksmiths, etc.," at the prison. If Wheeler were unsuccessful in his search, Potts nevertheless expected "some soldier boys here from Ohio" the next month. "If they [come] in time," the governor ordered, "I want you to make guards out of some of them for we must do something for them to give them a start in the Country."[58] Both the marshals and the wardens themselves had barely minimal penological experience, and they initially improvised disciplinary regimens to fit the impoverished provincial conditions.

But there now was a federal prison in Montana. Lynchings (except for a brief, though very intense flare-up due to cattle-rustling and the lack of *any* organized law enforcement within hundreds of miles in the remote central badlands in 1884) all but vanished.[59] The ritual of punishment, even in such an isolated and rural locale as Montana, had changed, and the prison symbolized that change starkly. New and broad social and cultural forces that reflected shifting attitudes toward criminality, deviance, and the involvement of the modern state in regulating incarceration in late nineteenth-century American society had converged upon the farthest reaches of the continent.

In Montana, the establishment of the federal prison was a direct response to the lawlessness perpetuated by both outlaws and vigilance committees and was a part of larger social and economic forces sweeping across the American West. Initially, in the 1860s, a preoccupied federal government acted inconsistently, even ineptly, in its efforts to establish a prison at Deer Lodge (and at Boise City, Laramie, Walla Walla, and elsewhere in the West where the United States built and maintained penitentiaries). But its efforts marked a decided shift from the seeming chaos of sporadic lynch law and the incarceration of lesser offenders in improvised and inadequate local facilities to a more rational and uniform system of state sanctioned and administered discipline. Was it the manifestation of total power? No. But it did alter the nature of criminal punishment substantially, and it did aid in a smoother and quicker transition to extractive and industrial capitalism in the region. Moreover, incarcerated individuals now found themselves in an altogether new relationship with the state and with its emerging power. In Montana, suspected criminals went from being notorious, albeit public, figures, whose harsh punishment served as a symbolic community ritual, to being anonymous, dehumanized into the all-too-familiar "other" so characteristic of modern society's perception (or lack of perception) of those it incarcerates, who rotted away in cramped, brick-lined cells in an impressive, half-finished building in a far-off western mountain valley.

3 / "The Accursed Thing"

The Territorial Penitentiary

I . . . shall avoid it as long as possible.
—GOVERNOR BENJAMIN F. POTTS

The United States penitentiary at Deer Lodge City officially opened its thirteen cell doors on July 2, 1871. In the ensuing several days, sheriffs from the five Montana counties brought in convicted criminals from their own over-crowded county jails, thus saving their respective counties the expense of maintaining them; that burden now fell on the territory and the United States. Nine young males, including two Chinese immigrants, a miner from Wales, and George Dixon, the former slave from Missouri, suffered the ignominy of being the penitentiary's first occupants. Over the course of the next eighteen years (until Montana achieved statehood in 1889), 602 other individuals would follow these initiates.[1] Between 1889 and 1921, approximately another 4,000 would follow them.

By the early 1870s the territorial judiciary had ensconced itself in Montana and took active steps to establish law and order. During the late 1860s, judges began sending individuals to local jails, or, if their sentences were longer than two years, to the Detroit House of Correction. Even short-term sentences, however, were extremely burdensome to the local, embryonic economies, and the threat of escapes was ever present. To the citizens of Helena, Virginia City, Missoula, and Deer Lodge (the county seats of the territorial judicial districts), in whose jails convicted individuals most

35

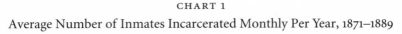

CHART 1

Average Number of Inmates Incarcerated Monthly Per Year, 1871–1889

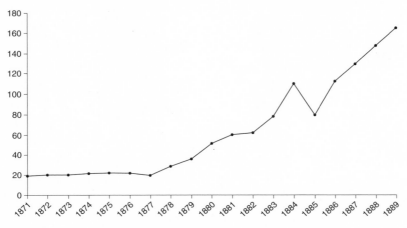

SOURCE: *Second Annual Report of the Board of Prison Commissioners,* 1892

often served their sentences, the gubernatorial order to transfer inmates to the penitentiary came as much-anticipated and welcome news.[2]

The Interior Department initially planned the territorial prison to hold forty-two prisoners in the one partially finished wing—fourteen cells per story—with plans to build an adjacent wing that would house another forty-two at some indeterminate point in the future. However, in 1871, due to the initially inadequate appropriation, only fourteen cells on the ground floor had been completed, one of which was designated as a washroom. Yet it quickly became apparent that the thirteen cells would be inadequate to meet the territory's needs. By July 30, 1871, twenty-eight days after the initial nine inmates christened the new penitentiary, six more joined them, thus officially overcrowding the penitentiary; it remained so throughout the territorial years.[3] Chart 1 represents the average number of prisoners incarcerated monthly per year during the territorial years of 1871 to 1889.

Government architects conceived and designed the western penitentiaries to follow a modified version of the Auburn penal philosophy. Although this approach and the necessary prison architecture had been widely used in New York and several other eastern institutions earlier in the century, it had already proven too expensive to sustain, and many states had begun to abandon the concepts and architecture in favor of other approaches; especially appealing were industrially based reformatories.[4]

It is virtually impossible to determine precisely the immediate deterrent effect the early prison had on crime in Montana. The territorial governor, Benjamin Franklin Potts (who was also the U.S. Superintendent of Indian Affairs within Montana), believed that at least it discouraged the pernicious Indian whiskey trade operating in northern Montana. As Potts informed Secretary of Interior Columbus Delano in September of 1871:

> At the last term of court held . . . two men were convicted for selling whiskey to Indians; one was sentenced to eighteen months imprisonment in the penitentiary, and the other to six months. . . . This had an excellent effect, and on the west side of the mountains, where these two men had been operating, a regular stampede took place out of that section of the country of "wolfers" and whiskey traders.[5]

In spite of such news, and as shown in Chart 2, the number of inmates continued to climb steadily for nearly fifty years, as Montana approached and achieved statehood in 1889.

Initially, territorial judges aggressively sentenced a wide range of offenders to prison terms, despite the lack of cell space. During the territorial years, Montana incarcerated its inhabitants at the third highest per capita rate in the nation. Certainly the territory's swelling population between 1871 and 1889 was a contributing factor. However, population increase alone cannot account for the dramatic rise in per capita incarceration, which exceeded in percentage the rise in the general population. The average monthly inmate census escalated from 19 per month in 1871, to 109 in 1884, to 163 by statehood in 1889. This was an 850 percent gain in eighteen years, while the general population in Montana increased by only roughly 600 percent. In 1880 and 1890 (years for which the U.S. Census Bureau calculated figures of incarcerated individuals both regionally and nationally), the number of prison inmates per capita in Montana was above the regional average and was more than double the national average during the same period, as Chart 3 graphically illustrates. Only Nevada and California ranked ahead of Montana during the 1870s and 1880s. Until the

CHART 2

Monthly Average Inmate Population (Annual Figures), 1871–1921

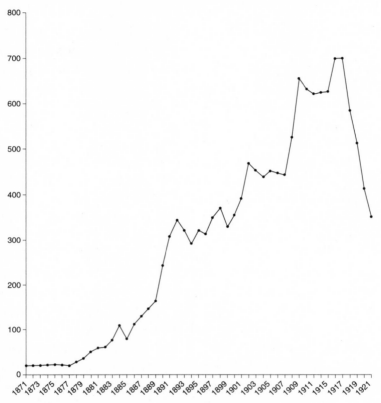

SOURCE: *Second Annual Report of the Board of Prison Commissioners,* 1892

1920s, Montana consistently imprisoned people at approximately double the national average rate and significantly above the regional rate.[6]

At least two factors could account for the meteoric rise in incarceration in Montana. First, because of the state's recent lynchings, self-conscious judges and juries sought to downplay the incidents and ape the customs of the ostensibly more civilized East.[7] As Potts had explained to President Ulysses Grant in 1870, "An able Judge has more power for good here than all the Federal officers put together."[8] Consequently, judges and juries vigorously sentenced individuals to prison terms. Second, and more practi-

CHART 3

Per Capita Incarceration Per 100,000: U.S., Montana, and West, 1880–1923

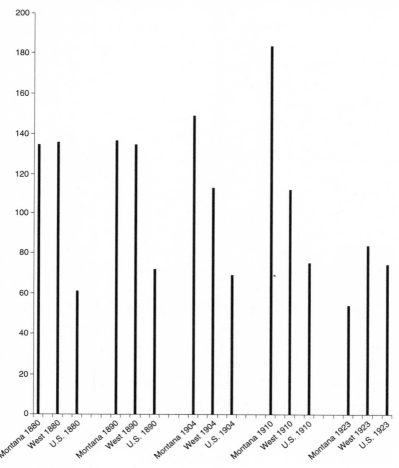

SOURCE: Cahalan, *Historical Corrections Statistics.*

cally, the handful of county governments had neither the cell space nor the money to hold criminals for more than a few days or weeks; officials were especially eager to rid themselves of territorial prisoners after Congress voted an additional appropriation enabling construction of another cell tier in the mid-1870s to increase (modestly) the institution's cell capacity by fourteen.

Austere budgets and constant squabbles between Department of Justice and territorial officials charged with the penitentiary's oversight continued after the prison opened in 1871 and persisted during the territorial period. Indeed, operating from Washington, D.C., a remote western prison in an area not served by rail or a reliable water route soon proved to be a source of endless complexity and bureaucratic headache. Under the provisions of the initial governing contract, Montana paid the federal government $1.00 per day per inmate to support prisoners convicted in territorial courts, while the Justice Department agreed to pay all other expenses associated with the prison. It became obvious, however, even before the penitentiary opened, that this amount would fall far short of adequately covering the operating costs of the penitentiary. Governor Potts admitted to U.S. Marshal William Wheeler that "$1.00 per day will be low for keeping convicts[,] but if [the] U.S. is to pay the expense of the prison we need not complain." Later he advised Wheeler to keep quiet about the arrangement. "You need not say anything about the cost of keeping the prisoners for the Territory[;] for that will be so gained to the Territory [if] the U.S. pays it and the Territory saves it."[9]

Despite penny-pinching and the $1.00 per day received from the territory, it still cost the United States $1.86 a day to maintain Montana's inmates, a cost 86 percent higher than the Justice Department had initially planned. Between April 1871 and November 1872, the federal government spent $21,429.46 to operate the prison; Montana contributed $8,271. By late 1872, the Justice Department, partially due to the expense it incurred in Montana, began reconsidering the federal government's involvement in financing the western penitentiaries.[10] As a result, both the Justice and Interior Departments took steps to rid themselves of the burden by turning over the financial and administrative operation of the penitentiaries to the respective territories. Though most western territories, Montana included, wanted to assume the economic benefits and prestige of statehood as rapidly as possible, the headache of running the federal penitentiaries was not an attractive prospect and did not sit well with the mostly financially strapped local administrations. In March of 1873, after Potts learned that he was now fully in charge of the Deer Lodge prison, he complained, "I don't want the accursed thing and shall avoid it as long as possible."[11]

Potts tried, unsuccessfully, to make good his threat. It did not take long for the territory, despite appointing a three-person prison commission board—chaired by Potts—and drafting specific by-laws to operate the penitentiary, to encounter its own financial problems running the institution. During the fifteen-odd months that the territory controlled the facility, the penitentiary's operating costs soared to $2.03 a day per inmate, more than double what it had been previously paying the federal government. In early 1874 the Montana territorial legislature petitioned Congress to reassume management of the institution because it had become too burdensome. Congress reluctantly assented.[12]

Between 1871 and 1874, Congress appropriated nothing to increase the cell capacity of the space-strained penitentiary, though the institution's inmate population had begun to swell substantially. Even the disinterested Potts began to take notice. In 1874, after a number of escapes and attempted escapes from the brick-lined cells, the governor announced to Martin Maginnis (the territory's nonvoting delegate to Congress), "I regard the increase of prison room as absolutely necessary for the safety and health of those who may be confined." Accordingly, Maginnis pressed Congress for money to complete another tier of cells and to line with iron those already constructed. In 1874, Congress finally conceded and appropriated $6,020 to complete an additional story with fourteen new cells.[13]

Despite the increased cell space, the capacity of the penitentiary—even with two inmates per cell—reached its peak and then passed it by the late 1870s. By January 1879, forty-four individuals occupied the twenty-seven cells. Two years later, there were fifty-four inmates (double the original and ideal maximum capacity). By January 1885 an astonishingly high number, 120, or nearly five individuals *per cell,* resided in the Montana prison. In keeping with the pioneer spirit, the warden forced many prisoners to camp out on the prison grounds while the territory hastily constructed log cellblocks and auxiliary buildings. The U.S. marshal, Robert Kelley, even purchased the old Deer Lodge county jail, dismantled the frame structure, and reconstructed it inside the prison compound in an attempt to relieve the overcrowding. Governor Potts, after receiving nothing from Congress to expand the prison, recommended to the territorial legislature that territorial prisoners be confined once again in the county jails.[14]

But these stopgap measures betrayed a level of need that even the most hardened and frugal could not overlook. The lack of prison space even exacerbated, at least indirectly, an outburst of shortlived, but intense, vigilance by central and eastern Montana cattle ranchers in early 1884.[15] Several rounds of bureaucratic hand-wringing then ensued as territorial officials repeatedly lobbied the United States for additional appropriations.[16]

The penitentiary vexed Potts's gubernatorial successor, John Crosby, as much as it had Potts. After assuming office in 1883, Crosby soon discovered that the administration of the penitentiary was conducted "most loosely and in a reprehensible manner," and he began to take immediate steps to meliorate the overcrowding. Crosby told the secretary of the interior that the prison's congestion "has been largely used as an argument for seeking and exercising executive clemency in years past, and the frequency of escapes is an undoubted cause of the growing tendency to resort to lynch law."[17] He recommended to Congress (to no avail) that Montana "authorities contract with the authorities in the older States for the keeping of its long-term convicts, at a considerable saving of expense and under better discipline."[18] However, when Congress finally relented in 1884 and allocated $15,000 for enlarging the prison, Crosby promptly authorized the funds to be used to construct central offices and warden's quarters. Alexander Botkin, the presiding U.S. marshal, considered Crosby's decision wholly "unwise and unwarranted." In defense of Crosby, one must note that a month previously a team of inspectors had deemed the walls and foundation of the existing wing too weak to support a third tier of cells (information unbeknownst to Botkin).[19] The remedy, the inspectors suggested, was to complete the other wing of the penitentiary (called for in the original specifications), which in turn required another round of pleading with Congress by Montana officials.[20]

Finally, in early 1885 the United States attorney general intervened and ordered a halt to a further increase in incarceration in Montana until the Department of the Interior could complete construction of the penitentiary it had begun in 1870, fifteen years previously. By mid-1885, Warden Botkin, obviously nearing his breaking point, warned that "unless increased accommodations are provided [soon] it will be impossible that the sentences of our courts [which met in the spring and fall] shall be executed" and that "any delay will result in serious embarrassments." Among these would be the fact that "some of the prisoners will be obliged to camp out next winter," Maginnis tersely wrote the U.S. attorney general.[21] Congress, after protracted pressure from the attorney general, assented and appropriated yet another $25,000 to the territory.[22]

In the meantime, while the Justice Department, the U.S. Treasury, the Department of the Interior, the Montana territorial delegate to Congress, the Montana territorial governors, the U.S. marshal, and the prison warden haggled for months over the appropriation, approximately fifty prisoners waited in county jails. Some waited for up to two years, while the prison population gradually declined, the appropriation cleared, and the new wing finally reached completion. By the spring of 1886, after feverish construction throughout the fall and early spring, the capacity of the prison was effectively tripled and the United States Penitentiary at Deer Lodge officially completed. Territorial judges subsequently wasted little time in refilling it. By year's end the prison had already exceeded capacity.

In light of these circumstances, the prison's financial situation came to influence the way the staff and the governor administered sentences. Most significant, the finances forced compromises in the length of time prisoners served their sentences, as Crosby candidly admitted to his superiors in 1883. In response to the chronic overcrowding, the various territorial governors resorted extensively to their executive power to commute sentences or to grant outright pardons. The immediate effect of such action, which governors and wardens quickly comprehended, was to limit the overcrowding within the penitentiary. One hundred and thirty inmates, or about 30 percent, received pardons between 1871 and 1885. Between 1871 and 1889, judges and juries condemned fourteen individuals to life sentences. Excluding one individual who escaped and was never recaptured, another who went to the insane asylum after a year, and another who refused a pardon, these prisoners served an average "life" sentence of 11.3 years. Only six inmates, just a fraction over 1 percent, ever served their complete sentences between 1871 and 1885.[23]

The various territorial governors were remarkably indiscriminate in their pardoning too. In most American prisons, receiving a pardon was conditioned primarily upon an inmate's friends, political influence, financial connections, and ability to gain an audience with the governor. These factors were all present in Montana, but during the periods of severe overcrowding the warden simply sent lists of candidates to the governor irrespective of political connections, class standing, race, or ethnicity.[24]

Nor did it matter how heinous a crime one committed. Sixty-three percent of incarcerated murderers received pardons during the territorial years, a higher percentage than among those who committed lesser crimes. Of the twenty-nine individuals convicted of murder between 1871 and 1885, only one served his complete sentence, and he could be considered an anomaly due to his failing mental health and repeated refusal of pardons bestowed by several governors. A Gallatin County jury had found Michael Foley guilty of an 1879 murder, and he spent the next forty-nine years in Deer Lodge, until his death in 1929; territorial and later state officials, at a loss when Foley refused pardons, simply kept him in prison.[25] As one Butte commentator caustically observed in 1890 (a few months after statehood):

> Only criminals convicted of capital offenses and whose hands are dripping
> with human blood, seem to have any chance for clemency nowadays. A man
> who steals a loaf of bread or a pair of blankets is seldom shown any mercy,
> but the assassin, who makes widows and orphans, often escapes the pun-
> ishment for his crime.[26]

The overcrowding also compromised the uniform application of the broadest behavioral incentive that the penitentiary staff had at its disposal—the good time policy, a method still widely used in contemporary American prisons. For each calendar month with no infractions and satisfactory work performance, the prisoner received two and one half days' reduction of sentence, with proportionately increasing amounts after the first year.[27] Any infraction of the internal rules, theoretically, would result in loss of accrued good time. But because the prison remained so critically overcrowded for so long, the administration rarely revoked inmates' accumulated good time. For example, in May 1883, George Wells, serving a ten-year sentence for a robbery in Madison County in 1879, brutally assaulted a guard and attempted to escape. Despite this infraction, Wells still received a *forty-*

five-month diminution of his sentence because of good time accumulation, and the warden released him just two years later.[28]

The overcrowded conditions, however, did not deter the prison staff from using other forms of internal discipline. Minor infractions resulted in reduced rations, days or weeks in "the dungeon" (a darkened cell dug into the ground floor), or, for the most obdurate cases, "tying up," a form of punishment indigenous to many nineteenth-century American prisons. This method of torture consisted of binding an inmate's wrists with a small cord and then lashing him to an overhead fixture. As one historian of nineteenth-century prisons has described the method, "The tension was then adjusted according to the degree of pain to be inflicted: the milder form allowed the subject to keep his toes on the floor; the severe case was hoisted in the air" for a protracted period, causing severe pain in the shoulders, back, arms, and eventually legs. Warden C. B. Adriance reported to Governor Potts and the prison's short-lived board of directors in 1873 that in the Montana penitentiary tying up "has never failed to accomplish the desired end."[29]

Even for those inmates who simply did their time peacefully and steered clear of the dungeon and tying up, daily life within the brick walls was hardly a pleasant experience. The summer heat, despite the Deer Lodge Valley's mostly salubrious northerly location, could be stifling, and at times the cellblocks became veritable ovens. The stench of diseased inmates in the cramped quarters wafted through the stale air of the cellblock much of the time.[30] Open buckets in each cell sufficed to hold human waste (and would until 1959 in one of the main cellblocks). During the winter, the majority of inmates were usually in poor health despite (or more likely because of) sleeping on a straw bed, wearing "garments of coarse material," and eating "sufficient plain and wholesome food," usually starch-laden with few vegetables and no fruit of any kind provided by the territory. During an inventory conducted in 1878, the warden listed on hand, among other things, "two boxes raisins . . . nine cans pears, eleven cans corn, seven cans peaches, eight cans apples, thirty pounds dried apples, and six pounds of dried peaches." Who received this food—the inmates or the guards and warden who also ate at the prison—is a matter of conjecture. By 1891 (some two years after statehood), however, inmates received no canned or dried fruit and very few vegetables of any sort (see Table 1).[31]

TABLE 1

Daily Bill of Fare for the State Prison, 1891

Monday

Breakfast:	Mush and milk, bread, coffee with sugar.
Dinner:	Baked beans with pork or bacon, bread, potatoes.
Supper:	Corned beef, bread, tea with sugar.

Tuesday

Breakfast:	Beef hash, cornbread, coffee with sugar.
Dinner:	Beef stew, potatoes, bread, boiled cabbage.
Supper:	Oatmeal and milk, bread, tea with sugar.

Wednesday

Breakfast:	Rice and milk, bread, coffee with sugar.
Dinner:	Roast beef, bread, potatoes, and carrots.
Supper:	Beef hash, bread, tea with sugar.

Thursday

Breakfast:	Oatmeal and milk, bread, coffee with sugar.
Dinner:	Baked beans, brown bread, potatoes, beets.
Supper:	Corned beef, bread, tea with sugar.

Friday

Breakfast:	Corned beef hash, cornbread, coffee with sugar.
Dinner:	Boiled codfish, potatoes, bread, turnips.
Supper:	Beef stew, bread, tea with sugar.

Saturday

Breakfast:	Mush and milk, bread, coffee with sugar.
Dinner:	Mutton stew, bread, potatoes, cabbage.
Supper:	Corned beef, bread, tea with sugar.

Sunday

Breakfast:	Rice and milk, bread, coffee with sugar.
Dinner:	Fresh roast pork, baked potatoes, bread, beets, turnips.
Supper:	Oatmeal and milk, bread, tea with sugar.

SOURCE: "Montana Prison Convict Register, March 1879 through November 1910" and "Descriptive List of Prisoners Received at State [sic] Prison, July 1, 1871–October 1, 1885. *Montana Prison Records,* Montana Historical Society.

First jail in Montana at the mining camp of Bannack in southwestern region of the territory. Constructed circa 1862. Photo by E. C. Schoettner. Courtesy Montana Historical Society, Helena

The result of vigilante justice, 1866. Courtesy Montana Historical Society

The United States Penitentiary at Deer Lodge City, Montana Territory, as it appeared shortly after initial construction in 1870 and 1871. Courtesy Montana Historical Society

Front Elevation.

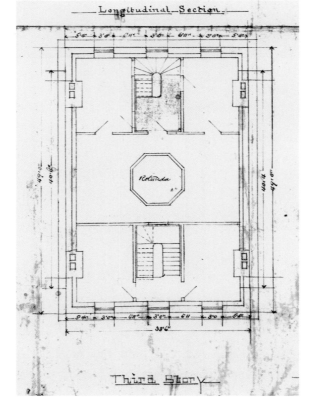

Longitudinal Section.

Rotunda

Third Story.

(*Facing page, top*) Federal architectural design for western territorial penitentiaries. Appropriations never matched the needs of the institutions based on the design. As such, institutions such as Montana's remained appallingly overcrowded during the territorial years. Courtesy Montana Historical Society

(*Facing page, bottom*) Ambitious design plan for the third story interior, begun in 1870, completed fifteen years later. Courtesy Montana Historical Society

After statehood the physical structures within the institution grew rapidly, including the addition—built by inmate labor—of a sandstone wall and new cellblocks. Photo taken sometime after 1912. Note the old territorial penitentiary in between the two cellblocks in the center of the photo. Courtesy Montana Historical Society

Overcrowding has plagued the institution throughout its history, consistently forcing officials to improvise, such as in this log cellblock constructed during the 1880s and used after statehood into the 1890s. Courtesy Montana Historical Society

(*Facing page, top*) The interior of the 1896 cellblock. No cell had running water or toilet facilities. Two buckets had to suffice: one for drinking water, one for human waste. Courtesy Montana Historical Society

(*Facing page, bottom*) "Turnkeys," or guards, patrol the catwalk in the 1896 cellblock. No date, but probably pre-1900. Courtesy Montana Historical Society

Montana State Prison — April-99—

Prison guards, 1899. Courtesy Montana Historical Society

(*Facing page, top*) An early view of Deer Lodge with the federal penitentiary inset. Note the board fence surrounding the institution. High winds periodically caused it to blow over. Sketch by J. Manz. Courtesy Montana Historical Society

(*Facing page, bottom*) A view from the west side of the prison taken between 1895 and 1906. Under the lease agreement with the state of Montana, lessees Frank Conley and Thomas McTague managed to increase the size of the buildings enormously, and inexpensively, using primarily inmate labor. Courtesy Montana Historical Society

Albert Shoemaker, age 20. Photo taken March 1, 1901, the day he entered the Montana State Prison to begin serving a one-year term for burglary. Upon incarceration prison officials quickly began transforming the individual. Inmates were shaved and required to wear the coarse, prison-striped garments. Courtesy Montana Historical Society

William Foster, age 31. Photo taken on February 25, 1901, the day he entered the Montana State Prison to serve a two-year term for grand larceny. Courtesy Montana Historical Society

Under Conley and McTague, inmates built state roads throughout western Montana, including this one on the east side of Flathead Lake in the early 1900s. Courtesy Montana Historical Society

An inmate in his rough prison garb, 1901. Courtesy Montana Historical Society

Frank Conley served as guard, lessee, then warden of the institution for over thirty-five years, from 1886 until his ouster in 1921. Courtesy Montana Historical Society

Montana Territorial Governor
Benjamin Franklin Potts, who tried
in vain to rid the territory of
financial oversight of the early
federal penitentiary. Courtesy
Montana Historical Society

Montana Governor Joseph M.
Dixon. Dixon, an early twentieth-
century progressive, removed
Frank Conley in 1921 and faced a
ferocious public relations and legal
backlash engineered by the
powerful Anaconda Copper
Company. Courtesy Montana
Historical Society

By the mid-1930s the old territorial building had been razed, replaced by a central administration building (white building in center). In the spirit of efficiency, prison officials converted nearly all recreational areas into vegetable gardens (foreground). Photo taken in 1952. Courtesy Montana Historical Society

Inmates had few employment options within the institution. This is the garment shop, February 1927. Courtesy Montana Historical Society

Another view of the interior yard during the 1950s. The 1912 cellblock, scene of the 1959 riot, is in the background. Courtesy Montana Historical Society

Damage to the 1912 cellblock, from a national guardsman's bazooka blast, still visible today. Courtesy of author

The state hired Floyd Powell to serve as warden and reform the aging institution in 1958. Floyd's reforms caused discord among hardened inmates who rioted in April 1959. Here Powell looks toward one of the guard's towers during the thirty-six-hour stand-off that eventually left three dead, including the deputy warden and the two inmate ringleaders. Courtesy of author

The Montana State Penitentiary, 2000. Courtesy Montana State Prison

Though the prison contracted a physician to attend the prison twice a week, he was "to supply all medicines required for the treatment of the convicts, without other compensation than stated as his salary." Surely this must have been a disincentive to prescribe any medicine. In the six-month period between May and November 1873, the physician reported sixty-seven diseases and illnesses out of a total population that never exceeded twenty-one— or approximately three maladies per prisoner. The doctor recommended an increase of cells to cut down on the spread of communicable diseases and that "boots be furnished during the winter months to those who work out of doors" to prevent colds. He apparently enjoyed some popularity among the prisoners. In 1873 fourteen of nineteen inmates, including two Chinese and two African Americans, signed a petition to the prison commissioners requesting that the physician, who was then under investigation for undetermined infractions, be retained.[32]

Throughout Montana's history, most prison inmates have come from the lowest economic stratum, mirroring the demographic pattern in nearly all prisons across time. The vast majority of individuals sentenced to the territorial prison, some 63 percent, were there for crimes they committed against property, chiefly grand larceny, theft, forgery, or arson, as indicated by Tables 2 and 3 below.[33]

Many prisoners were part of a large surplus labor force of unskilled young men and women buffeted by the boom and bust cycle of the extractive mining industry or the cattle ranching bonanza that dominated the region's economy during the territorial years. The most frequently stated occupation was "laborer," which accounted for 22 percent of the inmate population, with miners and farmers constituting approximately another 20 percent. A large number (18 percent) identified themselves by what might be considered semiskilled occupations—shoemakers, blacksmiths, tinsmiths, stonemasons, carpenters, and clerks—while a small number of individuals listed occupations that could be regarded as middle to upper-middle class at the time: engineer, veterinary surgeon, physician, and dentist.[34]

For women, who also tended to be from the lowest economic class, the predominant occupation—for 29 out of 63 listed on the prison registers between 1871 and 1910—was that of prostitution or its ancillaries.[35] The aver-

TABLE 2

Crimes for Which Males Were Incarcerated, 1871–1885

Crime	N	Percentage of Total (rounded)
Grand Larceny	173	46
Assault (various types)	42	11
Murder	29	7.7
Manslaughter	25	6.6
Robbery	18	4.7
Burglary	15	4.0
Breaking Jail	14	3.7
Forgery	10	2.6
Robbing U.S. Mail	9	2.0
Arson	5	1.3
False Imprisonment	4	1.0
Rape	3	.75
Conspiracy to Defraud	2	.50
Incest	2	.50
Mayhem	2	.50
Assisting Soldier to Desert	2	.50
Illegal Voting	2	.50
Extortion	2	.50
Counterfeiting	2	.50
Crime Against Nature	1	.25
Perjury	1	.25
Cattle Theft	1	.25
Receiving Stolen Property	1	.25
Bigamy	1	.25
Abortion	1	.25
Resisting Officer	1	.25
None Noted	1	.25
TOTAL	380	

SOURCE: "Montana Prison Convict Register, March 1879 through November 1910"
and "Descriptive List of Prisoners Received at State [sic] Prison, July 1, 1871–October 1, 1885.
Montana Prison Records, Montana Historical Society.

TABLE 3

Crimes for Which Females Were Incarcerated, 1878–1910*

Crime	N	Percentage of Total (rounded)
Grand Larceny	31	49
Assault	9	14
Manslaughter	7	11
Murder	5	8
Burglary	4	6
Forgery	2	3
Bigamy	2	3
Robbery	1	1.5
Arson	1	1.5
TOTAL	63	

*Because Montana incarcerated only four women during the territorial period, 1871–1889, I have extended the territorial data of this and subsequent tables in reference to female inmates to 1910 to elicit a wider and more representative range of data.

SOURCE: "Montana Prison Convict Register, March 1879 through November 1910" and "Descriptive List of Prisoners Received at State [sic] Prison, July 1, 1871–October 1, 1885. *Montana Prison Records,* Montana Historical Society.

age inmate age, for both males and females, was around thirty.[36] Many came from lower-class neighborhoods springing up in the few Montana towns— Butte, Missoula, Deer Lodge, Bozeman, Helena, and Virginia City—that had developed around the original rough mining camps and along the Northern Pacific Railroad line in the territory. Most had at least a few years of formal education.[37]

Both men and women entered and left prison with little or no money. For example, there were 107 inmates incarcerated on July 30, 1889, and they had an average of $9.54; 39 had less than $1.00.[38] For most, understandably, their finances improved little during their prison terms. In many instances, upon release inmates had barely enough money to purchase a train ticket out of Deer Lodge (after the Northern Pacific line arrived in 1883). Until statehood all proceeds of inmate labor went to pay for the expenses of incarceration; the territory forbade inmates from retaining any money they earned from their labor. Upon release, however, as the prison

TABLE 4
Stated Occupations, Males, 1871–1885

Occupation	N	Percentage of Total (rounded)
Laborer	85	22
Miner	39	10
Farmer	32	8.4
None	22	6.0
Cook	14	3.6
Teamster	14	3.6
Carpenter	9	2.0
Clerk	9	2.0
Machinist	9	2.0
Painter	8	2.0
Butcher	8	2.0
Blacksmith	7	1.8
Tailor	6	1.5
Saloon Keeper	5	1.3
Bookkeeper	5	1.3
Herder	5	1.3
Shoemaker	5	1.3
Barber	5	1.3
Plasterer	4	1.0
Hunter	4	1.0
Soldier	4	1.0
Hostler	4	1.0
Baker	3	.75
Sailor	3	.75
Horse Jockey	3	.75
Physician	3	.75
Stockraiser	3	.75
Merchant	3	.75
Engineer	3	.75
Tinsmith	2	.50
Harness Maker	2	.50

TABLE 4 *(continued)*

Occupation	N	Percentage of Total (rounded)
Druggist	2	.50
Lumberman	2	.50
Chairmaker	2	.50
Upholsterer	2	.50
Cigar Maker	2	.50
Musician	2	.50
Horsebreaker	2	.50
Cowboy	2	.50
Stonemason	1	.25
Ranchman	1	.25
Stage-Driver	1	.25
Washerman	1	.25
Driller	1	.25
Civil Engineer	1	.25
Indian	1	.25
Candymaker	1	.25
Tramp	1	.25
Hotel Waiter	1	.25
Rivetmaker	1	.25
Wagon Maker	1	.25
Mason	1	.25
Bricklayer	1	.25
Copyist	1	.25
Gambler	1	.25
RR Engineer	1	.25
Bartender	1	.25
Sheepherder	1	.25
Horse Trainer	1	.25
Cabinetmaker	1	.25
Cooper	1	.25
Sculptor	1	.25
Glassblower	1	.25

(continued)

TABLE 4 *(continued)*

Occupation	N	Percentage of Total (rounded)
Dentist	1	.25
Mechanic	1	.25
Veterinary Surgeon	1	.25
Brewer	1	.25
Axman	1	.25
Railroading	1	.25
Driver	1	.25
Wheelwright	1	.25
Brick Molder	1	.25
Steward	1	.25
Boilermaker	1	.25
Hair Maker	1	.25
TOTAL	380	

SOURCE: "Montana Prison Convict Register, March 1879 through November 1910" and "Descriptive List of Prisoners Received at State [sic] Prison, July 1, 1871–October 1, 1885. *Montana Prison Records,* Montana Historical Society.

regulations stipulated, a former inmate received "a suit of coarse clothes" not to exceed $15.00 in value, ensuring in all likelihood that he would stand out as a former convict by his clothing.[39]

In the face of persistent austerity, Montana's territorial officers hoped that inculcating habits of labor might also help to defray expenses. Governor Potts was especially determined to make the prison pay for itself. In his view, cost containment and not successful rehabilitation or low recidivism gauged the prison's effectiveness.[40] At one point he even pondered the necessity of paying for mittens for the inmates involved in outside labor during the harsh Montana winter. "As to the purchase of gloves at $22 per dozen for convicts," he wrote the warden, "I think it extravagant and can't . . . justify the expenditure." On second thought, the governor relented, but he cautioned the warden to dispense items "*only* as they are *absolutely* needed"—he "expect[ed] the *strictest economy* in *everything.*" Potts reminded the warden that "the Territory will insist on her

TABLE 5

Stated Occupations, Females, 1878–1910

Occupation	N	Percentage of Total (rounded)
Demimonde	20	32
Dressmaker	7	11
Streetwalker	5	8
Cook/Baker	5	8
Housewife	4	6
Unlisted	4	6
Housekeeper	3	5
Domestic	2	3
Sporting Woman	2	3
Candy Store Clerk	1	1.5
Capitalist	1	1.5
Milliner	1	1.5
Ranch Woman	1	1.5
Laundress	1	1.5
Servant	1	1.5
Sporting Woman Keeper	1	1.5
Storekeeper	1	1.5
Teacher	1	1.5
Waitress	1	1.5
None	1	1.5
TOTAL	63	

SOURCE: "Montana Prison Convict Register, March 1879 through November 1910" and "Descriptive List of Prisoners Received at State [sic] Prison, July 1, 1871–October 1, 1885. *Montana Prison Records,* Montana Historical Society.

right to get from the labor of her convicts every dollar that she can honestly realize."[41]

The bylaws of the penitentiary and the original congressional mandate, in fact, made it imperative that the administration attempt to recoup the cost of running the institution through contracting inmate labor outside the prison. In 1873, after the territory assumed control of the prison, the Mon-

TABLE 6
Ages of Male Inmates, 1871–1885

Age	N	Percentage of Total (rounded)
16–19	28	7.3
20–24	85	22
25–29	97	25
30–39	104	27
40–49	50	13
50–59	12	3
60+	2	.5
Not listed	2	.5
TOTAL	380	

SOURCE: "Montana Prison Convict Register, March 1879 through November 1910" and "Descriptive List of Prisoners Received at State [sic] Prison, July 1, 1871–October 1, 1885. *Montana Prison Records,* Montana Historical Society.

tana legislature ordered the board of directors "to keep as many convicts constantly employed on contracts . . . at the highest price that can be obtained for their labor, and the proceeds thereof shall be applied to the payment of the current expenses of the Prison." The warden at the time, C. B. Adriance, notified Governor Potts that he was "anxious to make all the money I can for the Territory." The directors reported to Potts in late 1873 that Adriance kept many inmates employed in "the art of turning, fitting, and finishing household furniture," while others were "engaged in sawing wood by machinery," but their optimistic prediction that "the day is not far distant when the institution may be self-sustaining" was never even remotely realized during the territorial period. Instead, inmate idleness at the prison was most often the norm because the local Deer Lodge economy was too primitive to create sufficient jobs for the burgeoning inmate population. Local individuals and businesses could contract with the warden to hire labor at $.75 a day. But as one warden complained in 1877:

> The greatest misfortune to the prisoners is that they have no regular employment, the town is so small that it does not find it profitable to hire prison

TABLE 7
Ages of Female Inmates, 1878–1910

Age	N	Percentage of Total (rounded)
16–19	9	14
20–29	26	41
30–39	21	33
40–49	4	6
50–59	1	1.5
Not listed	2	3.0
TOTAL	63	

SOURCE: "Montana Prison Convict Register, March 1879 through November 1910" and "Descriptive List of Prisoners Received at State [sic] Prison, July 1, 1871–October 1, 1885. *Montana Prison Records,* Montana Historical Society.

labor, because the prisoners cannot go outside of the prison yard and there is no manufacturing done in the town. All work on the improvements done about the prison has been done by the prisoners and only the materials paid for by the government. The prisoners make their own clothes, cook, saw wood, and do all that is done for the prison and themselves. They have a great deal of spare time.[42]

Because the institution remained habitually overcrowded and chronically underfunded while the inmates were generally under- or unemployed and lived in inhumane conditions, it is tempting to characterize Montana's territorial prison as an abysmal failure, or at least as a precursor to still more failure in the twentieth century. But from other perspectives and according to other standards, the territorial prison in Montana was effective on levels not immediately visible.

First, a leading benchmark that policymakers and politicians historically have employed to assess the impact the prison experience has on an individual is recidivism. In early Montana society, recidivism was very low, at least when compared to the strikingly higher figures of the next century. Only 2 percent of inmates returned (compared to current national levels as high as 65 percent); only ten individuals can be positively identified as repeat offenders between 1871 and 1885.[43] Certainly there were factors that may have contributed to the low recidivism rate besides the prison experience, such as death or simply movement out of Montana into another territory, state, or nation. But for whatever reason, the penitentiary does appear to have modestly succeeded in preventing recidivism—that is until the population and the economy stabilized during the decades surrounding the end of the century, and the number of those who returned to the prison began gradually to increase.[44]

Second, the Montana territorial government used its prison as a cheap means to attempt to instill in its lower-class criminals self-discipline and labor habits. This, in fact, was and has remained the chief goal of prison rehabilitation since the early nineteenth century. For example, the first rule in the "Rules and Regulations" guidelines promulgated by the territory after its brief control of the penitentiary in 1873 directed that prisoners "labor faithfully and diligently." There was an incentive: hard-working and obedient inmates were eligible for a diminution of sentence. Considering the extreme overcrowding of the penitentiary, this latter stipulation was of pivotal administrative importance. Nearly all territorial inmates received sentence reductions based on good behavior and apparently faithful labor. Thus it can be inferred that the inducement to labor, at least on the surface, appeared to have made something of an impression, particularly when the alternative was to sit in cramped, hot, stench-ridden cells all day. Yet given that any profits derived from their labor went to offset the costs of their incarceration and that the overcrowding required that nearly all be released early, one can well imagine the mixed message the territorial penitentiary inmates might have received about the benefits of hard work.[45]

Third, and most important but least visible, the penitentiary made manifest the growing power of constituted authority over individuals and moved the territory's judicial branch toward stability. The embryonic Montana criminal justice system, with assistance from the penitentiary staff, became more proficient in its ability to identify and classify deviant individuals— to create new knowledge about them by virtue of their incarceration and its subsequent documentation procedures. Perceptions and awareness of deviance have always been present in American history, particularly in rural

America—and this knowledge has always served as a way to measure and reconfirm one's own identity against those who are deviant—but such perceptions were decidedly heightened in the urbanizing and populated settings of nineteenth-century America. In armies, hospitals, asylums, and prisons, especially, techniques for categorizing, observing, and hierarchizing the deviant, delinquent, criminal, or insane became refined and widely implemented.[46] This mirrored a trend occurring throughout both Europe and Victorian America, in which a growing cadre of recently professionalized medical doctors, psychiatrists, asylum keepers, and penologists defined, shaped, categorized, walled off, and became generally hypersensitive to deviancy in its many manifestations.[47]

In an increasingly secular and commercial world, it was this newly professionalized class that came to define and treat deviancy almost exclusively. For the politically dominant whites, identifying and closely monitoring those deemed subversive or deviant became critical during this period, particularly in light of the immigration explosion in late nineteenth-century America, an America that felt increasingly threatened from both within and without. Foucault observed that "discipline is a political anatomy of detail."[48] Details, when the security of a nation, a race, and a way of life were at stake, became crucial. America's penitentiaries, asylums, and reformatories assisted by virtue of their detailed documentation of the criminally deviant and insane.

Certainly this documenting and identifying occurred in Montana and in other western territories that built federal penitentiaries and asylums. Remarkably, even considering the crude and chronically unfinished conditions of Montana's prison, penitentiary officials efficiently documented and categorized all their incarcerated individuals; no one in the penitentiary, or in the asylum at nearby Warm Springs, fell through the cracks. Upon entering, inmates had their heads shaved and received striped pants and a cap and a prison-made jacket, all part of the distinctive uniforms worn by most nineteenth-century convicted criminals.[49] On the prison register, the staff meticulously cataloged a plethora of specific identifying information about the new inmate that obviously could assist authorities in capturing him or her in the event of escape: height; weight; tattoos; hair, eye, and skin colors; date of imprisonment; and criminal history—all appeared on the register. But birthplace, date of birth, education level, religion, health, race, tobacco usage, shoe size, and occupation also became traits that the territory's officials recorded.[50]

Finally, imprisonment was uniform for all prisoners, irrespective of race or ethnicity. Although nativism and racism often characterized late nineteenth-century Anglo American attitudes, it appears, based on incarceration figures in territorial Montana, that judges and juries did not single out any particular racial or ethnic group for extended incarceration.

Most striking and surprising, the governor pardoned minorities without regard for their race, responding in many cases to local petitions signed by substantial numbers of upstanding citizens.[51] The experience minorities had with the Montana criminal justice system and particularly with the prison appears not to have been racially based or biased overall, a circumstance similar to what scholars elsewhere have discovered. Though the incarceration patterns in many institutions of the nineteenth-century West remain to be fully examined, Clare McKanna, who has analyzed Mexican, Mestizo, and Native American incarceration in California during roughly this same period, concluded "that the treatment of minorities by the [California] legal system seems to have been fairly equal [to that of Anglos] during the sentencing procedure." Paul Hietter has determined that this was also the case in territorial Arizona. In neighboring Idaho, as the historian Liping Zhu has noted, "Chinese immigrants were served by a relatively fair justice system," and the courts, "though hardly perfect, went out of their way to protect Chinese civil liberties and legal rights."[52] And in Montana itself, John Wunder, in his survey of a range of civil and criminal cases involving Chinese, has observed that in the face of regional anti-Chinese sentiment of the late 1870s and early 1880s "the legal institutions in Montana faced their task squarely and blunted the force of anti-Chinese public opinion . . . and judged them equitably."[53]

Nevertheless, discrimination was an unfortunate reality for racial and cultural minorities in some (if not all) territorial Montana towns—discrimination that often led to arrests and convictions on questionable grounds. A cursory review of the arrest and conviction of one Chinese inmate reveals that racism was a factor leading to his imprisonment. The

TABLE 8

Race and Ethnicity of Male Inmates, 1871–1885

Race/Ethnicity	N	Percentage of Total (rounded)
U.S. Native (white)	239	63
Foreign Born	101	27
(Canada and Europe)		
Native American	15	4.0
Chinese	13	3.4
African American	9	2.3
Mexican	3	.75
TOTAL	380	

SOURCE: "Montana Prison Convict Register, March 1879 through November 1910" and "Descriptive List of Prisoners Received at State [sic] Prison, July 1, 1871–October 1, 1885. *Montana Prison Records,* Montana Historical Society.

territorial court tried and convicted Ah Wah, a resident of Deer Lodge, in 1871 for assault with a deadly weapon against a white man, John Martel, in a dispute concerning the use of water in an irrigation ditch. Five of the twelve jurors who convicted Ah Wah admitted prejudice toward the Chinese race and did not believe "Chinese evidence"—the testimony of an Asian under oath—to be trustworthy. Despite these admissions, the judge did not excuse any of the jurors, and they convicted Ah Wah and sentenced him to a year in the territorial prison. Judging by a brief newspaper account, Ah Wah was probably already an object of racial scorn in the community: the local reporter happily informed the town that "the belligerous [sic] 'Chinee,'" and "his pig-tail will be imprisoned twelve months."[54] However, it is important to note that Ah Wah was sentenced to *only* twelve months (and subsequently received a month off for good behavior), the same sentence that Samuel Hughes, Frank Merrill, and Patrick Duane received—all white, all immigrants, all convicted of the same offense as Ah Wah in the early 1870s in Montana territorial courts.[55]

Though presumably such episodes occurred all too frequently, the racial and immigrant composition of those imprisoned prior to the 1890s closely mirrored that of the general population: about 11 percent of inmates

TABLE 9

Race and Ethnicity of Female Inmates, 1878–1910

Race/Ethnicity	N	Percentage of Total (rounded)
Unlisted	29	46
Negro	14	22
Mulatto	9	14
German	4	6
Irish	3	5
English	1	1.5
French	1	1.5
Scottish	1	1.5
Mexican	1	1.5
TOTAL	63	

SOURCE: "Montana Prison Convict Register, March 1879 through November 1910" and "Descriptive List of Prisoners Received at State [sic] Prison, July 1, 1871–October 1, 1885. *Montana Prison Records,* Montana Historical Society.

were either African American, Chinese, Mexican, or Native American.[56] Given the substantial ethnic minority population in Montana during this time and the concurrent Anglo nativism, one would expect to find comparable or even strikingly higher percentages of minorities incarcerated in the prison. This, however, was not the case. Foreign-born individuals made up 29 percent of the total Montana population in 1880 and 32 percent of the total prison population, a statistically insignificant difference. After the 1890s the presence of Irish immigrants—who came to the region in large numbers to work the profitable copper mines of nearby Butte—increased in the inmate population, but not disproportionate to their numbers in the general population.[57] While racial harassment was undoubtedly widespread in Montana, systemized incarceration on the basis of race did not occur in the Montana prison. It cost too much.

Only 4 of 611 individuals incarcerated in the Montana territorial prison were women, though at least two of these were from racial and ethnic minorities. The first woman prisoner, Felicita Sanchez (who went under several aliases), convicted of manslaughter in Missoula in 1878, was probably of Mexican descent. Prison officials initially housed Sanchez in the same cellblock as her male counterparts. Later, after another woman, Angelina (a.k.a. "Mary") Drouillard from Missoula arrived (convicted of murdering her abusive husband, a county sheriff), the territory quartered Sanchez and Drouillard in one of the separate and more primitive log facilities on the prison grounds. Drouillard arrived at the prison pregnant and was released temporarily to the charge of the local Deer Lodge hospital when she went into labor (the child was placed for adoption). Upon return to her log quarters she attempted suicide with drugs she had smuggled from her hospital stay.[58]

After statehood, and in the midst of Progressive efforts to curb prostitution, the number of women prisoners rose significantly. Between 1890 and 1910 fifty-nine women were incarcerated, a roughly 1,400 percent increase over the previous twenty-year period. The early dearth of women inmates may have been due to the absence of a permanent women's cellblock until after statehood. Anne Butler, in her study of black women incarcerated in the late nineteenth-century West, has determined that after statehood Montana, like other western territories and states, incarcerated a significant, and disproportionately high, number of African American women.[59]

But minorities, both men and women, in addition to receiving sentences similar to those of their white counterparts, also earned diminution of their sentences based on good time and executive pardons in roughly equal proportions to Anglos. Between 1871 and 1885, fourteen of the forty-one non-white inmates (34 percent) received an executive pardon, while 29 percent of the white prison population received pardons. These percentages should not mislead, however, as attesting to a lack of discrimination: they do not take into account ethnic and minority incarceration in local jails nor can they in any way reflect the minority inmate population's day-to-day relationships with the white guards and inmates—relationships that may very well have been as brutalizing as was placing women in an all-male institution. Certainly the attempt to reshape Native American values through rigid schedules and work routines and weekly doses of Protestantism must have been at the very least culturally and psychologically disruptive. Even worse, because of the cramped living conditions, inmates most susceptible to communicable diseases such as smallpox and measles, including several Chinese and Native Americans, died in prison. Ah Tung, aged forty and sentenced for murder in July 1871, died within six months of his arrival. Moy Toy, aged thirty-one, convicted of murder in 1872 (probably committed in self-defense), received a pardon within four months as he was "in a dying condition." San Pierre, a twenty-five-year-old Flathead Indian convicted of manslaughter in Missoula in 1878, died after twenty-seven months in prison. Another Native American, Pierre, twenty-nine, convicted of murder, died within three years of his 1881 incarceration. Worst of all, sixteen-year-old Axe Handle, a Northern Cheyenne and the youngest inmate Montana incarcerated in the territorial prison (dubiously convicted of an 1884 arson in Miles City along with White Bear, Howling Wolf, and Stand-to-One-Side), died before reaching his seventeenth birthday. Seven months later the territorial governor pardoned and released the remaining three Northern Cheyenne.[60]

Though local citizenry often petitioned for the release of these individuals so that the "ends of justice and humanity would be subserved," in many cases it was simply economically expedient for the governor to grant a pardon because it was much cheaper to release a dying inmate than to provide medical care. As the prison physician C. F. Musigbrod wrote Governor Potts about one sick and emaciated inmate, caring for him "would very likely become an expensive charge. I think the sooner this Territory gets rid of him so much the better it is."[61]

Though disease may have been discriminating, as mentioned, the various territorial governors were not. Nonwhites received gubernatorial pardons at a rate roughly equal to that of the general prison population.[62] At least in the eyes of budget-conscious territorial bureaucrats, every prisoner was equal in the amount he or she cost to incarcerate. Lower-class whites, Chinese, former slaves, Irish immigrants, Native Americans—all had had perhaps their most precious possession, their physical freedom, revoked by judges and juries representing the local Montana communities and society as a whole. Yet cultural, ethnic, and racial hierarchies most surely developed among Montana's inmates as they did in other territorial prisons in the West. But it is worthwhile to note that prisoners could occasionally cross cultural and racial boundaries and unite in a common cause, as indicated by their 1873 petition to the governor to retain the prison physician "as we are satisfied with his treatment."[63]

The successes and failures of any American prison, nearly all of which have been chronically underfunded and overcrowded, can and should be assessed in more complicated ways. To reiterate, the creation of a prison in one of the most remote areas in the American West was an effective and a relatively inexpensive way to bound vast physical space, socialize, however haphazardly, lower-class miscreants, and simultaneously broadcast the message of legal legitimacy and stability to the rest of the population scattered across the territory. In principle, the establishment of a prison in an area that previously had been characterized by lawlessness and episodic and increasingly embarrassing vigilantism reflected the emergence of more coherent and permanent law and order. It also reflected the growing power of central government, operating through local criminal justice authorities, in the American West. The ability of the state (that is, the United States working through its territorial officials in the West) to identify its deviants and punish them equitably and discreetly increased dramatically with the appearance of the penitentiary and its accompanying disciplinary procedures and routines.

But in practice, Montana's remote prison itself was hardly a bastion of rationality serving as a rural and western version of an all-seeing panopticon, ceaselessly surveying and controlling the population. Far from it. Due to its persistent overcrowding and early releases, poor hygiene, lack of uniform disciplinary procedures, inmate idleness, and occasional physical torture, Montana's prison was (and still is) a far cry from some perfectly efficient Foucauldian total institution. Chronic poverty consistently undermined penal discipline and punishment in territorial Montana. Like many of the other western territories, it was governed and administered by impoverished legislatures and distant and frequently misinformed or callously indifferent bureaucrats. Nor was the creation of the Montana territorial prison—or any other in the American West—a result of any logical, clear, or conscious decision of a territorial ruling class to use the institution as a subversive tool of social control with which those in power successfully subordinated, indoctrinated, and reformed recalcitrant members of the lower orders. One merely needs to reflect on the ever-increasing numbers of penitentiary inmates to see how ineffective the prison experience has been historically, if viewing the prison from a purely economic standpoint. It is anything but cost-effective.[64]

Nor did Montana's penitentiary disseminate a very powerful and persuasive message to potential wrongdoers as a means to deter crime. Though lynchings ended for the most part after the creation of the penitentiary in 1871, the crime rate in Montana did not decrease measurably. Instead, Montana incarcerated individuals at a remarkably high rate—significantly higher, in fact, than its territorial neighbors of Wyoming, Idaho, Washington, Utah, and Colorado.[65]

And yet the geographically removed territory of Montana, thousands of miles from Washington, D.C., and the center of national power, was able to quantify, categorize, and most important identify a number of its deviants with remarkable precision. And that ability also extended to the mentally infirm and to the criminally insane during this time. Procedures used at the penitentiary served the nearby insane asylum well, and its territorial history closely mirrors that of the penitentiary's in several key respects.[66]

In 1877 the territory contracted with a pair of local physician entrepreneurs, A. H. Mitchell and Charles Musigbrod, to provide custody and care for the territory's mentally ill at a site fifteen miles south of the penitentiary. Both men already had close ties to the territorial penitentiary— Mitchell had overseen its construction at several junctures, and Musigbrod had served briefly as its physician.[67] Like the nearby penitentiary, the asylum was austere in nearly all procedures and policies. The patients, like the prison inmates a few miles away, were with very few exceptions Montana's most indigent and incapable, committed from counties that did not wish to bear any expense for their care. As far as the State Board of Charities could judge in its 1894 tour of the asylum, "The persons there confined were, as a rule, originally of a low grade of intelligence and belong to the pauper and criminal classes." "This fact," board members concluded cryptically, "gives a peculiar character to the institution, while it keeps the management within narrow limits."[68]

Between 1877 and 1881 (the period for which the contractors maintained the earliest statistics), of the eighty admitted patients, forty-five, or 60 percent, were immigrants. The average age was around thirty-five.[69] Mirroring numbers in the early prison, the asylum confined only four women during those first four years, three of whose occupations were listed as housekeeper and the other as courtesan.[70] The stated occupations of both genders indicate their lower-class status: thirty-one identified themselves as laborers and another nineteen as miners, with such occupations as sailors, farmers, shoemakers, and blacksmiths constituting most of the remainder. Over 50 percent admitted that the duration of their present conditions extended back at least two years or more. Of the thirty-nine patients in residence on January 1, 1881, Dr. Mitchell reported that thirty-five were incurable.[71]

By the late 1880s, patient numbers began to increase concurrent with the territory's population increase. In 1889 alone the asylum admitted 104 patients. Between 1877 and 1891 it had admitted nearly 750 people and subsequently discharged approximately 54 percent of them. During the territorial years, nearly 17 percent of the patients died. For many people, confinement to Warm Springs was akin to a death sentence.[72]

All of the official reports emanating from Warm Springs over this twenty-plus-year period, 1877–1900, paint a rosy, even a glowing, picture. Even those individuals who strove to reform the system—the members of the State Board of Charities primarily—were pleased with the level of care, conditions, and treatment provided to the patients. The patients were well fed, the staff generally cheerful, the grounds well maintained. Of course, conditions that society may have considered humane and sanitary a century ago are deemed appalling now; the justifications for confining many of the individuals listed above is shocking enough. To compound matters, the staff permitted bathing, undergarment changing, and laundering only weekly. Over time, the coarse clothing the inmates wore became thoroughly soiled and ragged. Save for Native Americans starving to death on reservations during this period, those confined at Warm Springs were indeed Montana's, possibly even the American West's, most pitiable.[73]

The two physicians based their treatments on the concept of moral guardianship pioneered at the turn of the century by Philippe Pinel, combined with strong narcotics and daily doses of physical labor, even if the work had no economic value.[74] Mitchell and Musigbrod firmly believed in the efficacy of hard outdoor work, perhaps in part because whatever food their landholding produced could be used to feed the growing patient population and freed the monthly inmate lease payment to be invested in other ventures. Mitchell believed that "work—active out door employment—of some kind, is more important than all other treatment to the chronic insane," including, in his words, "indiscriminate drugging." As a result, "an effort is made to give as many of the inmates employment as is practicable. This is found in gardening, working on [the] farm, on walks and grounds, in graveling, cutting wood, etc." Rarely, Mitchell reported to the governor in 1881, did he have to resort to "mechanical restraint" or "the dark room," and only "during periods of excitement."[75]

Because there are no extant patient diaries, letters, complaints, reminiscences, or journals from this early period, it is difficult to contradict these official or quasi-official observations. On balance, the asylum was an adequately humane place *relative* to other nineteenth-century institutions. But there is evidence that contradicts the official reports. Beginning in 1894 the staff photographed every patient and included the photo in that person's medical record. Hundreds and eventually thousands of Montanans were photographed in their asylum-issued uniforms—uniforms made of rough material manufactured at the prison—striped uniforms exactly like those worn by convicted criminals. It was yet another attempt of the state to impose regimentation and order upon the disordered for which it cared. Yet in photo after photo, the uniforms are filthy and in tatters and hint at just exactly what conditions were like at the asylum.[76]

This much can be surmised. From 1877 to at least 1900 and beyond, the Montana Asylum for the Insane served mostly as a custodial institution providing minimal care for some of Montana's most helpless. Like the prison, it identified inmates, categorized them, examined them, made judgments about them, fed them, clothed them—in a matter of speaking—and photographed them. It kept them alive and relieved families of the burdensome chore of care. From one angle, the asylum served as a symbol of humanitarianism in a remote and rugged corner of the American West.[77]

Yet on the other hand, no one could resist his or her initial confinement and forfeiture of freedom. No person confined was in a position to refuse medical procedures. All had to wear the rough-textured and striped, prison-woven garb. Neither the state nor the proprietors ever compensated the patients for their labor in and around the institution; like those governing the prison, the asylum's rules stipulated merely that patients were to receive a suit of clothes, a hat, shoes, and twenty dollars upon discharge.[78] The contractual arrangement that the state maintained with the asylum's proprietors—long after it was fiscally necessary—enabled men of some wealth and modest power to become wealthier and a bit more powerful because of the unfortunate plight of the mentally ill in Montana. After 1889—and undoubtedly well before—the institution was chronically overcrowded, underfunded, unsanitary, and isolated from much of the rest of Montana and the urban areas whence came the majority of patients. It was, until 1912, managed by private individuals who stood to make significant profit from high numbers of patients and cost-saving measures.

The Warm Springs asylum, like the prison, was a response to disorder and irrationality in an age when a thinly populated, politically insignificant western territory and, eventually, state such as Montana self-consciously sought approval and respectability. The asylum, like the prison, was a means to help construct order out of disorder, normality out of abnormality, rationality out of irrationality as distant Montana moved into the twentieth century.[79]

The power of the United States's appointed judicial officers and contracted medical personnel to punish and confine became natural and legitimate while lynching and putative inhumanity quickly became both anachronistic and anathema. In Montana, certainly, and in the American West in general, the constituted government's power to incarcerate and to identify deviance became more widely and discreetly diffused through creation of federally funded territorial penitentiaries and, immediately on their heels, mental asylums. This reflected a movement from the chaos of sporadic lynch law and the incarceration of lesser offenders in improvised local facilities to a more uniform system of societally sanctioned and administered discipline and medical observation and procedures. Incarcerated individuals now found themselves in an altogether different and much closer relationship with societal power in the supposedly wide-open, wild, and woolly American West.

In Montana Territory criminals, the deviant, and the "abnormal" generally went from being public figures, whose punishment served as an important and symbolic community ritual, to being anonymous, dehumanized into the all-too-familiar "other" so characteristic of modern society's perception (or its desire not to be overly perceptive) of those it incarcerates and confines. With the establishment of a prison and asylum, the identification, disciplining, and punishment of criminal deviance and the segregation of the mentally infirm underwent a profound alteration in just a few short years. It transformed from a very public, political, and ceremonial spectacle of vengeful, violent physical force exacted upon a criminal's body by local communities to a more broadly diffused, more "economical," discreet, efficient, and state-run event carried out in secrecy behind (eventually) stone walls in remote institutions with affectations toward the reformation of criminality and the treatment of deviance. It was a means for an inchoate society to circumscribe a vast physical space and impose, at the minimum, institutional stability (arguably an essential precondition to the development of a capitalistic economy) where none had previously existed. In a historical instant, Montana's rituals moved from the sixteenth century to the late nineteenth. As a result, for better or worse, a remote territory began to assume some of the characteristics of a modernizing society.

4 / No Warden More Efficient: Frank Conley

There is no warden in the United States more efficient.

—WILLIAM A. CLARK, JR.

In March 1886, a twenty-two-year-old, nondescript undersheriff from remote Custer County in far-off eastern Montana delivered to the penitentiary Fred Choate, E. L. Hallenbeck, and Lincoln Lee, tried and convicted by the spring term of the territorial district court of assault, forgery, and grand larceny. Hitherto, the officer's brief claim to law enforcement notoriety had been as a member of the central Montana vigilance committee in 1884.[1] When he learned that one of the prison guards had recently quit, he decided to take the position and quickly relocated to Deer Lodge.

Though his prisoners all served their time and subsequently left the penitentiary within three years, Frank Conley stayed at the institution for the next thirty-five. He worked first as a guard and then, after Montana achieved statehood, he—along with Thomas McTague, another local undersheriff—ran the prison for eighteen years under a contracted lease agreement with the state. After Montana abandoned that arrangement and took over control of the prison, Conley became the warden in 1908. He remained as warden until 1921, when a progressive governor, Joseph M. Dixon, unceremoniously removed him.

During Conley's tenure, Montana's prison underwent a remarkable and dramatic transformation fueled by a huge increase in inmates and an equally substantial infrastructure expansion. Between 1890 and 1917, as Chart 4 reflects, the average monthly inmate population nearly tripled, from 242 in 1890 to a high of 698 in 1917.[2] The prison's physical layout and architecture changed accordingly, with numerous construction projects completed during the Conley era. And the state's position on inmate rehabilitation transformed as well, loosely mirroring national trends and progressive reform. Most significant, Frank Conley amassed such personal power over the administration, rehabilitation goals, and daily life of the inmates that his values, mostly fueled by a stubborn right-wing political ideology, overrode all others for more than thirty years. He controlled nearly all aspects of the prison's culture, and he enormously influenced penology in the state, while amassing a tidy personal fortune, until scandal finally caught up with him in 1921.

In March 1890, four months after Montana achieved statehood, the United States turned over its federal penitentiary at Deer Lodge to the new state. The 1889 Montana constitution created a board of prison commissioners, consisting of the governor, secretary of state, and the attorney general, to oversee the administration of the penitentiary. Because there was no longer any warden at the institution—the United States had supplied one between 1871 and 1890—the board entered into a contractual lease arrangement (an increasingly common management practice in many territories and states at the time) with Frank Conley and his business partner, Thomas McTague, each of whom had already begun to profit from local real estate investments.[3]

Under the terms of the arrangement, the state owned the land, prison buildings, and property within the prison. It paid Conley and McTague $.70 per prisoner per day for the first one hundred, and $1.00 for every prisoner per day above that number. The commissioners had the prerogative of inspecting the prison at any time, and they published an annual report (based on information supplied by the lessees). Conley and McTague, however, ran the prison, administered discipline, purchased supplies, and erected structures on the prison grounds as they saw fit.[4]

Almost immediately, the state benefited from the arrangement. The Montana government essentially washed its hands of the responsibility of

CHART 4

Average Number of Inmates Incarcerated Monthly, 1890–1920

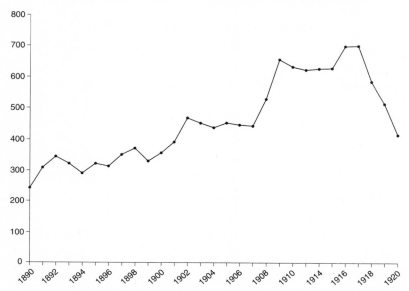

SOURCE: *Annual Report of the Board of Prison Commissioners, 1891–1906* and *1914–1932* (Helena: State Publishing Company, 1906 and 1933).

incarceration: it had only to pay the two lessees a set fee based on the numbers within the prison population. In fact, as the state grew—due in large measure to an economic boom in the 1880s fueled by the railroad and the mining industry—and the courts incarcerated more residents, it became cheaper for Montana to house prisoners. Accordingly, Conley and McTague could lower the rate they charged the state. By 1893 they had dropped the fee to $.40 a day per prisoner.[5] With the new state's ever-increasing population, it was apparent that the prison population would not decline. Indeed, since 1886 the population of the prison had never fallen below one hundred, and it had steadily risen since the expansion in 1885. As long as the lessees agreed to use the funds to care for (however loosely that could be defined), feed, and clothe the prisoners and to keep the physical plant in good and secure order, then the arrangement seemed beneficial to all parties.

In fact, the venture at Deer Lodge soon became such an economic bonanza that it became increasingly difficult for the prison commissioners—or any other state official—to look too objectively at the management of the institution under the lessees. By 1893 Conley had inmate work crews constructing buildings on the prison grounds and assisting in other public works projects. He devised a trustee program that allowed inmates to work outside of the prison proper. They even built roads in the rugged mountains around Flathead Lake, some 120 miles west of Deer Lodge, and in surrounding counties. All of this construction came at a considerable savings to the state. Montana now managed to identify and incarcerate its criminals and deviants *and* cheaply enlarge its prison and the asylum at Warm Springs and build roads and bridges in the rough, mountainous, western Montana terrain. With Conley in charge, the prison finally began, literally and figuratively, to work.[6]

Under the lease arrangement, idle inmates, long a problem during the territorial years, now had steady employment because Conley and McTague had a personal and vested economic incentive to employ them. In nearly all nineteenth-century American prisons, wardens and other administrators used physical labor, a fundamental, if not *the* fundamental, element of the capitalist ethos, as the chief means of punishment and reformation.[7] In the very literal sense, work set one free as the staff inextricably tied an inmate's productivity to his or her chance for early release. When promulgating its extensive initial rules for governing the prison in 1891, the Board of Prison Commissioners stated, "It will be incumbent upon the contractors of the prison to give the strictest attention to the conduct and character of every prisoner, and to advise themselves as to the behavior of every prisoner," particularly "his industry, alacrity and zeal *in the execution of any work* that may be assigned to him."[8] In 1892 in their annual report, the commissioners justified increased labor at the prison:

> Industry is one of the first lessons that should be taught in a prison. Work
> is one of the greatest reformers and the chief aid to the reformation of a man
> is to teach him to make his living. The thing to be attained, if possible is such
> an employment or trade.[9]

Conley was even more candid:

> The work done by the men in the way of road construction is itself of ines-
> timable value to the state and counties; and greater still are the benefits derived
> by the prisoners. The outside work, the absence of physical restraint, and
> the trust and confidence instill in each man a sense of pride, both for him-
> self and for his work. He values his advantages and his privileges. He does
> not brood and ponder over his sufferings and wrongs, his failures and dis-
> appointments. He awakens to a new appreciation of life and determines to
> make a better future.[10]

As the Board of Prison Commissioners noted in its annual report in 1893,
"Both the morals and the health of convicts can be improved by the mind
and muscles being interested in employment. There is no place where more
evil can arise by reason of enforced idleness than in a prison." Idleness, commissioners concluded, led to "physical decay, moral weakness, and insanity."[11] Indeed, work might even alleviate the dreaded "moral weakness" (a
euphemism for homosexuality), which officials had long considered the
scourge of penitentiary life. In 1905 a special legislative investigating committee touring the prison recognized that there was "foundation to the
charge" that "immoral practices and unmentionable crimes exist to a certain extent" within the penitentiary. The committee was of the opinion,
shared by "the wardens[,] that a practical solution as a means of stopping
or diminishing" the homosexual behavior "would be to give the men outdoor hard work to occupy their minds." Hard, "manly" labor, apparently,
could "cure" homosexuality.[12]

Besides its alleged curative and masculinizing powers and its assist to
Montana's economy, inmate labor directly benefited the penitentiary in its
day-to-day operation. By 1892 Conley and McTague had purchased a
ranch outside of Deer Lodge and used inmates to raise produce to feed the
burgeoning prison population, which, by 1893, stood at over 300. Conley
and McTague thus could run the prison still more cheaply and underbid
any potential competition, or at least make any buyout prohibitively
expensive, during periodic renewals of the lease, particularly after they purchased their own equipment and used it at the prison.[13]

Despite the fact that Montana (and much of the rest of the nation) languished during the down years after the Panic of 1893, the prison had skipped nary a beat as Conley and McTague had inmates construct a sandstone wall, two new cellblocks, and numerous storage facilities on the prison grounds (and at the ranch) between 1892 and 1896. The expansion of the cellblocks and the wall were particular sources of pride for both the lessees and state officials. One block housed 164 inmates, and the other, completed in 1896, had space for 256. There were four tiers and 32 cells per tier. Each cell was six feet wide by eight feet long by seven feet four inches high. Imposing gothic-style guard turrets stood at each of the four corners. The wall rose an imposing twenty-four feet high, bore four and half feet underground, and was two feet thick aboveground and three and half feet wide underground. Additional guard towers stood every 300 feet along the wall. There could be no possibility of escape over—or under—the wall.[14]

The facilities could now accommodate more prisoners, and the courts obliged; between 1890 and 1893 the inmate population rose over 33 percent, and Montana now had an even larger pool of free labor. The lease system, of course, saved the cash-strapped state the heavy expense of paying contracted labor—a remarkable feat considering that the nearby copper-mining center of Butte contained "one of the strongest labor bastions in America," according to one labor historian. But there is no evidence to suggest that organized labor paid much attention to the escapades at the prison; throughout the 1890s and after the turn of the century it remained curiously silent on the issue. This stood in marked contrast to other states where big labor challenged and vigorously opposed the use of inmate labor.[15]

The arrangement was beneficial to the town of Deer Lodge, too. Many of the local merchants and politicians, for good reason, were especially supportive of Conley's endeavors and the expanded prison. Conley purchased goods from their stores, and they were able to hire cheap labor at a moment's notice. Inmates performed minor city service tasks, such as landscaping public grounds, and built and repaired roads in the surrounding valley.[16]

When rumor spread in 1893 that the state was contemplating building a companion to the Deer Lodge institution in Billings (an Eastern Montana State Prison) as a brazen political bribe to entice that city's support for locating the permanent state capitol in Helena, some merchants in Deer Lodge believed, incorrectly, that the state planned to close the Deer Lodge penitentiary.[17] They petitioned the legislature and vigorously argued that "to remove the prison to any other place would entail an enormous and wholly unnecessary expense; to remove it to Billings would be the acme of unwise and recklessly extravagant legislation, which neither your consciences nor your constituents would approve."[18] Nearly every one of the petition signers had some sort of economic or political association with Conley and did business with the penitentiary. In the end, the dual prison scheme failed, mostly due to the economic difficulties Montana faced in the wake of the larger national economic depression of 1893. But in Deer Lodge, even the fleeting rumor of the loss of such an important economic asset was enough to set off shock waves.

But above all else, the lease arrangement was beneficial to Conley and McTague, and they quickly set about consolidating their personal power in Deer Lodge. They ensured that their prison operation was so successful that the state would be hard-pressed and unwise to follow any other course with any other party. Within a few months of securing their initial contract in 1890, Conley and McTague purchased and leased prime ranch property west of Deer Lodge. Ultimately their ranch holdings encompassed some 23,000 acres in the Deer Lodge Valley.[19] Quickly they diversified and began raising hogs, chickens, cattle—both dairy and beef—grain and hay, and vegetables, using inmate labor. Eventually Conley assumed more of the daily administrative responsibilities of the prison, while his personal financial and political interests expanded.[20]

Though he was often tactless and lacked social sophistication, Conley's rapid and hardnosed rise to wealth brought him into an ever-expanding circle of the economically powerful in the state, including the ruthless Butte mining magnate, self-made multimillionaire, and former Deer Lodge banker William Andrews Clark and his sons. Conley married a socialite from Missoula and took on all the trappings of a gentleman. In addition to acquiring vast tracts of prime Deer Lodge valley real estate, he traveled by an inmate-chauffeured limousine, developed a taste for racehorses and purebred livestock (and he even had a racetrack constructed by inmate labor outside of Deer Lodge), hosted private prizefights for his friends and associates, and entertained guests in an opulent $30,000 bungalow across from the prison, "finished," as one newspaper reported, "in solid mahogany and the dining room paneled in walnut from the forests of Russia." Eventually a logging camp, sawmill, icehouses, and a brickyard appeared on the Conley and McTague ranch, as did a lake—complete with summer homes for both men—a trout hatchery, and a private game reserve. Conley managed all of this on a salary that never exceeded $4,000 per year.[21]

Yet Conley and McTague saw nothing improper in their use of inmates to acquire their personal Montana fiefdoms; they could easily rationalize by claiming that overall they were saving the state a considerable amount of money and they were rehabilitating inmates. Because of the wealth now at stake, inmates, already on the lowest social stratum, became fungible— mere cogs in Conley's money-making and the state's road-building machines. Based solely on economic considerations, the Montana prison had become what many observers considered a successful institution. For the state of Montana, the community of Deer Lodge, and for Frank Conley and Thomas McTague, crime did, indeed, pay.

Even more important to him, Conley—because of his increased wealth, status, and financial clout and despite being "unencumbered," as one Montana historian has described him, "by more than a modicum of formal education"—soon became the town's (and surrounding area's) boss politician.[22] He won the Deer Lodge mayoral office in 1892, serving through 1893, again from 1895 to 1903, and then again from 1907 until 1929. Because of Conley's expanding financial and political muscle, his flourishing relationship with big business in the state, his blustery personality, as well as his sheer imposing physical stature (he stood six feet six inches tall and weighed more than 300 pounds), few dared cross him. As a journalist advised U.S. Senator Thomas Carter prior to his re-election bid in 1912, "Conley seems to be the real boss of Deer Lodge and his methods have made him many enemies in the town." For obvious reasons, "the union men dislike him, . . . and yet he seems to be the really big man in the town. He should be very valuable to you if you can keep him from using loud-mouthed and strong-arm methods."[23]

Obviously, the lease system in the hands of someone such as Conley was well-suited for abuse, and problems should have been apparent to the state government from the start. In late 1891 the newly created board of prison commissioners formally entertained a complaint from Thomas Powers, who had served a year in the penitentiary after being convicted of grand larceny in 1890. After an uneventful prison stay, Powers leveled a variety of charges against the proprietors, reserving most of his criticism for Conley.

The former inmate told the board that during his sentence he witnessed Conley and McTague provide themselves with inmate cooks at their private residences and that inmates supplied free labor for various minor construction projects around Deer Lodge, including a shooting gallery for Mr. Conley and associates. He also detailed how inmates built a store for an anonymous "college graduate," cut wood, and shod horses—free of charge—for Deer Lodge residents. More damaging, Conley's brother, James, Powers revealed, took a group of women fishing for two nights, accompanied by an inmate (ostensibly used as a servant). Finally, and perhaps most harmful, Powers accused Conley of submitting false warrants to the state in relation to clothing monies. Apparently not all released prisoners were being issued their suit of free clothes, a tradition since the territorial period and mandated by state regulations, and some prisoners had to furnish their own. Powers, evidently an experienced inmate, told the board that Deer Lodge "does not compare with [prisons] back east, and that they believe in moral suasion in eastern institutions, and that men receive so much schooling, and when they are released they are not in a worse condition than when they went in."[24] Powers also related how the prison physician was selling medical supplies to prisoners, and he described a "dungeon," a "bullring in the middle of the floor; and a ring in the ceiling." At one point, Powers revealed, a piqued Conley made the remark, within earshot of inmates, that "he would show some of these smart ducks what punishment was."[25]

Naturally, the grousing of disgruntled former convicts must be viewed skeptically, but it is beyond dispute that Conley did indeed show prisoners punishment. Reports of a severe disciplinary regime began trickling out of the institution nearly from the outset of Conley's tenure. Guards logged punishments for dozens of infractions ranging from the minor and benign—"dancing in cell," "talking at table," "refusing to work"—to the more serious and deadly—"possessing knife" and "assault." Offenders could expect, on the average, a week to ten days in a darkened cell on bread and water, though particularly recalcitrant inmates could receive as much as seventy-five days of such punishment.[26] After a mostly glowing report of all the efforts the contractors had made on behalf of the physical improvements of the penitentiary, a journalist from nearby Anaconda, after a tour of the prison in 1895, reported:

> Alas for the poor devil at Deer Lodge whose perversity earns him repeated terms of solitude in the dungeon. One cannot resist the conclusion that such a man is in the right place when he is a prison's inmate—he must be utterly wrong. You go into the cellar of the main building to reach the dungeon. It is a black hole, unspeakably gloomy. Its wall and floor and top are cold-looking blocks of stone. Light is excluded: two massive doors shut out the inmate from the world—no human being is within calling distance. At intervals, an attendant passes in the daily allowance of bread and water. It is a bare cell, its only furnishing is a little straw scattered over the floor. A man of sensibility or self-respect must feel that indeed he is under the grinding of the iron heel when the hours crawl along that measure his time in this horrible solitude. I saw a poor wretch released after twenty-one days of dungeon punishment. His garb was in tatters, his beard an ugly stubble, his eyes bloodshot. He had the gauntiness [sic] in feature of a wasted consumptive. He was shackled. He was a man of stalwart frame, but his bony hands looked ugly. He might as well have been three weeks out of the world. . . . Brought out of the gruesome companionship of darkness, the glorious light of the early afternoon seemed to daze the man. For a time, in the prison yard, he acted like one who was an utter stranger to this earth. In a place with every inch of which a long term of service had made him familiar, he seemed at first to have no idea of his bearings.[27]

Several years later another former inmate, Thomas O'Brien, went so far as to publish a book, *Infamy Immortal,* which, among other things, described his stay in the penitentiary. O'Brien charged Conley with assaulting an inmate with a blackjack to the point of causing his subsequent death; utilizing inmate labor for his own personal gain while punishing those who refused to go out and work; employing inmates as servants in private dwellings in Deer Lodge (echoing Powers's earlier charge); striking a sweetheart deal with a Deer Lodge lawyer employed solely to secure pardons for inmates; bribing a member of the State Board of Charities to make a favorable report on the penitentiary; releasing O'Brien (and other inmates) without sufficient clothing and with worn-out shoes; and, finally, allowing a female prisoner to become pregnant while incarcerated and then getting her quietly pardoned.[28]

Perhaps these inmates held grudges and their stories are unreliable, though neither their respective testimony nor their demeanor while in prison revealed such. Both served their sentences without documented incident, and neither had broken any of the disciplinary rules; each received an early release. Their stays were average in all respects. The Board of Prison Commissioners did not comment publicly on Powers's allegations and considered ultimately "all the grievances complained of" as "covered by rules."[29] A special joint committee of investigation appointed by the Montana House of Representatives in 1905 determined, categorically, that O'Brien's charges were baseless.[30] The matters then faded, and no other inmates came forward during the 1890s to corroborate Powers's accusations or, after the turn of the century, to bolster O'Brien's.

But both were portents of larger problems the state was to encounter later during Conley's reign, rumored though never fully substantiated until his ouster in 1921, namely his chronic use and abuse of state property for his own private gain.[31] The protracted sweetheart deal at the prison reveals the wide latitude the Montana government was willing to allow in its profitable marriage with Conley and McTague. Not surprisingly, various legislative investigating committees, charged by the state constitution with periodically investigating the prison, rarely found anything amiss. Though as early as 1891 a senate committee admitted, "The prison [is] very much crowded" and "the present buildings . . . entirely inadequate to accommodate the prisoners now confined therein," it had "not but words of praise for the present managers of the prison in the way they are fulfilling their contract with the State." It urged "the continuance of the Contract System in the management of the prison and keeping of the prisoners, as being more economical, and the best, in many other ways."[32] Clearly, it was economical.[33]

By the late 1890s, the appalling state of prisons and mental institutions increasingly captured the attention of progressive reformers and prompted a transformation in the administration of social and criminal justice. Unquestionably, improving prison conditions became central to many local and national initiatives.[34] The reformers, both male and female, advocated, among other things, professionalization of the police forces and later reform of the court system, its judicial officers, and eventually wardens and prison staffs.[35] The key, ultimately, was the reformation of the criminal so he or she might be assimilated into society as a productive and nonrecidivist citizen. Juvenile justice, particularly, was a progressive focus. But adult reformation also captured the attention of progressive-spirited penologists such as Thomas Mott Osborne, chairman of the New York State Prison Reform Commission in the early years of the twentieth century, and members of the National Prison Congress, which had met periodically since the 1870s, publishing a journal and holding conventions. Even Theodore Roosevelt in 1913 chimed in with ideas on punishment and penology and dubbed the movement "the New Penology."[36]

Probably the most striking deviation from past practices was the attention this new penology placed on individualized treatment, reflected most dramatically in the changing methods judges used to sentence individuals to prison. Until the 1890s in most states—Montana included—judges sentenced individuals to fixed terms for specific crimes based on the severity of the infraction and regardless of the individual's character or past record. In Montana, for example, conviction for grand larceny usually meant a sentence of one year in prison, and second-degree murder brought twenty years. Judges were bound by these codified, set punishments and sentenced individuals during the 1870s through the 1890s accordingly.[37]

But progressive reformers, in sharp contrast to their predecessors, generally held that individuals were products of their social environments. Biological, social, or psychological factors, and not some innate sinfulness or lack of character, conspired against these individuals in their descent into crime. Thus, each person was to be judged and subsequently sentenced according to a variety of factors: the individual's past criminal record, his or her home life, the presence of alcohol or addictive drugs in the commission of the particular crime, remorse exhibited by the individual, amount of education, and so on. These determinants and variables allowed prison specialists, or penologists as they were more often referred to now—reflecting another strain of progressivism, the increasing reliance on educated specialists or technicians to solve social problems—wider discretion in their dealings with prison inmates.

In the field of jurisprudence, the indeterminate sentence, buttressed by newer concepts of parole and probation, gradually came to replace the fixed sentences previously meted out by jurists. Judges eventually began sentencing criminal offenders to sentences with minimum and maximum terms. By the late 1890s, a conviction of grand larceny, depending on the gravity of the crime, the age of the individual, and his or her background, carried a sentence of not fewer than six months to no more than eighteen, or twenty-four, again depending upon judicial discretion. In 1900 the National Prison Association formally adopted the philosophy of indeterminate sentencing and advocated its usage throughout the United States.[38] Montana, slow to act, finally adopted the practice officially in 1915 by legislative fiat.[39]

Education was also a cornerstone of progressivism, and many reformers vigorously championed the benefits of a rigorous, rational, and comprehensive education for all of society's members as a means by which society could overcome its myriad ills. Not surprisingly, a new emphasis on educating and reforming both the criminal and ultimately society's evils within the prison walls became increasingly prevalent around the turn of the century.[40]

This new ideology fundamentally altered the way prison staffs viewed and dealt with the incarcerated individual. Primarily, they placed much greater emphasis on a person's behavior in prison than had been the case in the past. It also restructured the relationship between inmate and warden. In Montana, because the staff consisted of Conley and McTague and a handful of guards, prison officials accumulated an enormous amount of discretionary *personal* power over an individual's fate while incarcerated. Learning to accept work in Conley's system— cheerfully—now became a means for an individual to prove that he or she was reformed and deserving of an early release.

Almost from the state's inception, policymakers had begun incorporating some of the new philosophy about the nature and function of the penitentiary in society. During the state constitutional debates in 1889, Judge Hiram Knowles of Silverbow County voiced his strong opposition to altering section 23 of Montana's revised legal code, which stated: "Laws for the punishment of crime shall be founded on the principle of reformation and prevention, and not of vindictive justice." "I hope that we will not strike out that provision," Knowles enjoined, because

> it does mean a good deal. It means that the punishment for crime shall be with the view of reforming the criminal, and with the view to prevent in the future, his committing the same crime. Instead of incarcerating him simply as a punishment, without any other object in view than to simply punish a man is a kind of spirit of revenge, he is put there for the purposes of reformation and prevention. That is all there is to it. The idea is that the punishment shall be somewhat with a view to reform the man, making him a better man. . . . If we are to put a man there, simply for the purpose of punishing him . . . [that] seems to me to be a preposterous proposition.[41]

Delegate Bickford from Missoula concurred. Punishment without vengeance, he declared, "is one of the progressive ideas of our present civilization, and one of the ideas which perhaps will shine as brightly in the years to come as any other—that our laws are based upon principles of humanity and not upon principles of revenge."[42] The section stood, and the convention ultimately incorporated it into the state's legal code.

Progressive ideology at the prison itself trickled slowly into Conley's thinking. After a benefactor donated some musical instruments, he allowed the inmates to create a concert band, and thereafter over the years they serenaded the Deer Lodge community with occasional public concerts. The lessees and the Board of Prison Commissioners also established a sort of school within the prison in 1895. Inmate instructors taught English grammar, bookkeeping, penmanship, typewriting, telegraphy, and photography. In 1899 a Chicago newspaper described the school in glowing terms:

> It is rather unusual to see within prison walls hundreds of men of all ages and nationalities patiently mastering the various branches, from reading and

spelling up to higher mathematics, to hear the click of typewriters and the hum of recitation classes, interspersed with lessons in music, vocal and instrumental, but this is what may be seen and heard in the state penitentiary.[43]

Nonetheless, the state spent very little money during these years on educating inmates, preferring donations of books—William A. Clark, a Butte millionaire and by now Conley's personal friend, bestowed some 4,700 volumes in 1901.[44] When Conley did purchase a few books for the prison library, he made sure "that miscellaneous fiction comprise[d] the most popular" and that "socialist literature" or any kind "carrying a tinge of anarchism [was] absolutely prohibited."[45] Mainly the prison school became a halfhearted attempt to assimilate foreigners. By 1916 only forty students were taking active part in classes, most of them in English language classes.[46]

By and large, even as early as 1891, many of the 114 rules and regulations the state created to govern the administration of the penitentiary were progressive in nature. For example, according to rule 17, "it will be incumbent upon the contractors . . . to give the strictest attention to the conduct and character of every prisoner, and to advise themselves as to the behavior of every prisoner; his industry, alacrity and zeal in the execution of any work that may be assigned to him within the prison walls." And rule 17 also outlined the conduct of the contractors in regard to the internal punishment of prisoners. "In awarding punishment," it admonished,

> [the contractors] shall take into consideration the age, previous conduct, habits, and disposition of the offender; . . . and in the administration of punishment, they shall take special care to deprive it of all appearance of personal vindictiveness; even under great provocation.[47]

And thus, on balance, the changing public attitudes, embodied in progressivism, may have had a positive influence on the regime at the new Montana State Prison: prisoners at least had more opportunity to relieve the tedium of life inside their cells through outside labor, though it might have entailed, ironically, building their own cellblocks, as it did in both 1896 and 1912. Conley did allow musical expression and some education. Clark even donated funds in 1917 for the creation of small movie theater, which Conley wholeheartedly endorsed, though he used it as a disciplinary tool immediately (refractory inmates lost theater-going privileges). These were all changes that, arguably, improved and meliorated the monotony of prison life. And Conley, partially as a result of the increasingly enormous personal stake he had in the prison, took an individualized, paternalistic approach to inmates, as his partner, McTague, pursued other business interests. Conley held a warden's court daily to address inmate infractions and to hear grievances, and he used his extensive business contacts on the outside to find employment for some released inmates. But in regard to progressive-based innovations or imaginative, cutting-edge approaches, Conley was impervious.

Following the tradition at the prison, it was solely Conley's decision whether or not to release an inmate early for good behavior or to recommend that the prison commissioners or governor pardon or commute an individual's sentence. Allowing the warden such wide license in determining what constituted a reformation of character of a particular individual left significant latitude for Conley's personal bias to intrude. Conley had always had a patronizing attitude toward prisoners. As he told one reporter, "The longer I am here the more convinced I become that 50 percent of the men sent to prison for crime are not criminal at heart, but are of defective mentality. Most of the prisoners are like children and need supervision."[48] Furthermore, he believed that "the logical medium for the cultivation of respect for law and order is the home and the public school," because "from my experience with criminals I have learned that a large percentage owe their downfall . . . to the lack of a moral code."[49]

After the turn of the century, his attitude toward the state's inmates became less paternalistic and more distant. In 1908 during a warden's court, an inmate attacked Conley and his assistant, killing the latter and wounding Conley severely. As a reporter recalled, after that "Conley's attitude toward the prisoners changed. . . . When a real tough prisoner came to Deer Lodge, Conley would assure him that if he behaved and caused no trouble he would see that he was paroled long before he otherwise would."[50]

Conley also had little use for any type of legislated prison reform. "All over the United States," he told another newspaper:

there is at present going a steady agitation for prison reform, and interest in the improvement of prison life seems to be in the air. Many fantastic and unprofitable, so-called reforms and innovations are being tried; a system of coddling inmates of prisons seems to be the most popular. Reforms on the whole do not sufficiently emphasize the importance of awakening the latent moral sense of the criminal which would show him the futility of the viola- tion of a law with the consequent loss of liberty.[51]

Conley managed to attend at least one American Prison Association meeting, in 1916. Afterward, he described the gathering as a place "where long-haired men and short-haired women sought to reform prisoners by prayer," and he felt that his attendance had been a waste of time.[52]

Worse still, Conley was racist, nativist, and, by the beginning of the twen- tieth century, openly anti-union. Montana passed some of the most repres- sive antisedition legislation in the nation in 1917, aimed primarily at muzzling the Industrial Workers of the World (I.W.W.), German immi- grants, and the primarily ethnic-minority working-class miners in the crit- ical Butte copper mines.[53] Conley did his part for the state and the war effort by denying parole and release of individuals whom he unilaterally deemed threats to society, regardless of their comportment in the penitentiary. Much of his correspondence during the war is revealing.

In response to a letter from an attorney regarding the release of his client, Conley responded, "From what I have seen of him I think he is pro-German and ought to stay here. Any man who has been in the United States as long as he has ought to talk English at least."[54] After the gover- nor inquired about the status of another German, Fred Rodewald, Con- ley replied, "[I] will say he will be eligible to parole the 1st of September. I have offered him several chances to go to work on the outside but he refuses. He seems to be one of these Germans who are dissatisfied with conditions of this country."[55] To an immigration agent he wrote: "Inclosed find copy of letter sent by Fred O. Christensen. He is the party I phoned you about yesterday; you can readily see by the tone of this letter that he better be returned to the old country at once. If I had my way this kind of people would be stood up against the wall and shot."[56] To an individ- ual who complained to Conley about an insulting letter he received from an inmate, the response was: "This man Reber is a foreigner and is very ignorant."[57]

The Montana judicial system agreed that such prisoners were not only ignorant but security threats as well. In 1918 alone, judges sentenced dozens of individuals to the penitentiary on dubious evidence, and the prison population soared.[58] On July 5, 1918, at the height of American military involvement in Europe, 726 individuals resided in the Montana prison, the largest number in the prison's forty-seven-year history and the highest population until the late 1960s.[59]

Perhaps because of his big-business sympathies and connections, Conley held a special and open disdain for those individuals affiliated with the I.W.W., known as Wobblies. And without doubt he was not alone in his hostility toward the I.W.W. The Montana legislature—through the passage of the 1917 antisedition act—practically declared open season on anyone affiliated with the Wobblies.[60] Conley once described an inmate as "lazy and an agitator . . . certainly the earmarks of an I.W.W."[61] To the wife of an inmate convicted of sedition during the height of the ultra-patriotic hysteria he wrote:

> In some cases it is possible to obtain a parole after serving half of the minimum sentence, but in the case of Seditionists it is different. If this country is not good enough to make a man loyal, he is certainly not entitled to its freedom. A man guilty of sedition will receive no favors from me. Your husband will have to do at least half his maximum sentence.[62]

Conley refused to recommend parole for Fritz Lang, convicted for "seditious talk," because, as the warden explained to the Board of Prison Commissioners, "there are a lot of Germans on the outside who ought to be in and when we get one in, we are going to keep him."[63] To another immigration inspector he wrote, "I have several I.W.W.s here that should be deported."[64] He reassured John H. McIntosh, a Butte businessman, that "if any of the I.W.W.s start any rough stuff here we will tend to them and tend to them good."[65] Finally, the warden begrudgingly admitted to the governor that William Dooley's conduct in prison "was good while here," surprising, as Conley "always considered him an I.W.W."[66]

Conley held black inmates in equally low regard. To a chief of police in Alberta he wrote:

> Enclosed find photo and description of a nigger Charles Smith who was released from here Feb. 6th, on parole. Shortly after he was paroled he with four others burglarized my summer home about five miles from here. I am very anxious to get a hold of him. If you will get a hold of him and deport him to the line I will guarantee to have an officer get him. He is a bad nigger and should be taken care of.[67]

In a letter to a woman who was contemplating a romantic relationship with a black man, he informed her that the man was "a half-baked nigger and I wouldn't waste any time with him."[68] Conley entrusted a black inmate, Oscar Johnson, as a local mail carrier outside the prison in 1918, but he soon learned that Johnson "sent a white woman a note and tried to make a date with her and if he had been successful in getting her to keep the appointment, I feel sure I would have had a rape case on my hands." Conley quickly reassigned Johnson back inside the prison.[69] Even the few Mexican Americans incarcerated in the prison did not escape Conley's disparagement. In a prerelease hearing for Fred Albo, the Board of Prison Commissioners could not decide whether to continue holding him or release him. The following exchange occurred:

> *Governor:* Hold him I think.
> *Secretary of State:* Go to it.
> *Attorney General:* It makes no difference if he is a Mexican?
> *Clerk:* The Warden hates Mexicans and recommends him. He must be a good
> man.
> *Governor:* All right, don't hold him.

Conley held a special disdain for homosexual inmates, considering them "degenerate punk[s] of the lowest type"; outdoor work could be their only salvation.[70]

There were other abuses, more long-lasting and much more encompassing than those exhibited by Conley's pettiness and strong-arm tactics toward inmates. Conley's failure to embrace reform would ultimately prove his undoing and result in the collapse of his suzerainty in the early 1920s. The context and complexities extended back decades.

Though a regional parvenu, Conley achieved a rapid rise to wealth and gentlemanly affectations, which brought him into an ever-expanding circle of the economically powerful in the state. His association with the upper echelons in Montana began shortly after he and McTague became lessees of the penitentiary in 1890. To protect itself financially, the state required that Conley and McTague find individuals willing to sign surety bonds to back them. S. E. Larabie, a prominent Deer Lodge banker and merchant, Frank Higgins, a Missoula merchant and capitalist, James A. Murray, a Butte banker, and Marcus Daly of Butte and later Anaconda's largest mine owner (and putatively, for a time, Montana's wealthiest man) each signed $50,000 surety bonds backing Conley and his enterprise at the state prison.[71] He had also gained some social credibility after marrying a Missoula socialite and the daughter of western Montana financier, C. P. Higgins, in 1902.

With the wealth came a degree of regional political clout, and the warden eventually became a force within the Republican party. Nevertheless, he managed to remain just bipartisan enough to garner occasional local Democratic support, and he even orchestrated a fete for the Democratic vice presidential candidate Franklin Roosevelt in 1920 at his Deer Lodge residence.[72] Other prominent national figures, including Theodore Roosevelt and Secretary of the Treasury William McAdoo, also paid visits. Lesser lights, such as the Montana governors Samuel V. Stewart and Edwin L. Norris and at least two Montana judges, William F. Clancy and Edward Harney, frequently enjoyed Conley's hospitality. In addition to these prominent guests, the warden entertained Cornelius "Con" Kelley, John G. Morony, and J. Bruce Kremer, executives of the powerful Anaconda Copper Mining Company, as well as the multimillionaire mining and banking magnate William A. Clark and his son, William A. Clark, Jr.[73]

Conley's connections were mainly a result of the emergence of Butte, some forty miles east of Deer Lodge. By the 1890s the formerly rough mining camp had established itself as one of the most powerful metal-mining centers in the world and a regional economic and political colossus. Butte mines produced some 41 percent of the world's copper by the 1890s. Large "copper kings," the famous ruthless millionaire capitalists Clark, Marcus Daly, and F. Augustus Heinze, in order to drive up the price of their own holdings, variously attempted to corner the world market on copper, subjugate each other, and eventually ward off a takeover of the fabulously profitable Butte and Anaconda mines by the world's largest monopoly, John D. Rockefeller's leviathan Standard Oil, which moved into the copper arena around the turn of the century.[74]

Clark, one of the world's wealthiest men by the turn of the century, had gotten his financial start by opening a bank in Deer Lodge in 1872. He and his sons, who increasingly controlled the Clark fortune by the turn of the century, and Conley had forged something of a friendship during Conley's lessee years.[75] At various points Clark donated musical instruments, books, and a movie theater to the prison, and apparently he had taken at least a passing interest in the affairs of the prison. He attended the gala for Roosevelt at Conley's house in 1920, as well as other Conley social functions, and he and his sons occasionally frequented concerts performed by the prison band.

Beyond their interest in the prison, what both men shared was a close relationship with the Amalgamated Copper Mining Company and later with its corporate successor, the Anaconda Copper Mining Company, owned and controlled by executives from John D. Rockefeller's Standard Oil empire after 1906. The "A.C.M." or simply "the Company," as it was known throughout the state, had been taken over by executives from Standard Oil after a protracted legal battle, and the corporation moved quickly to gain a stranglehold on Montana public opinion, economics, and politics. By 1915 Rockefeller's minions had bought out and outmaneuvered (and outlasted) the copper barons, cornered most of the state's important newspapers, and generously financed sympathetic local politicians (including Conley) and judges—nearly all of whom were Republican. In short order, the Company had successfully created an "invisible government" within the state.[76] Because of Conley's political sway in the Deer Lodge Valley, he easily fell into the A.C.M. camp. As one observer noted, by 1908 Conley was "hand in glove with the Anaconda Company," and the warden freely admitted to "being friendly with the Amalgamated."[77]

Did Conley use the state prison as part of the invisible government? Though the extent of Conley's culpability may never be fully known, he did purchase all of the prison electrical, plumbing, and sundry construction supplies from the Company-owned supply business in Butte (but then, so did almost everyone else). He did entertain, frequently and lavishly, Company executives at his Deer Lodge residence, where inmates cooked and served food produced on the prison ranch.[78] As warden, he did his best to ensure that union radicals—particularly those affiliated with the I.W.W. and active in nearby Butte and especially vocal in their opposition to corporate Montana—would remain in prison, even beyond the expiration of their sentences. And there is even some indirect evidence that he offered the use of inmates to the A.C.M. to break the 1914 Butte Miners Union strike then paralyzing the Butte mines and impeding corporate profits. The governor at the time, Sam Stewart, declared martial law in September of 1914 and enlisted Conley as the city's provost marshal. The local paper assured its readers that the warden, "terror to evil-doers," would "round up the gang of ex-convicts, dynamiters, I.W.W. agitators, and a large number of plug-uglies and hold-up men who terrorized Butte for months."[79]

By about 1920 Conley's brazen financial transactions at the prison had become a source of embarrassment and growing controversy in progressive political circles around the state. Most damaging, and the subject of speculation for years, Conley used the prison, its various ranches, and its free labor to further his own personal gain, a circumstance not lost on the state's increasingly militant working class. In an especially damaging exposé in 1919, a Great Falls–based daily, the *Montana Nonpartisan*, openly charged what was widely rumored throughout the state:

> In Deer Lodge . . . 'Inside Friends' of the Warden and of the 'Powers that be' can get all the farm and other help they need from the institution—Gratis. It is also currently reported and seemingly on A1 authority that scads of men from the institution are used during the haying season on the Big Hole ranches of the Copper Barons.

Furthermore, "our fat friend [Conley] also has a fine farm of his own, but his help costs nothing." The paper concluded that "a full investigation of the methods used" at the penitentiary was in order because, most damning, "this immense overfed Colossus is the Real Governor of the State."[80]

By the early 1920s Conley's cheeky association with the A.C.M. and his freewheeling tactics were egregious enough for Governor Joseph M. Dixon to act. Dixon had been a force in both national and regional politics, having served as Montana's U.S. senator from 1907 to 1913 and then losing his re-election bid on a "put the Amalgamated out of Montana politics" platform in 1912.[81] It was in the Senate that he caught the eye of President Theodore Roosevelt, who enlisted him as campaign manager of his failed 1912 progressive, Bull-Moose party presidential campaign. During this time, Dixon had gradually become one of the more powerful and visible progressives in the state, gaining popularity by the late teens through his advocacy of mining taxation reform and open criticism of the Anaconda Company, increasingly popular stances among Montana's growing numbers of working-class and anticorporate activists.[82] Dixon, elected the Republican governor in 1920 over his Democratic opponent, Burton K. Wheeler, saw in the Conley situation an opportunity to clean up and make more efficient state government (twin progressive themes) *and* use a backdoor approach to attack the A.C.M.

In early 1921, embarrassed by Conley's presence in his new administration and despite having received "an indirect warning from 'the Big Outfit,'" (as Dixon termed the A.C.M.) not to remove Conley, the new governor resolved "to restore government in Montana to normal conditions and away from supervisory control by any form of invisible government" by removing the longtime warden.[83] Publicly, his pretext was a $138,000 budget deficit at the prison the previous year. Privately, in a letter to Conley, Dixon justified his actions thus:

> I had first hoped that matters might be so adjusted as not to make it necessary to make any change in the wardenship, but, in the situation I am facing and some of the forces that are apparently determined to handicap me in the state administration, I feel that in order to carry out the work of the administration it will be better for everyone concerned if the man in charge of the State Prison should be one with whom I could work in perfect harmony without any mental reservation.[84]

Immediately Dixon faced a firestorm of opposition from the A.C.M., its "interlocking state press" as the governor rightly coined it (complete with its sensationalist headlines), and its high-powered legal team. William A. Clark, Jr., excoriated Dixon from his Los Angeles mansion, asserting that "there is no warden in the United States more efficient and more beloved than Mr. Conley." It was obvious, Clark charged, that Dixon's "antagonism toward the Anaconda Company is responsible for this one." The million-aire, who had financially assisted Dixon in his hard-fought gubernato-rial race against his fellow progressive Burton K. Wheeler, warned that if Dixon did not "reconsider" his decision and "reinstate Frank Conley," Clark would "withdraw all support of [Dixon] politically and of [his] adminis-tration."[85] Dixon responded by curtly advising Clark that as governor he was "necessarily in a position to know more in detail the actual needs at the Penitentiary" than Clark could be, sarcastically adding that he was "aware . . . that Mr. Conley has a great many warm friends whom he has entertained in the years past and who were adverse to seeing a change made in the wardenship."[86]

Dixon may have underestimated the intensity of opposition to his move. The Company papers churned out story after story, many of them of dubi-ous factual value, on Conley's success in running the prison and the incom-petence of his successor, M. W. Potter.[87] It was later established, nonetheless, that under Conley the prison cost Montana $342,428 to run in 1920. In 1921 under Potter it operated for $177,478.[88] Of course, in order to achieve such dramatic savings, Potter paroled several hundred inmates during late 1921 and 1922, inmates that the state had incarcerated during the war and the early years of Prohibition.[89]

Reports from Potter and others during the summer of 1921, as well as the ferocity of response from the A.C.M., began to rouse Dixon's suspicions even further about the extent of Conley's corrupt dealings with the prison, the Company, and the state. As a result, Dixon, over the strong opposition of several of his key advisors, including the state's attorney general, the influential Wellington Rankin (brother of Montana's famous congress-woman, Jeannette Rankin), ordered an investigation of the prison during Conley's long tenure. He appointed a supporter and attorney, T. H. Mac-

Donald, who, daunted by the enormity of the project, reluctantly agreed, leading what became a five-month investigation into Conley's finances and the prison's administration, focusing closely on purchasing contracts made by Conley.

MacDonald concluded his scathing summary report in November 1921 with a blunt assessment: "No man can make reasonable inquiry into the history of the Montana State Prison without being appalled that such a state of affairs has been permitted to exist. Every avenue of curtailment of expenses has been diverted into the private treasury of the former Warden and every industry at the Prison has been prostituted to his enrichment." MacDonald believed that Conley had bilked the state out of some $200,000 over the course of his tenure at Deer Lodge. The governor quickly ordered a full audit and pressed his reluctant attorney general for legal action.[90]

The investigator's report was not shocking—many had long suspected Conley was corrupt—but it startled readers with the scope of the former warden's abuse. The report implicated Conley in a number of unlawful acts between 1908 and 1921, including:

1) gutting the penitentiary's warehouse, garage, and machine shop just prior to his removal;

2) appropriating beef, assorted groceries and produce, cream, and butter for his private use in the amount of some $8,330;

3) using over a half *million* tons of state coal for his private residence;

4) using and maintaining thirteen private autos at state expense, running up a gas, oil, and maintenance bill of over $12,000 per *year* on the vehicles;[91]

5) using the prison's ranch to feed his private dairy herd and employing free inmate labor to care for and feed his livestock;

6) selling to the state (for use in the prison), dairy products and beef produced by the herd, at market rates;

7) selling pork to the prison, from his own herd, which had been fed on prison swill.[92]

After learning of the magnitude of the investigator's findings, Dixon, true to his progressivism, could "not escape the conviction that this institution has for years been run on a most extravagant basis with little regard for economic administration."[93] In the course of the ensuing winter, the governor, aware of the political firestorm that would follow, nevertheless pressed for, and received, a criminal indictment.

Incredibly, Conley responded, through his Company-supplied lawyer, the former Montana attorney general C. B. Nolan, by countersuing the Montana government, charging that the state owed *him* $120,000 in unpaid claims.[94] William Clark, Jr., keenly following the case from Los Angeles, stepped up the pressure on Dixon by warning the governor to "retire from the attitude you have taken regarding former Warden Conley; otherwise you are politically a back number."[95] Company-run papers across the state blasted Dixon's actions. The Anaconda *Standard,* in typical Company-controlled editorializing, lamented that it was "unfortunate that politics should interfere with so splendid a public servant [as Conley], and that years of patience and diligence and an intimate knowledge of a technical profession should be disregarded in order to reward a political follower or vent a petty spleen."[96]

After months of litigation, mainly engineered by Conley's lead lawyer to cloud the issues and inflame the public against Dixon, the case was tried in a Helena district court before Judge A. J. Horsky without a jury. Several dozen witnesses, including two former governors, Dixon himself, a former state attorney general, former inmates, and former guards, testified about the nature of the prison operation between 1908 and 1921.[97] Most of those who came to Conley's defense cited the fact that any agreements Conley made were often oral in nature, and it was difficult to recall the specifics. Conley himself took the stand for a full two weeks, explaining that he had never broken any written laws and that he had kept the state apprised constantly of the administration of the prison. At one point, in a jocular attempt to redirect criticism toward Dixon, Conley responded to cross-examination on his financial state:

> *Attorney General:* How much money did you have when you started in at the penitentiary?
>
> *Conley:* Just as much as Governor Dixon had when he went to Congress. We were both broke.[98]

The trial bore out the fact that after Conley spent thirty-five years at the prison as guard, contractor, and finally warden, his personal dealings—and property—had become indistinguishable from the state's. Attempts to replace Conley had been fruitless. In 1908, when the Board of Prison Commissioners opened bids for new contractors, F. A. Henderson and Jack Wyman from Butte actually underbid Conley and McTague. But after inventorying the property at the prison, state auditors discovered that the pair had amassed personal property that encompassed several dozen pages of inventory sheets and was worth thousands of dollars—property that was essential to the prison's daily operations and that the state could not afford to pay for. Conversely, the state's property filled only one page, and most of that was a listing of the physical structures. Montana, thus, was forced to stay in its marriage with Conley, abandon the contract system, and retain him as warden.[99]

Meanwhile, Judge Horsky determined that the issue was not whether Conley had illegally absconded with state funds but whether he had violated any written laws. Because the state never clearly delineated the nature of its relationship with Conley after 1908—it had terminated the lease arrangement but retained Conley and his property—the judge ruled that indeed no laws existed for Conley to violate. He acquitted Conley of virtually all of the state's charges. The judge also dismissed all but $632 of Conley's counter-claims, but Horsky ordered the state to pay the enormous cost of the lengthy trial. In a 25,000-word closing statement, Horsky concluded that "every act of Conley . . . was in the interest of the state of Montana."[100]

The executives of the A.C.M., despite their public support of Conley and despite Conley's cozy relationship with them, really cared little for his personal fate. Through the trial they used their press to attack Dixon, whom they viewed as eminently dangerous to their corporate vice grip on Montana's politics and economy because of his intractable and implacable desire to reform the tax code to their ultimate fiscal detriment. In the end, to them Conley was merely a blustering and disposable pawn in a much larger struggle for political hegemony in the state—hegemony the A.C.M. more or less maintained in Montana until well after World War II. Judge Horsky's verdict was a Pyrrhic victory, of sorts, for a discredited Conley and only a temporary one for the A.C.M.; Dixon ultimately threw his support behind a citizen-backed tax-reform initiative that passed in 1924. For the governor, as his biographer asserts, the verdict "became a vital link in the succession of events leading to [Dixon's] political destruction," namely, his 1924 re-election defeat.[101]

As for Conley, he remained in Deer Lodge until his death in 1939, his imprint indelibly stamped on the prison. For over three decades, almost single-handedly and without precedent, he influenced the course of incarceration, rehabilitation, and punishment in Montana. A new Montana prison, constructed in the 1970s, sits on Conley's former ranchlands—land acquired, in many ways, through the sweat of inmate labor—three miles outside of Deer Lodge.

5 / Getting Tough on Crime

1921 to the Present

"It was a hellhole there . . . the worst I'd ever seen."
—FLOYD POWELL, Montana State Prison warden, 1958–1962,
after his initial tour of the prison in 1958.

Frank Conley's greatest source of professional pride had been the amount of construction and physical improvements that inmates had accomplished during his long tenure. Under his reign the prison infrastructure, particularly cell capacity, had expanded enormously. Of course, the more cell space the state had, the more room it—or more precisely, the more its judges and juries—now had for convicted criminals. But there were now more facilities for the state to maintain, at least minimally. By the late 1920s, however, Montana's economy declined sharply because of falling wheat and copper prices. The prison simply was no longer the bargain it had been during Conley's administration. With the onset of the Great Depression the inmate population rose dramatically, and legislative appropriations to support imprisonment in Montana began to decrease even more sharply. By 1930, after a sluggish economic decade and stagnating general population growth, the prison census stood at 710, the highest it had been since the antisedition hysterics during World War I. The next year, 1931, it dropped only marginally, to 684. Slowly, the numbers declined, and they would not be equaled or surpassed until the 1960s (see Chart 5).

During the Depression, however, legislative appropriations from the

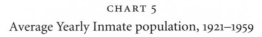

CHART 5

Average Yearly Inmate population, 1921–1959

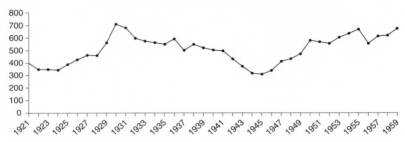

SOURCE: State Board of Prison Commissioners Annual Reports (Helena), 23rd–28th Reports, MHS.

cash-starved state did not keep up, and in fact declined; the physical plant itself—a source of pride after statehood—began to deteriorate markedly, particularly the 1896 cellblock, one of the two constructed by inmates during Conley's years.[1]

The older cellblock never had the luxury of interior plumbing; two buckets had to suffice in each cell: one for drinking water and the other for human waste. The electrical wiring, installed after the turn of the century, was woefully inadequate and could barely support a single, dim twenty-five-watt bulb in each individual cell; inmates could not even read by the light.[2]

In 1931 a legislative committee toured the prison and was shocked. It commented that the 1896 cellblock was "an eyesore to the state and is crying out in its filth and unsanitary condition. . . . The roof . . . is wood and makes the enclosure a veritable fire trap. In case of fire . . . each cell would have to be unlocked separately instead of modern, up-to-date lever systems. . . . The air is very foul for better ventilation is not possible." Inmates, moreover, were "lying idle, rotting away in stink and stench. The place as it is, is lousy with bed bugs and the cells are dark and grimy." Most appalling to the touring members were the cells themselves. "The cells are small and poorly lit with the aperture in the door barely large enough [to] look out from. No toilet accommodations are available to the inmates at night and they are forced to defecate and urinate in cans under their cots." After viewing the newer cellblock, the committee described the isolation area hewn from beneath the ground floor as "a hideous place to throw a man." These cells, which Conley had constructed for troublemakers, totaled six in number and were "right down in the bowels of the earth—mere cold, dark holes cut in solid stone." Even in the austere days of 1931 the committee recommended appropriating $300,000 to gut the structures and using inmates to perform the remodeling. Its recommendation, however, never made it to the legislative floor.[3] In the meantime, thousands of inmates passed through the institution in the ensuing decades.

After Conley's dismissal in 1921, Montana governors began to appoint men, as Dixon had explained to Conley, with whom they "could work in perfect harmony without any mental reservation."[4] The prison disappeared from the public eye for much of the next forty years. The warden's job became a political patronage position for the various governors, and a series of political hacks held the post. The various governors between 1924 and 1958 did not all take the business of running the prison seriously. Their warden appointees ranged from those with some passing experience in law enforcement (two rural county sheriffs and a sergeant in the Montana Highway Patrol) to those completely unprepared for the position (a state highway commissioner and road engineer, a postmaster from the tiny eastern Montana town of Baker, a cattle rancher, a conductor for the Milwaukee Railroad, and a former salesman with the Folgers Coffee Company).[5]

None had any professional penological experience, and few had the necessary administrative acumen required to run such an increasingly complex and sprawling organization as a modern state prison. Yet because of the precedent Conley had set, and simply because of the nature of the position, almost exclusive financial and administrative control of prison affairs rested with the warden. He implemented policy, he lobbied for new building projects (though other than razing the old territorial prison in 1931 and replacing it with a central administrative building, there were no new substantive building projects between 1931 and 1959), he formulated budgetary needs, and he hired and fired staff.

Warden Faye O. Burrell, who ran the institution from 1953 until early 1958, is a case study in the type of administrative incompetence that dominated between the 1930s and 1950s. Burrell was especially amateurish at managing both personnel and the prison budget, which was not surprising considering that his previous penal experience had been as the Ravalli County sheriff in charge of the two-cell county jail. In the early 1950s, the Montana legislature, aware of the rapidly advancing decrepitude of the prison, began to appropriate modestly increased funds for the upkeep of the physical plant. However, Burrell, frugal to a fault and administratively inept, simply did not spend his appropriations, allowing thousands of unspent dollars to revert to the general legislative fund. In 1955, for example, the legislature appropriated $105,000 to build a desperately needed minimum security building on Conley's old prison ranch outside of Deer Lodge. By late 1957 Burrell had spent only $125 of the money on the project. In the meantime, the prison population swelled and conditions worsened.[6]

The staff—the guard force and support personnel—were nonprofessional, poorly trained, and even more poorly paid. A visiting consultant observed in late 1957 that the Montana State Prison suffered with "the lowest employee morale" he had "ever encountered in a penal institution."[7] According to a study conducted in 1946, the pay of a prison guard in Montana ranked 115 out of 120 state and local institutions surveyed. Only several Arkansas and North Carolina facilities, each of which used inmate trustees as guards, ranked lower. The average starting salary nationally that year was $2,000 for a prison guard. In Montana, guards earned $1,200, some 40 percent less than the national average.[8] As one of the wardens complained to Governor Sam Ford in 1941, "The salaries paid to the Guards here are merely 'sheepherders wages,' and the sheepherder doesn't have to live in town and wear brass buttons and a uniform that he has to furnish himself."[9] In the mid-1950s, 80 percent of the guards at Deer Lodge were retirees over age fifty-five. Some of the guards were drifters who stayed in the position only temporarily; in 1957 alone the prison experienced a 75 percent turnover of the guard force.[10] The warden often performed no background check on an applicant, and prospective employees took no written examination. Once hired, prison guards received no formal training. It is miraculous that the prison remained as quiescent for as long as it did in the three decades after the Conley imbroglio.[11]

For inmates, there was hardly a less appealing prison in which to do time than the one offered by Montana by the mid-twentieth century. Vestiges of the old Auburn system began to creep back into the prison by the 1930s. The 1931 legislative subcommittee recorded the daily prison routine:

> The men file into the dining room when the gong sounds, with their arms crossed in front of them and in silence. They eat three times a day and seemed to observe the strictest kind of obedience to prison regulations. They file in, approximately 579 men, and sit on benches eight on a bench and two benches wide. They all sit facing the same way, looking into the throat of a formidable looking machine gun, perched on the top of a cage in front of the room.[12]

Despite Conley's personal enrichment and abuses of inmate labor during the course of his long tenure, prisoners could at least look forward to some type of outside employment to break the monotony of their sentences. Yet even before the Conley fiasco, the state had begun to curtail road-building and reduce the use of inmate labor outside of the prison; furthermore, legislation enacted during the Depression in order to protect organized labor prohibited the open sale of inmate-made goods, such as leather, shoes, or garments. The penitentiary did acquire Conley's ranch—which some inmates worked—and the state could offer employment for a handful of trustees as clerks in the Registrar of Motor Vehicles office adjacent to the prison. Yet few jobs existed within the prison compound itself, because Conley had focused inmate activities outside of the prison on his ranch properties or on road-building. The few jobs that were available were strictly of a service nature. Only garment and shoe shops, a laundry, a toy repair shop, the state's license plate plant, and a few positions in the infirmary employed inmate workers between 1930 and 1960. At any given time, only 200 or so inmates worked out of a total prison population averaging nearly 550. Idleness and lengthy cell time—often twenty-two hours a day—were commonplace by the 1940s and 1950s. The silent system dominated in the workplace too, as inmates were to "avoid all laughing and unnecessary noise, and to preserve entire silence except when it may be necessary to speak in relation to their wants, and in all such cases to speak in a low voice and respectful manner."[13]

Complicating both inmate life and the overall prison administration was the establishment of a process allowing inmate toughs to control the meager job opportunities inside the walls. The prison had no professionally trained or experienced managers to oversee inmate labor. Instead, prisoners, who bullied, cajoled, or bribed their way into the positions, ran the few industries. These "con-bosses," as they were known, had complete freedom in determining which inmates they wanted working in their shops. And, for obvious reasons, the few jobs were highly coveted; an employed inmate could break his monotonous routine through regular work and more important could receive additional good-time credit. As might be expected, the con-boss control, combined with an untrained and mostly unqualified staff, eventually led to flagrant abuses, rampant favoritism, inefficiency, and dangerously low prisoner morale by the mid-1950s.

Despite the national reforms and changes in penal philosophy instigated originally by progressive penologists in the early 1900s in other states, no classification system had ever been developed in Montana. The staff, operating under some procedures in place since the territorial days and constantly battling the ubiquitous problems of overcrowding and underfunding, rarely separated inmates based on age, types of crime, or sexual proclivities. The overwhelming majority of the prison population consisted of younger, heterosexual male inmates, aged twenty to thirty-five. Yet oftentimes the administration forced them—wittingly or unwittingly—to share cells with older, sometimes homosexual, hardened cons. Furthermore, no parole system existed prior to 1955, and an ambiguous, inconsistently administered good behavior policy that often deprived inmates who had honestly served their time of a legitimate early release placed an additional strain on the system. No educational or rehabilitative training was available in the penitentiary until the 1960s, and only a small, cramped library, which had not been significantly updated since the copper baron William A. Clark's original donations, served to augment inmate education. There was no full-time doctor or dentist on the premises until the 1970s. By the late 1950s, tensions within the prison had notably increased, particularly as news of prison uprisings in other states began to spread.[14]

In the hot days of late July 1957, the years of restiveness and bureaucratic inattention and ineptitude finally boiled over. The incident began when members of the prison band refused to shell peas, and it then erupted into a full-scale sit-down strike by hundreds of inmates. The inmates were particularly upset over the tyrannical rule of the deputy warden, Vern Lockwood, and presented a hastily drawn-up list of demands and grievances to the state attorney general. Included among them were "allowance of good time toward parole for time spent in cell due to lack of available work"; "better preparation of food"; "abolish silence system in dining room"; "better lights in cells"; "elimination of the convict boss system"; "better hospitalization"; and a "federal investigation of the prison as a whole."[15] Governor Hugo Aronson, a party-line Republican, after public prodding by his youthful and progressive Democratic attorney general, Forrest Anderson, who had negotiated with the inmates during the two-day strike, promised changes—much to the chagrin of a generally conservative Montana public that viewed any improved prison conditions as the mere coddling of hoodlums.[16]

Aronson, who had initially balked at changing the status quo, finally agreed in the spring of 1958 to professionalize the warden's position and employ an experienced and trained penologist to administer the prison for the first time in its nearly ninety-year history.[17] In the fall of 1958 the state hired Floyd Powell, a tough but honest and skilled administrator from the Wisconsin state prison system, who, along with his deputy warden and fellow Wisconsinite, Theodore Rothe, promised a sweeping reform of the mess in Deer Lodge. Immediately, the pair, with lukewarm blessings from the Board of Prison Commissioners and several concerned citizens' groups (though with no increased funding), began a systematic cleanup of the prison.

Powell and Rothe attempted to abolish the con-boss control of the prison industries, classify inmates, systematize internal discipline, and modestly train the guard force. They began by initiating a process to remove rifles the guards carried inside the prison on the internal catwalks. Naturally their changes met with fierce resistance from both inmates and guards. The older inmates resented any curtailment of their power, and the guards were unnerved by the idea of patrolling the penitentiary without their high-powered rifles. As one inmate recalled later, "There is a definite pecking order in prison. When you upset that, a shit storm [i]s bound to follow."[18]

Tensions exploded in April 1959, when a group of inmates, led by a career criminal, overpowered several guards, captured their rifles, took twenty-five hostages (stabbing a guard in the process), and subsequently killed Deputy Warden Rothe. Incredibly, they even managed to lure Powell, whose office sat across the street from the main gate, into the prison, where they made him a hostage briefly. Miraculously he escaped, though not before inmates paraded him through the prison kitchen and then threatened to slit his throat and hang him upside down in a window so that outsiders knew that the rioters were serious. As the national news media descended upon tiny Deer Lodge and after two days of ultimately fruitless negotiations, members of the Montana National Guard, firing World War II–vintage bazookas, machine guns, and tear gas, stormed the prison. The two inmate ringleaders died in a hail of gunfire before the riot ran its course. Thousands of dollars of damage resulted to the aging prison from inmates ransacking the institution during the two-day takeover.[19]

The riot, like all prison uprisings, made sensational national and international news: the *New York Times, Life* and *Time* magazines, even the *London Times,* all ran photos and comprehensive stories. Though some changes had occurred after the 1957 disturbance, the 1959 insurrection focused public attention on the dangerous conditions that existed in the state's underfunded and neglected prison. The riot forced the issue of long-overdue prison reform into the contemporary political conversation; the penitentiary once again became a contentious and visible public policy issue in Montana. The influential Mike Mansfield, one of Montana's U.S. senators, even intervened to ensure ample federal money was provided to the state to fund research and architectural plans for a new, ostensibly safer prison.[20]

In 1960 a $5 million bond issue made it to the ballot for voters to decide whether the state should levy bonds financed by increased property taxes to construct a new facility at Deer Lodge. Only a few civic groups supported the measure, and on election day the issue failed miserably, with 70 percent of the electorate opposed.[21] Despite the swirl of publicity surrounding the aging institution and its numerous ailments in the late 1950s, most Montanans were simply ill versed or misinformed about the prison's long history and myriad problems. A large percentage of Montanans believed that criminals in Deer Lodge did not deserve the comforts of a new facility; they were there to serve hard time and should not expect any form of pampering—be it better light bulbs in the cells or an entirely new facility.

Governor Aronson may have been the most uninformed of all. Despite having received extensive written reports on the 1959 disturbance at the time, several years later he admitted, "I'll never know just exactly what caused it. I think probably a lot of men wanted individual TVs in the cells and some other conveniences and comforts."[22]

This simply was not true. The prisoners were not demanding luxuries. Yet they faced appalling conditions in an antiquated facility, and the fact of two disturbances within three years was a strong message to the public about the situation at Deer Lodge. Unfortunately, any improvement would cost money and the hard reality was that Montana property owners were the most heavily taxed of all those in the western states in 1959. This tax burden coupled with the public's ignorance of prison conditions doomed the bond issue. The funding of a new prison would become one more piece of baggage in the already heavy load that Montana's taxpayers shouldered; a new prison was obviously a burden that few cared to bear.[23]

Though voters did not invest in a new prison in 1960, the 1959 riot did increase legislators' awareness of the prison and its host of problems. Within a year of the riot, officials reverted to an old and successful formula. They used inmates to complete several minor building projects on the prison ranch outside of Deer Lodge to ease overcrowding at the main facility, particularly after a major earthquake in August of 1959 significantly damaged the 1896 cellblock. As William Crowley, an assistant to the attorney general in 1959 and one who investigated the riot, reflected years later, "After 1957 a lot of people weren't convinced that anything was needed" to change the system. "I think that when this thing [the riot] came along in 1959 . . . it actively convinced everybody that something had to be done. It acted as a catalyst, that's its true historical importance."[24]

In the mid-1960s the state commissioned feasibility studies and architectural plans for a new prison. Finally in 1971, after a final push from the Democratic governor Forrest Anderson, himself a hardened veteran of the political struggles surrounding the prison in the late 1950s, the state secured $3.8 million in federal revenue-sharing funds to construct a new facility.[25]

In 1979 the Montana Department of Corrections (a new department created in 1972 when voters ratified a new state constitution) moved the last male prisoners five miles outside of town into the new Montana State Prison that sits on former Conley and prison ranchland. After debate about the fate of the old prison—it had been slated for demolition—the Powell County Museum and Arts Foundation managed to save it and turn it into a regional tourist attraction. Visitors who trickle in from nearby Interstate 90 can see Conley's imposing 1893 sandstone wall, the turreted guard posts, and the mammoth 1912 cellblock with the bazooka-blasted hole dating from the 1959 riot.[26]

By the early 1990s, new controversies—with familiar shades to them—began to envelop the prison system and the state bureaucracy overseeing it. State-of-the-art technology and late twentieth-century prison architecture are now parts of the security systems of the newer men's prison outside Deer Lodge. Yet even bulletproof Plexiglas, automated controls, and computerized technology have failed at the institution. In September of 1991, inmates managed to overpower a security station in the maximum-security section of the prison. Guards escaped, but the inmates then systematically tortured and murdered five informants kept in the wing for protection. A federal study found that staff professionalism was wanting, the "inmate disciplinary system was poorly designed and inconsistently administered," and "policies and procedures were sometimes inappropriate and more often ignored." In short, the federal investigation concluded that "the Prison had not been running well prior to the riot."[27] Multimillion-dollar lawsuits stemming from the state's culpability in the mismanagement that led to the disaster were still being litigated ten years after the event.

In the wake of this bloody riot and in the face of a sluggish economy in the early 1990s, the Montana legislature mandated both statewide budget rescissions and that the Department of Corrections take steps to begin reducing the inmate population at the Deer Lodge facility by attempting to move less serious offenders to cheaper, community-based correctional programs.[28]

Yet by 1994, as both the Republican "Contract with America" and the bipartisan "War on Drugs" were in full swing, the mood of the country—

and particularly that of Montana—had begun to veer markedly toward harsher punishments of criminals, seemingly with no regard for what that might cost. In the wake of this conservative national shift, state legislatures began to pass a number of mandatory sentencing laws abrogating in the process traditional judicial discretion. Judges were now constrained to sentence offenders to long prison terms even when they felt it was in the best interests of neither society nor the offender to do so. In the fall of 1994, Montana voters swept into power substantial conservative majorities in both houses of the legislature, augmenting the power of a moderate Republican governor and former county prosecutor and attorney general, Marc Racicot (elected in 1992). True to their history, Montanans were about to get *really* tough on crime once again.

Prosecuting attorneys, in particular, had initially reacted strongly to attempts to downsize the prison numbers in the wake of the 1993 legislative mandates. During a late 1993 state convention of county attorneys and their deputies, Dennis Paxinos, the county attorney from the state's most populous county, Yellowstone, blasted both the legislature and a complicitous Racicot for trying to "balanc[e] the budget on the back of victims." Paxinos's remedy sounded like rhetoric from the 1890s rather than the 1990s, as he argued that "we should be tripling our prison population," not downsizing it.[29] He would soon get his wish.

Despite a mid-1993 plan by the Department of Corrections to comply with the legislative mandate to reduce inmate population in the prison (from around 1,200 to 850) over a fourteen-month period, there were actually, as one study indicated, "fifty percent more prison admissions, ten percent fewer paroles granted, and thirty-three percent fewer direct discharges, than originally projected" by mid-1994.[30] The war on crime in the state had already begun in earnest, but it would get an enormous boost because of a chance encounter in a Billings restaurant just prior to the pivotal fall 1994 election.

During the late summer of 1994, the state had begun a long-overdue transfer of its handful of women inmates from dilapidated facilities at the state mental hospital at Warm Springs (site of the former asylum) to a new complex of buildings in Billings in the eastern part of the state. As part of an incentive program to assist smoothing over inmate difficulties and dis-

ruptions during the transition, the staff created an inmate advisory council. As a reward for their efforts on the council, several of the women received
supervised meals outside of the prison in Deer Lodge at a local restaurant.
The program continued with the move to Billings. In late October 1994,
Governor Racicot's chief corrections department administrator, James
"Mickey" Gamble, a vocal and hitherto successful advocate within the
department for increased funding to support community-based corrections
and inmate incentive programs such as those offered to the women on the
inmate advisory council, dined with three of the women at a Billings Red
Lobster restaurant. It would turn into a nightmarish public relations disaster that would reverberate for years.

Among the inmates dining with Gamble were twenty-seven-year-old
Becky Richards, from Missoula County, who was serving a life sentence
for murdering her husband in 1992; Renee Doiron, twenty-one, of Helena,
convicted of attempted mitigated deliberate homicide for slashing another
woman's throat; and Deborah Evans, a forty-one-year-old bail-jumper from
Helena.[31] Chance would have it that the statewide teachers convention was
being held in Billings that same weekend. Richards's former high school
teacher saw the group dining and immediately contacted the murdered husband's family in Seeley Lake, located in western Montana. Outraged that
their son's murderer was enjoying a meal outside of the prison less than
two years after her conviction, the family members then contacted the prosecuting attorney in the case, Fred Van Walkenburg in Missoula County,
and then later Governor Racicot personally.

The story broke in the state press a week before the general election in
November 1994. Van Walkenburg, a longtime Democrat, blamed Racicot's
"extremely liberal corrections policy" for the embarrassing affront; pre-
dictably, the public outcry was swift and venomous. Within days, Gamble
tendered his resignation due to a "serious judgment error" on his part.[32]

If there had been any life left in community corrections—in which
inmate incentives to rehabilitation (such as meals out in exchange for coop-
erative behavior) were viable alternatives to more expensive incarceration—
the Richards/Gamble incident snuffed it out entirely. Within several
months of the Gamble episode, too, a convicted murderer brutally assaulted
and nearly killed a female staff member at a low-security prison boot camp

near Swan River in western Montana. The facility had been created as an inexpensive alternative for low-risk, youthful offenders and could claim some degree of success at sending young men back into the community to lead crime-free lives. But it was clear by mid-1995 that the public had no wish for new alternatives and desired instead a return to the old, though comfortable traditions of Draconian punishment for its criminals.[33] The Racicot administration was more than willing to comply.

Racicot and his Department of Corrections head, Rick Day (a former Bozeman policeman), then embarked on an enormous prison expansion project of historic proportions, all but abandoning the goal of downsizing the state's prison population gradually in favor of alternative sentencing and community-based rehabilitation. Within six years the legislature doubled the Department of Corrections budget, authorized three regional prisons in the state with another to be run privately by Corrections Corporation of America, and began transferring some of Montana's convicted felons out of state to other privately run prisons.[34] The male prison population in Montana increased by some *90 percent* during this period, from 1,521 in 1993 to 2,881 by 2000, though the crime rate did not diminish correspondingly. Indeed, policymakers were oblivious to the fact that the violent crime rate in Montana in 1998 was actually *double* that of 1989.[35] As was the case at Deer Lodge, prison expansion had done nothing to deter crime in the state, and the long-term incarceration has continued to accelerate unabated. By mid-2002 Montana's incarceration rate was growing at the sixth fastest clip in the nation (as measured from June 2001 to June 2002), accelerating even faster than during the meteoric previous twenty-year period.[36]

And, unlike times in the past, the state has chosen to incarcerate substantially greater percentages of ethnic minorities than it has hitherto. In 2000 Native Americans constituted 6.2 percent of state's population but 20 percent of the prison population. By contrast, whites made up 91 percent of the general population but only 79 percent of incarcerated individuals within the system.[37]

For Native women, the figure is even higher; nearly one-third of the 429 incarcerated women in the state in early 2002 were Native American. Grinding, chronic poverty, the lack of meaningful or in some cases *any* employment on Montana's remote reservations, and the hopelessness caused by drugs and alcohol are all factors in Native people turning to crime. Yet, as the University of Montana sociologist Jim Burfeind has observed, an offender with close connections in and to the community—a family, children, or relationship to and with a civic organization—is less likely to serve jail time. "It could be that Native Americans often have less going on for them in the community," which then makes them more likely to receive a prison sentence.[38]

Moreover, not only is the prison historically *not* an effective deterrent, the recent move to "get tough on crime" has come at a substantial cost. The state's annual per capita income ranks variously between forty-seventh and fiftieth nationally; it is nearly 30 percent below the national average. Expansion during the prosperous 1990s was relatively stagnant too (except, of course, in the prison); between 1990 and 2000, per capita income growth was 5 percent lower than the national average. The state spent more per capita than thirty other states between 1980 and 2000, and by 1996 Montana's average yearly expenditure per inmate ranked twenty-eighth nationally and was 3 percent *above* the annual national average. Translated, it simply costs Montana a much greater percentage of its total wealth to sustain the zeal for incarceration. Other crucial areas of state spending have suffered grievously as a result.[39]

While prison spending skyrocketed in the late 1990s, state support for education, at all levels, from primary grades though higher education, dropped significantly. By 2002 Montana ranked forty-eighth nationally in teachers' salaries and forty-seventh in the nation in state revenue support for higher education. In 1995, K-12 public education spending accounted for 52 percent of the overall state general fund budget. In 1999 that figure had shrunk to 46.5 percent. During that same period, corrections funding more than doubled.[40] In 1990 the state spent $49.73 per resident from the state's general tax revenue for prisons and $173.73 per resident to support higher education. A decade later those numbers had shifted dramatically; the state now spends $108.68 per resident for prisons and $140.06 per resident for higher education. Put yet another way, between 1980 and 2000, prison spending per resident rose 195 percent, while spending per resident for higher education during that same twenty-year period declined 10 percent (and most of that since 1990). A recent Department of Justice report notes that three out of every four prison inmates have not earned a high school diploma. The correlation between the lack of education and the increased likelihood of criminal behavior and eventual, costly incarceration has been clearly established.[41]

Montanans, as they have so many times in the past, have set as a priority warehousing thousands of their citizens in cramped and increasingly expensive prison cells. The prison system and the societal power that it projects have always come at a steep price. From the inauspicious beginning of a fourteen-celled brick-lined building in 1871, to a capacious postmodern system of corrections, the prison in the small state of Montana has always exacted a toll on those who inhabit it, those who run it, and those who pay for it. As long as Montanans continue with an increasingly expensive punishment ritual from the distant past, the people of the Treasure State will remain chained to an uncertain future.

Notes

1. Until the 1970s, a single institution served both men and women at Deer Lodge. During Montana's territorial years, the institution's official name was the United States Penitentiary at Deer Lodge City, Montana, Territory. After statehood it became the Montana State Prison. Historically, officials and the public have referred to the institution variously as the "prison" or the "penitentiary." Its function was to incarcerate convicted criminals and to attempt to rehabilitate them through various means. I use the terms *prison* and *penitentiary* interchangeably throughout this study.

2. Recent statistics testify to this attitude. In the year 2000, for example, Montana led the other Pacific Northwest states (Alaska, Washington, and Oregon, but not Idaho) in the number of individuals it incarcerated per capita, at 348 per 100,000 residents. Alaska imprisoned 341 people per 100,000; Washington, 251 per 100,000; Oregon, 316 per 100,000; and Idaho, 430 per 100,000. Nationally, Montana ranked thirty-second in the number of incarcerated individuals per capita, while ranking forty-sixth in population and forty-eighth in per capita income. From 1980 to 2000, the period that marked the largest increase in the incarcerated population in American history, Montana outstripped the national percentage growth. Its per capita imprisoned population has grown some 370 percent; the national figure for the same period was 332 percent. "Rate (per 100,0000 resident population) of sentenced prisoners under jurisdiction of State and Federal correctional authorities on December 31," Table 6.28, *Sourcebook of Criminal Justice Statistics 2000*, Bureau of

Justice Statistics On-Line, http://www.albany.edu/sourcebook (accessed May 5, 2002).

3. *Weekly Independent* (Deer Lodge City), July 7, 1871.

4. Numerous penological and sociological studies debate the success or failure of prisons in modern America. For representative recent selections, see Joel Dyer, *The Perpetual Prisoner Machine: How America Profits from Crime* (Boulder, Colo.: Westview Press, 2000); Marc Mauer, *Race to Incarcerate* (New York: The New Press, 1999); Steven R. Donziger, ed., *The Real War on Crime* (New York: HarperCollins, 1996); and Wendy Kaminer, "Federal Offense," *Atlantic Monthly* (June 1994): 102–109.

5. Until the mid-1970s, the state incarcerated women and men separately at one facility in Deer Lodge. By 1991, the state housed women offenders in another facility at Warm Springs, fifteen miles away.

6. Bureau of Justice Statistics, "Prison Statistics, Summary Findings," http://www.ojp.usdoj.gov/bjs/prisons.htm (accessed May 7, 2003).

1 / THE MAJESTY OF THE LAW

Chapter epigraph: Wallace Stegner, *Wolf Willow: A History, a Story, and a Memory of the Last Plains Frontier* (New York: Penguin Books, 1990), 5.

1. Thomas Dimsdale, *The Vigilantes of Montana* (Virginia City, Mont.: 1865; reprint, Norman: University of Oklahoma Press, 1953), 194–205.

2. Information on Slade's life comes from Lew L. Callaway, "Joseph Alfred Slade: Killer or Victim?" *Montana Magazine of History* 3 (January 1953), 5–34.

3. Dimsdale, *Vigilantes of Montana,* 196.

4. Ibid., 15.

5. Ibid., 199–201, 205.

6. Historians have examined exhaustively vigilantism's place in both American and Montana history. For contemporary Montana accounts, see Dimsdale, *Vigilantes of Montana,* and Nathaniel Pitt Langford's apologia, *Vigilante Days and Ways* (1890; reprint, Missoula: University of Montana Press, 1957). For recent scholarship focusing on vigilance and the nature of crime and violence in the American West, consult Roger D. McGrath, *Gunfighters, Highwaymen and Vigilantes: Violence on the Frontier* (Berkeley: University of California Press, 1984); Richard Maxwell Brown, *Strain of Violence: Historical Studies of American Violence and*

Vigilantism (New York: Oxford University Press, 1975); Richard Maxwell Brown, *No Duty to Retreat: Violence and Values in American History and Society* (New York: Oxford University Press, 1991); William C. Culberson, *Vigilantism: Political History of Private Power in America* (New York: Greenwood Press, 1990); Richard Maxwell Brown, "The History of Vigilantism in America," in *Vigilante Politics,* ed. H. Jon Rosenbaum and Peter C. Sederberg (Philadelphia: University of Pennsylvania Press, 1976), 79–109; David Johnson, "Vigilance and the Law: The Moral Authority of Popular Justice in the Far West," *American Quarterly* 33 (1981): 558–86; Richard Slotkin, "Apotheosis of the Lynching: The Political Uses of Symbolic Violence," *Western Legal History* 6 (Winter/Spring 1993): 1–16; and Richard Maxwell Brown, "Violence," in *The Oxford History of the American West,* ed. Clyde A. Milner II, Carol O'Connor, and Martha A. Sandweiss (New York: Oxford University Press, 1994), 395–98. For a broader treatment of the scope of criminal justice in American history, see Samuel Walker, *Popular Justice: A History of American Criminal Justice,* 2d ed. (New York: Oxford University Press, 1998); for the evolution of capital punishment in America, consult Louis P. Masur, *Rites of Execution: Capital Punishment and the Transformation of American Culture, 1776–1865* (New York: Oxford University Press, 1989).

7. Dimsdale, *Vigilantes of Montana,* 199–201, 205.

8. George Dixon pardon request of Governor Benjamin Potts, September 27, 1874, in Records of the Montana Territory Executive Office, Montana Historical Society (hereafter MHS), Helena, Montana.

9. *Daily Herald* (Helena), January 20, 1871.

10. Ibid., January 21, 1871.

11. The full text of the confession is in ibid., January 24, 1871.

12. Ibid., January 23, 1871.

13. *New North-West* (Deer Lodge), January 27, 1871.

14. Ibid., March 21, 1871.

15. Sociological and demographic data on these and other Montana inmates comes from the original untitled log book maintained chronologically at the prison from 1871 to 1885 and the log book entitled "State Convict Register," maintained from 1891 to 1895 but containing data for prisoners from 1885 to 1889, both in Montana Prison Records, MHS. Both cited hereafter as Record of Prisoners.

16. Potts quoted in the *Daily Independent* (Helena), January 15, 1881. Dixon had written Potts in 1874 detailing his coerced confession and requesting a pardon.

17. Lee Silliman, "1870: To the Hangman's Tree," *Montana, the Magazine of Western History* 28 (Autumn 1978): 50–57.

18. Johnson, "Vigilance and the Law," 562. Emphasis added.

19. David Rothman, *Conscience and Convenience: The Asylum and Its Alternatives in Progressive America* (Boston: Little, Brown, 1980), 4.

20. Jesse Lemisch originally coined the phrase "history from the bottom up" in "The American Revolution Seen from the Bottom Up," in *Towards A New Past: Dissenting Essays in American History,* ed. Barton J. Bernstein (New York: Random House, 1968), 3–45.

21. In Montana, confinement in the prison was historically reserved for those convicted of felony offenses. As Mark Ellis notes in "Law and Order in Buffalo Bill's Country: Crime and Criminal Justice in Lincoln County, Nebraska, 1868–1910," Ph.D. diss., University of Nebraska–Lincoln, 1999, of the 105 individuals sentenced to the Nebraska state penitentiary between 1868 and 1910, 84 were there for crimes committed against property (447–50, appendix 2). While similar, specific localized evidence remains to be uncovered in Montana, the vast majority of Montana's prison inmates were incarcerated for crimes considered to have been committed against property. See Tables 1 and 2 in Chapter 3, this work.

22. And indeed, a number of pardons issued in the nineteenth century stipulated that pardoned inmates were required to exit the territory and pledge never to return.

23. Southern prison historiography is especially rich. See, for example, Mark Carleton, *Politics and Punishment: The History of the Louisiana State Penal System* (Baton Rouge: Louisiana State University Press, 1971); Michael Hindus, *Prison and Plantation: Crime, Justice, and Authority in Massachusetts and South Carolina* (Chapel Hill: University of North Carolina Press, 1980); Paul Keve, *The History of Corrections in Virginia* (Charlottesville: University Press of Virginia, 1986); Donald Walker, *Penology for Profit: A History of the Texas Prison System* (Austin: Texas A&M Press, 1988); Mathew Mancini, *One Dies, Get Another: Convict Leasing in the American South, 1866–1928* (Columbia: University of South Carolina Press, 1996); David M. Oshinsky, *Worse than Slavery: Parchman Farm and the Ordeal of Jim Crow Justice* (New York: The Free Press, 1996); and Mary Ellen Curtin, *Black Prisoners and Their World, Alabama, 1865–1900* (Charlottesville: University Press of Virginia, 2000).

24. Quoted in Alexander Piscotta, *Benevolent Repression: Social Control and the*

American Reformatory-Prison Movement (New York: New York University Press, 1994), 150.

25. The list of scholarly and popular books that address the role of western myth in the American imagination, and the myth of the western outlaw in popular culture, particularly, is lengthy. The cultural historian Richard Slotkin suggests that the western outlaw has become the foundation of the western myth, and that figure shapes everything from movie depictions to foreign policy and American self-image. See Richard Slotkin, *Gunfighter Nation* (New York: Atheneum, 1992). For representative recent work, consult Richard Maxwell Brown, *No Duty To Retreat;* Brown, "Violence," 393–426; Robert V. Hine and John Mack Faragher, *The American West: A New Interpretive History* (New Haven: Yale University Press, 2000), 472–511; and Richard Maxwell Brown, "Western Violence, Structure, Values, Myth," *Western Historical Quarterly* 24 (February 1993): 5–20. For the most illuminating recent debate on myth and frontier violence, consult Stewart Udall, Robert Dykstra, Michael Bellesiles, Paula Mitchell Marks, and Gregory Nobles, "How the West Got Wild: American Media and Frontier Violence," *Western Historical Quarterly* 31 (Autumn 2000): 277–95. For a recent overview of the transmission of western myth into popular culture, consult Anne Butler, "Selling the Popular Myth," in Milner, O'Connor, and Sandweiss, *Oxford History of the American West,* 771–802.

26. The oversight in the Pacific Northwest region prompted the historian Roland De Lorme to note in 1985 that the phenomenon of crime and punishment and specifically "the history of penology . . . remains almost untouched." De Lorme, "Crime and Punishment in the Pacific Northwest Territories: A Bibliographic Essay," *Pacific Northwest Quarterly* 76 (April 1985), 48.

27. A significant amount of recent scholarship on the embryonic western legal systems and case studies of local and evolving historic responses to violence and crime can augment, and have already, research on western prisons. See McGrath, *Gunfighters, Highwaymen and Vigilantes;* Robert Percival, *The Roots of Justice: Crime and Punishment in Alameda County, California, 1870–1910* (Chapel Hill: University of North Carolina Press, 1981); Clare V. McKanna, Jr., *Homicide, Race, and Justice in the American West, 1880–1920* (Tucson: University of Arizona Press, 1997); and Paul T. Hietter, "A Surprising Amount of Justice: The Experience of Mexican and Racial Minority Defendants Charged with Serious Crimes in Arizona, 1865–1920," *Pacific Historical Review* 70 (May 2001): 183–220. For specific Northwest case studies, see Charles A. Tracy, "Race, Crime and Social Policy: The Chi-

nese in Oregon, 1871–1885," *Crime and Social Justice* 11 (Winter 1980): 11–25, and
Joseph Laythe, "Bandits and Badges: Crime and Punishment in Oregon, 1875–1915,"
Ph.D. diss., University of Oregon, 1996.

John Wunder, in *Inferior Courts, Superior Justice: A History of the Justices of the
Peace on the Northwest Frontier, 1853–1889* (Westport: Greenwood Press, 1979), systematically examines the cases before and actions of the local justice of the peace
courts in the region as well as the social backgrounds of the justices of the peace
in much of the region during these years. For a more general view of the development of law and a legal culture in the West, see Gordon Morris Bakken, ed., *Law
in the Western United States* (Norman: University of Oklahoma Press, 2000); for
specifically the intermountain West, consult Gordon Morris Bakken, *The Development of Law on the Rocky Mountain Frontier: Civil Law and Society, 1850–1912*
(Westport, Conn.: Greenwood Press, 1983); John D. Guice, *The Rocky Mountain
Bench: The Territorial Supreme Courts of Colorado, Montana, and Wyoming,
1864–1912* (New Haven: Yale University Press, 1972); John R. Wunder, "Persistence
and Adaptation: The Emergence of a Legal Culture in the Northern Tier Territories, 1853–1890," in *Centennial West: Essays on the Northern Tier States,* ed. William
Lang (Seattle: University of Washington Press, 1991), 104–21, and Robert Harvie,
Keeping the Peace: Police Reform in Montana, 1889–1918 (Helena: Montana Historical Society Press, 1994).

For the earliest overview on western penology, consult Blake McKelvey, "Penology in the Westward Movement," *Pacific Historical Review* 2 (November 1933):
418–38. For more contemporary analyses on topical areas, consult Anne Butler, *Gendered Justice in the American West: Women Prisoners in Men's Penitentiaries* (Urbana:
University of Illinois Press, 1997); Anne Butler, "Women's Work in Prisons of the
American West, 1865–1920," *Western Legal History* 7 (Summer/Fall 1994): 201–22;
Anne Butler, "Still in Chains: Black Women in Western Prisons, 1865–1910," *Western Historical Quarterly* 20 (February 1989): 20–35; James Wilson, "Frontier in the
Shadows: Prisons in the Far Southwest, 1850–1917," *Arizona and the West* 22 (Win-
ter 1980): 323–42; Ward McAfee, "The Formation of Prison-Management Phi-
losophy in Oregon, 1843–1915," *Oregon Historical Quarterly* 91 (Fall 1990); Shelly
Bookspan, *A Germ of Goodness: The California State Prison System, 1851–1944* (Lin-
coln: University of Nebraska Press, 1991); Elinor McGinn, *At Hard Labor: Inmate
Labor at the Colorado State Penitentiary, 1871–1940* (New York: Peter Lang, 1993);
Paul Knepper "Imprisonment and Society in Arizona Territory," Ph.D. diss., Ari-

zona State University, 1990; Judy Johnson, "For Any Good At All: A Comparative Study of State Penitentiaries in Arizona, Nevada, New Mexico, and Utah from 1900 to 1980," Ph.D. diss., University of New Mexico, 1987.

28. In a self-conscious revisionism of western history, Richard White lumps crime and criminals mainly into categories of "social banditry" and "vigilantes" and concentrates, briefly, on the exploits of a few noted "gunfighters." Richard White, *"It's Your Misfortune and None of My Own": A New History of the American West* (Norman: University of Oklahoma Press, 1991), 328–51.

29. Michael Malone, Richard Roeder, and William Lang, *Montana: A History of Two Centuries*, rev. ed. (Seattle: University of Washington Press, 1991), passim.

30. Department of Justice, Bureau of Justice Statistics, *Historical Corrections Statistics in the United States, 1850–1984*, by Margaret Cahalan (Rockville, Md.: Westat, 1986), 30. On federal attention, see Clark C. Spence, *Territorial Politics and Government in Montana, 1864–89* (Chicago: University of Illinois Press, 1975).

31. Only an out-of-print study, Jules Karlin's *Joseph M. Dixon of Montana, Part 2: Governor versus the Anaconda, 1817–1934* (Missoula: University of Montana Press, 1974), 87–117, addresses the scandal in depth; recent texts ignore his findings.

32. According to the 2000 census, the state incarcerates 1.5 percent of the total Native American population (847 out of 56,068). This figure seems low, but it is three times higher than the average for the general population, .45 percent. Native Americans make up 6.2 percent of the total Montana population but 20 percent of those residing in correctional institutions. U.S. Census Bureau, *Census 2000 Redistricting Data* (P.L. 94-171) Summary File, Tables PL1 and PL2 (Available as a publication and in PDF format at www.census.gov/clo/www/redistricting.html; the report was issued in July 2000); U.S. Census Bureau, American Fact Finder, Detailed Tables, Montana, PCT16, "Group Quarters Population by Group Quarters Type," and PCT17C, "Group Quarters Population by Sex, by Age, by Group Quarters Type (American Indian and Alaska Native Alone)" http://factfinder .census.gov (accessed February 26, 2002). Also see "Prison's Racial Disparity: Native Americans Make up Disproportionate Percentage of Inmates," *Billings Gazette*, January 14, 2002.

33. See William Deverell, "The Significance of the American West in the History of the United States," *Western Historical Quarterly* 25 (Summer 1994): 185–206.

34. See, specifically, William G. Robbins, *Colony and Empire: The Capitalist Transformation of the American West* (Lawrence: University of Kansas Press, 1994),

121–42 and passim (Mumford quote, 122). Richard Maxwell Brown, "Law and Order on the American Frontier: The Western Civil War of Incorporation," in *Law for the Elephant, Law for the Beaver: Essays in the Legal History of the North American West*, ed. John McLaren, Hamar Foster, and Chet Orloff (Saline, Mich.: McNaughton and Gunn, 1992), 74–89. Other scholars also place the notion of incorporation at the center of their recent histories of specific regions during this period. Consult John Walton, *Western Times and Water Wars: State, Culture, and Rebellion in California* (Berkeley: University of California Press, 1992); David Alan Johnson, *Founding the Far West: California, Oregon, and Nevada, 1840–1890* (Berkeley: University of California Press, 1992), 1–11 and passim; and Robert Weibe, *The Search for Order, 1877–1920* (New York: Hill & Wang, 1967), esp. chap. 2. This struggle was a process not indigenous simply to the American West, as Brown correctly notes, but was occurring throughout much of late nineteenth-century America. For a broad overview of this struggle in other American regions, see Alan Trachtenberg, *The Incorporation of America: Culture and Society in the Gilded Age* (New York: Hill and Wang, 1982). Brown, "Law and Order on the American Frontier," 74.

35. The West as a colonial extension of the United States has a long historiography. Two classic studies are Bernard DeVoto, "The West: A Plundered Province," *Harper's Magazine* (August 1934): 355–64, and Earl Pomeroy, *The Territories and the United States, 1861–1890: Studies in Colonial Administration* (Philadelphia: University of Pennsylvania Press, 1947). For representative Montana works, consult Joseph Kinsey Howard, *Montana: High, Wide, and Handsome* (Lincoln: University of Nebraska Press, 1943), and K. Ross Toole, *Montana: An Uncommon Land* (Norman: University of Oklahoma Press, 1959).

36. As the historian Richard Bensel has noted, "The very process of secession, war, and reunification both strengthened the American state in every dimension of institutional design and substantive policy and committed the entire apparatus to the promotion of northern industrial development and western settlement." Immediately after the war, Bensel believes that "the state experimented with policies as statist and far-reaching as any in American history . . . including the commitment of the American state to modernizing policies associated with the industrial and financial sectors of the North." Richard Franklin Bensel, *Yankee Leviathan: The Origins of Central State Authority in America, 1859–1877* (New York: Cambridge University Press, 1990), 2.

37. Trachtenberg, *The Incorporation of America,* 4 and 7.

38. Christopher Lasch has argued that the entire enterprise of identifying and incarcerating societal miscreants and malcontents was one of the fundamental "preconditions of modern capitalism" and aided western society in its massive efforts to organize individuals into productive cogs in a new economic system. Christopher Lasch, *The World of Nations: Reflections on American History, Politics and Culture* (New York: Alfred Knopf, 1973), 316. Thomas Dumm, in *Democracy and Punishment: Disciplinary Origins of the United States* (Madison: University of Wisconsin Press, 1987), has applied these concepts to early nineteenth-century America. For a sweeping overview that places prisons and punishment in their historic sociological contexts, see David Garland, *Punishment and Modern Society: A Study in Social Theory* (Chicago: University of Chicago Press, 1990).

39. For the relationship between capitalism and prisons, see Michel Foucault, *Discipline and Punish: The Birth of the Prison,* trans. Alan Sheridan (New York: Vintage Books, 1977), 167–87 and passim. The relationship between capitalism and imprisonment has been of special interest to a range of social and cultural theorists. A classic work on the relationship of prisons and economics is Georg Rusche and Otto Kirchheimer, *Punishment and Social Structure* (New York: Columbia University Press, 1939). Other scholars have provided correctives and supplements since. See Christopher Adamson, "Toward a Marxian Penology: Captive Criminal Populations as Economic Threats and Resources," *Social Problems* 31 (April 1984): 435–58; and Christopher X. Adamson, "Hard Labor: The Form and Function of Prison Labor in Nineteenth Century America," Ph.D. diss., Princeton University, 1982. Also see John Conley, "Prisons, Production and Profit: Reconsidering the Importance of Prison Industries," *Journal of Social History* 4 (Fall 1980): 257–75; John Conley, "Revising Conceptions about the Origin of Prisons: The Importance of Economic Considerations," *Social Science Quarterly* 62 (1981): 247–58; and John Conley, "Economics and the Social Reality of Prisons," *Journal of Criminal Justice* 10 (1982): 25–35.

40. See the classic work of Gustave de Beaumont and Alexis de Tocqueville, *On the Penitentiary System in the United States and its Application in France* (Philadelphia: Carey, Lea & Blanchard, 1833).

41. For a broad discussion of the definition and evolution of state power in the American West, see Karen Merrill, "In Search of the Federal Presence in the American West," *Western Historical Quarterly* 30 (Winter, 1999): 449–73.

42. Some western historians have viewed and explained the compressing and

managing of spatial territory, the creation of political constitutions where none previously existed, the subduing of a hostile and unforgiving environment, and attempted cultural suppression as part of the general process of conquest playing out in the late nineteenth-century American West. Consult William G. Robbins, "The 'Plundered Province' Thesis and the Recent Historiography of the American West," *Pacific Historical Review* 55 (November 1986): 577–97; Donald Worster, "New West, True West: Interpreting the Region's History," *Western Historical Quarterly* 18 (April 1987): 157-76; and Walter Nugent, "Frontiers and Empires in the Late Nineteenth Century," *Western Historical Quarterly* 20 (November 1989): 393–408. For a sampling of new western history with the notion of regional conquest at its core, consult Patricia Nelson Limerick, Clyde A. Milner II, and Charles Rankin, eds., *Trails Toward a New Western History* (Lawrence: University Press of Kansas, 1991).

43. David Rothman, *The Discovery of the Asylum: Social Order and Disorder in the New Republic* (Boston: Little Brown, 1971), and Thomas Bender, *Toward an Urban Vision: Ideas and Institutions in Nineteenth-Century America* (Lexington: University of Kentucky Press, 1975), 131–35.

44. Charles Loring Brace, *The Dangerous Classes of New York, and Twenty Years' Work Among Them* (New York: Wynkoop and Hallenbeck, 1872). For other nineteenth-century expressions and attitudes toward what the Bureau of the Census director labeled the "defective classes," see Eric Monkkonen, *The Dangerous Class: Crime and Poverty in Columbus, Ohio* (Cambridge: Harvard University Press, 1975), 1–5 and 76–105; and Paul Boyer, *Urban Masses and Moral Order in America, 1820–1920* (Cambridge, Mass.: Harvard University Press, 1978), 67–175. It was during these latter decades, too, that curbing both prostitution and narcotic use became linked with the national assault on criminality and deviance identification. For the criminalizing of western prostitution, see Anne Butler, *Daughters of Joy, Sisters of Misery: Prostitutes in the American West, 1865–1890* (Urbana: University of Illinois Press, 1985), 96–121.

45. For the expanding role of the federal law enforcement apparatus after the Civil War, see Homer Cummings and Carl McFarland, *Federal Justice: Chapters in the History of Justice and the Federal Executive* (New York: Macmillan, 1937); and Robert J. Kaczorowski, *The Politics of Judicial Interpretation: The Federal Courts, Department of Justice and Civil Rights, 1866–1876* (Dobbs Ferry, N.Y.: Oceana Publications, 1985). For the Northern Tier region specifically, see De Lorme, "The Long Arm of the Law," 122–42.

46. Enoch C. Wines, *The State of Prisons and Child Saving Institutions in the Civilized World* (1880; reprint, Montclair, N.J.: Patterson Smith, 1986), 88.

47. See Paul Keve, *Prisons and the American Conscience: A History of Federal Corrections* (Carbondale: Southern Illinois University Press, 1991), 18–50 and 227–46.

48. U.S. House of Representatives, *Report on the Defective, Dependent, and Delinquent Classes of the Population of the United States,* 47th Cong., 2d sess., 1880, House Misc. Doc. 42, pt. 21, xlvi and liii.

49. Kate Brown, "Gridded Lives: Why Kazakhstan and Montana Are Nearly the Same Place," *American Historical Review* 106 (February 2001): 46.

50. Foucault, *Discipline and Punish,* 216 and 233.

2 / PENITENTIARY ON A SHOESTRING

Chapter epigraph: Nathaniel Hawthorne, *The Scarlet Letter* (New York: Harper Row, 1967), 42.

1. The most in-depth source on this period of Montana's history is Spence, *Territorial Politics and Government in Montana,* 212–31; also see Clark Spence, "We Want a Judge: Montana Territorial Justice and Politics," *Journal of the West* 20 (January 1981): 7–13.

2. Idaho Territory at the time comprised nearly all of present-day Wyoming, Montana, and Idaho.

3. See Ronald Limbaugh, "Attitudes of the Population of Idaho Toward Law and Order, 1860–1870," M.A. thesis, University of Idaho, 1962; and Ronald Limbaugh, *Rocky Mountain Carpetbaggers: Idaho's Territorial Governors, 1863–1890* (Moscow: University of Idaho Press, 1982), 17–18, 32, 45–66, 75, 124–25, 178.

4. See the *Montana Post* (Virginia City), November 8, 1867, and Spence, *Territorial Politics,* 219–20.

5. Not only were these Montana vigilantes aided by the memory of the public spectacle of what happened to miscreants, but they also developed a cryptic code, perhaps Masonic in origin, "3-7-77," which they scrawled on tents, cabin doors, or coffins of victims or potential victims as a symbolic reminder of their power. See Rex C. Myers, "The Fateful Numbers 3-7-77: A Reexamination," *Montana, the Magazine of Western History* 24 (Autumn 1974): 67–70. For other treatments of Montana's vigilantes, see Merrill G. Burlingame, "Montana's Righteous Hangmen: A Reconsideration," *Montana, the Magazine of Western History* 28

(October 1978): 36–49; Lew L. Callaway, *Montana's Righteous Hangmen: The Vigilantes in Action* (Norman: University of Oklahoma Press, 1982); and John Smurr "Afterthoughts on the Vigilantes," *Montana, the Magazine of Western History* 8 (Spring 1958): 8–20.

6. Johnson, "Vigilance and the Law," 572; *Rocky Mountain Gazette* (Helena), April 30, 1870; and *Daily Herald* (Helena), April 18, 1870.

7. Johnson, "Vigilance and the Law," 572.

8. "Spectacles of Suffering" comes from the title of Pieter Spierenburg's work *The Spectacle of Suffering: Executions and the Evolution of Repression: From a Preindustrial Metropolis to the European Experience* (New York: Cambridge University Press, 1984); Johnson, "Vigilance and the Law," 572.

9. Johnson, "Vigilance and the Law," 562.

10. Indeed, as Masur argues, in many eastern states the propriety of execution as a legitimate, legally sanctioned punishment was widely questioned and contested in the middle nineteenth century and faced, by 1870, stiff opposition (*Rites of Execution*, passim). For a history of both support of and opposition to capital punishment in Montana, see Robert O. Raffety, "The History and Theory of Capital Punishment," M.A. thesis, University of Montana, 1968.

11. Spence, *Territorial Politics*, 218-20; *Congressional Globe*, 39th Cong., 2d sess., 1866–67, 1816–17.

12. Thomas F. Meagher (Virginia City) to Andrew Johnson, January 20, 1866, in *The Papers of Andrew Johnson*, ed. Paul Bergeron, vol. 9 (Knoxville: University of Tennessee Press, 1991), 621.

13. Benjamin Franklin Potts (Helena) to James A. Garfield, June 3, 1871, Garfield Papers, Library of Congress, Washington, D.C. Potts wrote just a few months after two lynchings (described above) occurred within view of the district courthouse in Helena, of the prospective territorial capitol. For details of this incident, see Silliman, "1870: To the Hangman's Tree," 50–57.

14. Quoted in Guice, *Rocky Mountain Bench*, 137.

15. Lyman E. Munson, "Pioneer Life in Montana," *Contributions to the Historical Society of Montana*, Vol. 5 (Helena: Montana Historical Society Press, 1904), 209.

16. Henry Burdick to Attorney General E. R. Hoar, October 10, 1869, U.S. Department of Justice, Records of the Attorney Generals, Letters Received, 1809–1870, Record Group 60, Box 1, Montana, 1864–1870, National Archives, College Park, Md.

17. William F. Wheeler to Governor B. F. Potts, January 5, 1870, U.S. Department of Justice, Records of the Attorney Generals, Letters Received, Source Chronological Files, 1871–1884, Record Group 60, Box 829, Montana, January 1871–June 1872, and Governor B. F. Potts to Attorney General Ackerman, January 23, 1871, ibid.

18. Munson, "Pioneer Life," 236 and 210.

19. *Montana Post* (Virginia City), December 10, 1864.

20. "Territorial Governor Green Clay Smith's Message to the Legislature of Montana Territory," in *Montana Post* (Virginia City), November 9, 1867. Emphasis added.

21. Ibid.

22. Ibid.

23. Also see Judge Hosmer's "Charge to the Grand Jury of August 7th, 1866," in *Montana Post*, August 11, 1866.

24. Acting territorial governor, Thomas Francis Meagher, et al. (Virginia City) to Secretary of the Interior, April 18, 1867, U.S. Department of Interior, Territorial Papers, Montana, Letters Received, February 5, 1867–November 25, 1889, Record Group 48, National Archives, College Park, Md. (hereafter cited as Territorial Papers). Also see A. H. Esler et al. (Bannack City) to Secretary of the Interior, April 18, 1867, ibid. Unfortunately no scholar has undertaken a comprehensive examination of local jails in the American West. A popular, though factually dubious, survey of some nineteenth-century western jails can be found in Fred Harrison, *Hell Holes and Hangings* (Clarendon, Tex.: Clarendon Press, 1968). For a descriptive overview of selected local jails in the nineteenth-century middle-border West, see Philip Jordan, *Frontier Law and Order* (Lincoln: University of Nebraska Press, 1970), 140–54. For early California jails, see John Joseph Stanley, "Jailing the Elephant: The Early Jails of California," 81–85, in Bakken, ed., *Law in the Western United States*. For a description of the Virginia City jail, see J. M. Moynahan, "They've Hanged the Sheriff! Montana's First Jail," *American Jails* (January/February 1994): 55–62.

25. *An Act Concerning the Disposition of Convicts*, U.S. Statutes at Large 13 (1864), 74–75.

26. Munson, "Pioneer Montana," 212–13; on the expense of transporting prisoners, see *Congressional Globe*, 41st Congress, 3d sess., 1870–71, 60.

27. Thomas F. Meagher to Montana Territorial legislature (March 6, 1866), Ter-

ritorial Papers. Also see Wheeler to Potts, January 5, 1870, Records of the Attorney
Generals, Letters Received, Source Chronological Files, 1871–1884.

28. Hubert Howe Bancroft, *The History of Washington, Idaho and Montana,
1846–1889* (San Francisco: The History Company, 1890), 653.

29. Green Clay Smith (Virginia City) to O. H. Browning, April 18, 1868, Territorial Papers.

30. For the complicated interplay and relationship between the western territories and the federal government after the Civil War, see White, *"It's Your Misfortune,"* 155–78.

31. For Hauser's rise in territorial Montana, see Robbins, *Colony and Empire,*
103–20; also see John Hakola, "Samuel T. Hauser and the Economic Development
of Montana: A Case Study in Nineteenth Century Frontier Capitalism," Ph.D. diss.,
Indiana University, 1961, 36, 37–74, and passim.

32. Ibid., 44.

33. S. W. Batchelder, C. S. Ream, and William Sturgis (Argenta) to Secretary
of the Interior, April 18, 1867, Territorial Papers.

34. See George Thomson, "The History of Penal Institutions in the Rocky Mountain West, 1846–1900," Ph.D. diss., University of Colorado, 1965, 24–38; Knepper,
"Imprisonment and Society," 52–61; Thomas G. Alexander, *A Clash of Interests:
Interior Department and Mountain West* (Provo: Brigham Young University Press,
1977), 12–25; and Butler, *Gendered Justice,* 13.

35. *An Act Concerning the Disposition of Convicts,* 74-75; U.S. House of Representatives, *Annual Report of the Secretary of the Interior,* 40th Cong., 2d sess., 1867–
68, H. Exec. Doc. 1, p. 21.

36. For representative memorials for financial assistance in constructing these
prisons within the territories, see U.S. House of Representatives, *Wisconsin Penitentiary,* 25th Cong., 2d sess., 1837–38, H. Doc. 332; U.S. House of Representatives,
Penitentiary, Iowa, 26th Cong., 1st sess., 1839, H. Rep. 297. For congressional debate,
see *Congressional Globe,* 39th Cong., 2d sess., 1867, p. 432.

37. For the historical background to this first federal penitentiary, consult Paul
Keve, *Prisons and the American Conscience,* 36; U.S. House of Representatives, *Report
of Charles Bulfinch on the Subject of Penitentiaries,* 19th Cong., 2d sess., 1828, H. Rept.
98; William Crawford, *Report on the Penitentiaries of the United States* (London:
House of Commons, 1834), 101–103; Stephen Dalsheim, *The United States Penitentiary for the District of Columbia, 1826–1862* (Washington, D.C.: Records of

Columbia History Society, 1945), vols. 1953–56; and Laurence F. Schmeckebier, *The District of Columbia: Its Government and Administration* (Baltimore: Johns Hopkins Press, 1928), 88–90.

38. Alexander, *A Clash of Interests,* 1. Also consult Norman O. Fornes, "The Origins and Early History of the United States Department of the Interior," Ph.D. diss., Pennsylvania State University, 1964, and Wilson, "Frontier in the Shadows," 324.

39. *Congressional Globe,* 39th Cong., 2d sess., Appendix, Laws of the United States, Chap. 9, Approved January 22, 1867, 180. The full title of the act was *An Act Setting Aside Certain Proceeds from Internal Revenue for the Erection of Penitentiaries in the Territories of Nebraska, Washington, Colorado, Montana, Arizona, and Dakota, U.S. Statutes at Large,* 14 (1867), 377.

40. Ibid.

41. A. B. Mullett, Treasury Department to O. H. Browning, Secretary of the Interior, in U.S. Senate, *Letter of the Secretary of the Interior,* 40th Cong., 3d sess., 1868–69, Sen. Ex. Doc. 35.

42. Roland De Lorme discusses the ambivalent philosophy the federal government assumed during these years in the Northern Tier region of Minnesota, Dakota, Wyoming, Montana, and Idaho. See De Lorme, "The Long Arm of the Law: Crime and Federal Law Enforcement in the Northern Tier Territories," in Lang, ed., *Centennial West,* 122–42.

43. Alexander, *A Clash of Interests,* 12–25, especially 21–22; Governor B. F. Potts to Attorney General A. T. Ackerman, April 5, 1871, Records of the Attorney Generals, Letters Received, Source Chronological Files, 1871–1884.

44. U.S. House of Representatives, 41st Cong., 2d sess., 1870–71, H. Exec. Doc. 286; A. T. Ackerman, U.S. Attorney General, to William F. Wheeler, U.S. Marshal, Helena, March 3, 1871, Department of Justice, Letters Sent by the Department of Justice, "Instructions to U.S. Attorneys and Marshals, 1867–1904," RG 60, National Archives, College Park, Md.

45. *New North-West* (Deer Lodge City), June 7, 1870. Also see A. H. Mitchell to J. D. Cox, Secretary of the Interior, June 7, 1870, *Territorial Papers.* The cornerstone contained copies of the local newspaper, U.S. coins and currency, and a bottle of Old Crow whiskey. *New North-West,* June 3, 1870.

46. A. H. Mitchell (Deer Lodge), to W. J. Otto, Acting Secretary of the Interior, October 29, 1870, Territorial Papers.

47. *New North-West,* October 21, 1870.

48. Ibid., April 21, 1871.

49. Ibid., October 21, 1870; Potts to A. L. Ackerman, Department of Justice, January 23, 1871, Records of the Attorney Generals, Letters Received, Source Chronological Files, 1871-1884.

50. Ibid., May 5, 1871. The wall, actually a wooden fence, eventually was constructed—five years later.

51. McGinn, *At Hard Labor,* 37.

52. The other main competitor of the Auburn-style prison was the one developed in the early nineteenth century in Philadelphia at the Walnut Street penitentiary. There inmates were confined in complete silence in individual cells with special, compartmentalized exercise yards to prevent interaction with other prisoners for the duration of their confinement. Such prisons, though for a time popular, quickly became economically impracticable, and most states adopted the competing Auburn plan. A number of sources address the origins of nineteenth-century American disciplinary techniques and technologies. See de Beaumont and de Tocqueville, *On the Penitentiary System in the United States;* Lewis, *The Development of American Prisons and Prison Customs;* David W. Lewis, *From Newgate to Dannemora: The Rise of the Penitentiary in New York, 1796–1845* (Ithaca: Cornell University Press, 1965); Adam Hirsch, *The Rise of the Penitentiary: Prisons and Punishment in Early America* (New Haven: Yale University Press, 1992); Rothman, *The Discovery of the Asylum,* 79–108; Joel Schwartz, "The Penitentiary and Perfectibility in Tocqueville," *Western Political Quarterly* 38 (March 1985): 7–26; Glen A. Gildemeister, *Prison Labor and Convict Competition with Free Workers in Industrializing America, 1840–1890* (Garland: New York, 1987), 1–42; Larry E. Sullivan, *The Prison Reform Movement: Forlorn Hope,* Twayne's Social Movement Series (Boston: Twayne Publishers, 1990), 1–20; and Dumm, *Democracy and Punishment,* 113–40. For an architectural analysis of the neighboring Idaho and Wyoming territorial penitentiaries, see William Tydeman, "The Landscape of Incarceration: Idaho's Old Penitentiary," *Idaho Yesterdays* 38 (Summer 1994): 3–12, and Jeffrey L. Hauff, "Wyoming's First Penitentiary: Archaeology of a Victorian Era Correctional Institution," *Wyoming Archaeologist* 31 (3–4): 59–65.

53. The staff designated one ground-floor cell as a washroom.

54. See Jeremy Bentham, *The Works of Jeremy Bentham,* Vol. 4: *Panopticon; Or, the Inspection House* (New York: Russell and Russell, 1962); Foucault, *Discipline and Punish,* 195–230 and passim.

55. For further details, see William F. Wheeler to H. H. Bancroft, October 23, 1877, Wheeler Papers, MHS, and Chapter 3, this volume.

56. *Weekly Independent* (Deer Lodge City), July 7, 1871.

57. On authorization for marshals as wardens, see *Congressional Globe*, 41st Cong., 3d sess., 1871, Appendix 12, 330. The politics of appointments were not confined simply to the local level. The initial penitentiary commissioners, elected by the Democratic territorial legislature and appointed by the Democratic territorial governor in late 1867, were all, not surprisingly, influential Democrats. See the *Montana Post* (Virginia City) December 28, 1867.

58. Benjamin Potts to William F. Wheeler, April 19, 1871, Wheeler Papers, MHS.

59. For this last round of vigilance, see Oscar O. Mueller, "The Central Montana Vigilante Raids of 1884," *Montana, the Magazine of Western History* 1 (January, 1951): 23–35.

3 / "THE ACCURSED THING": THE TERRITORIAL PENITENTIARY

Chapter epigraph: Governor Benjamin Potts to William Wheeler, March 5, 1873, Wheeler Papers, Montana Historical Society (MHS), Helena.

1. Record of Prisoners, MHS.

2. See Territorial Governor Benjamin F. Potts to Sheriff of Madison County et al., June 24, 1871, in Letters of Governor Benjamin Potts, Montana Governors Papers, MHS.

3. Incarceration figures for the first few years remained fairly constant, averaging about 19 to 21 per month. *Second Annual Report, Montana Board of Prison Commissioners* (Helena: n.p., 1892), table 23.

4. For a succinct overview of nineteenth-century penal philosophies, see David J. Rothman, "Perfecting the Prison: United States, 1789–1865," in *The Oxford History of the Prison: The Practice of Punishment in Western Society*, ed. Norval Morris and David J. Rothman (New York: Oxford University Press, 1995), 100–16, and Mark Colvin, *Penitentiaries, Reformatories, and Chain Gangs: Social Theory and the History of Punishment in Nineteenth-Century America* (New York: St. Martin's Press, 1997). For the reformatory movement, see Pisciotta, *Benevolent Repression*.

5. U.S. House of Representatives, *Report of the Secretary of the Interior*, 42d Cong., 2d sess., 1871, House Ex. Doc. 1, p. 826.

6. In 1880, for example, Nevada incarcerated its population at a rate of 241 per 100,000; California at 173 per 100,000; Montana at 135 per 100,000. The national average in 1880 was 61 per 100,000. Department of Justice, Bureau of Justice Statistics, *Historical Corrections Statistics in the United States, 1850–1984,* ed. Margaret Werner Cahalan (Rockville, Md.: Westat, 1986), 30. In 1870 the population of Montana Territory was 20,595; in 1880, 39,159; in 1890, 132,159. *Montana Almanac* (Missoula: Montana State University Press, 1957), 175; Department of Justice, *Historical Corrections Statistics,* 30.

7. For self-conscious attempts to emulate the judicial traditions of eastern America, see, for example, Munson, "Pioneer Life in Montana," 236; Acting Territorial Governor Thomas Francis Meagher to General F. Wheaton, October 20, 1865, Territorial Papers, Montana, Department of State, National Archives, College Park, Md.; *Montana Post* (Virginia City), December 11, 1865, and August 11, 1866; and Decius Wade, "Charge to Grand Jury," Decius S. Wade Papers, MHS. Also see Spence, *Territorial Politics,* 218–20. John Wunder has determined that in Montana the appellate court was extremely active compared to other Northern Tier territories, producing twice as many civil and criminal law opinions between 1864 and 1890 as any other territory. Wunder, "Persistence and Adaptation," 108. For concurrent judicial developments in other western states and territories, see Bakken, *Development of Law in Frontier California;* Bakken, *Practicing Law in Frontier California,* esp. 99–113; Lawrence M. Friedman and Robert V. Percival, *The Roots of Justice: Crime and Punishment in Alameda County, California* (Chapel Hill: University of North Carolina Press, 1979); and Guice, *Rocky Mountain Bench.*

8. Quoted in Guice, *Rocky Mountain Bench,* 137.

9. Governor Potts to W. F. Wheeler, April 19, 1871, Wheeler Papers, MHS; Potts to W. F. Wheeler, April 20, 1871, ibid.

10. Both the Idaho and Colorado territorial penitentiaries were costing substantially more than had been anticipated. During the initial sixteen-month operating period, it cost the United States $11,085.42 to sustain the Colorado penitentiary and $6,569.32 to maintain Idaho's prison, both constructed and opened at approximately the same time as Montana's. *Congressional Globe,* 42d Cong., 3d sess., 1874, 409–10.

11. On relinquishing control, see ibid. and *U.S. Statutes at Large* 17 (1873): 418; Governor Benjamin Potts to William Wheeler, March 5, 1873, Wheeler Papers, MHS. Federal penury affected (and compromised) other aspects of the territorial judi-

cial system in Montana. See Clark Spence, "The Territorial Bench in Montana: 1864–1889," *Montana, the Magazine of Western History* 13 (January 1963): 25–32.

12. "Report of the Board of Directors to Governor Potts, November 1873," Montana Territorial Prison Records, MHS; *U.S. Statutes at Large* 18 (1874): 112. Also see Potts to Martin Maginnis, April 6 and May 12, 1874, Martin Maginnis Papers, MHS.

13. B. F. Potts to Martin Maginnis, February 17, 1874, Maginnis Papers, MHS; U.S. House of Representatives, *Annual Report of the United States Attorney General,* H. Exec. Doc. 1, 43d Cong., 2d sess., 1874–75, 17.

14. "Descriptive List of Prisoners Received at State [sic] Prison, July 1, 1871–October 1, 1885," Montana Prison Records, Montana Historical Society, Helena; *Daily Herald* (Helena), February 14, 1883. A log kitchen, which burned in 1883, and a log hospital also constituted part of the physical plant in the 1880s. Governor Potts recommendation, *Territory of Montana House Journal,* 12th session (1881), 40.

15. For the genesis of vigilante activities during this period, see Mueller, "The Central Montana Vigilante Raids of 1884," 25–35. Some thirty-five individuals were believed to have been lynched on the eastern Montana and northern Wyoming cattle ranges during this time.

16. See John Schuyler Crosby (Montana Territorial Governor, Helena) to Benjamin Brewster (Washington, D.C.), June 3, 1883, Source Chronological Files, Montana, Papers of the United States Attorney General, Department of Justice, (1881–1883), National Archives, College Park, Md.; S. F. Phillips (Washington, D.C.) to John Schuyler Crosby, August 3, 1883; and Benjamin Brewster (Washington, D.C.) to John Schuyler Crosby, October 16, 1883, Department of Justice, Letters Sent, General and Miscellaneous (1818–1904), Papers of the United States Attorney General, National Archives, College Park, Md.

17. "Report of the Governor of Montana," October 5, 1884, *Annual Report of the Secretary of the Interior, 1884,* House Exec. Doc. No. 1, 48th Cong., 2d sess., 1884–1885, 559.

18. Quoted in Spence, *Territorial Politics,* 268. Also see U.S. House of Representatives, *Report of the Governor of Montana, 1883,* H. Exec. Doc. 1, 48th Cong., 1st sess., 1883–84; *Report of the Attorney General, 1884–85;* and Alexander Botkin, U.S. Marshal, to S. F. Phillips, Acting Attorney General, October 2, 1884, ibid. B. P Carpenter, Crosby's short-term successor, spent much of his six-month tenure unsuccessfully lobbying other states to board the territory's convicts. Spence, *Territorial Politics,* 158. Also see Helena *Herald,* June 5, July 6, and August 17, 1885.

19. Alexander C. Botkin to Benjamin Brewster, U. S. Attorney General, October 11, 1884, Territorial Papers; W. Y. Simonton and John Trigg to territorial governor John Crosby, September 6, 1884, Territorial Papers, quoted in Spence, *Territorial Politics*, 268 (also see 220).

20. See Benjamin Harrison, Chair, Senate Committee on Territories, to Hugh McCulloch, Secretary of the Treasury, February 6, 1885; A. H. Garland, United States Attorney General, to the Secretary of the Interior, July 2, 1885; Z. Montgomery, Assistant United States Attorney General to the Assistant Secretary of the Interior, July 14, 1885; R. S. Kelley, U.S. marshal, to A. H. Garland, July 7, 1885; R. S. Kelley to Martin Maginnis, July 27, 1885; Martin Maginnis to A. H. Garland, July 25, 1885; S. J. Hauser, territorial governor, to L.C. Lamar, Secretary of the Interior, August 13, 1885; Robert Kelley to S. J. Hauser, August 3, 1885; and J. M. McConnell to S. J. Hauser, August 10, 1885, all in Territorial Papers.

21. Territorial Governor B. P. Carpenter to A. H. Garland, United States Attorney General, June 24, 1885; Alexander Botkin to James K. Toole, June 22, 1885; and Martin Maginnis to A. H. Garland, July 25, 1885, all in Territorial Papers.

22. *Statutes at Large* 23, 510.

23. "Descriptive List of Prisoners."

24. Ibid.

25. For number of murders, ibid. See *Anaconda Standard*, (Anaconda), October 6, 1895, and June 19, 1910, for profiles of Foley.

26. *Daily Inter Mountain* (Butte), March 17, 1890.

27. The provisions of the policy are detailed in "An Act to Regulate and Govern the Montana Penitentiary passed May, 1873," *Laws, Memorials and Resolutions of the Territory of Montana, Passed at First Extraordinary Session of the Legislative Assembly, Convened by Proclamation of Governor of Said Territory at Virginia City, April 14, 1873, to May 1873* (Helena: n.p., 1874).

28. "Descriptive List of Prisoners"; for an account of the incident, see the *Daily Herald* (Helena), May 14 and May 18, 1883.

29. Rothman, *Conscience and Convenience*, 19; C. B. Adriance to the Board of Directors, Montana Penitentiary, November 17, 1873, Montana Territorial Prison Records, MHS.

30. William Wheeler to Governor Potts, June 28, 1872, Montana Executive Office Records, MHS.

31. "Inventory of U.S. Property Transferred by W. F. Wheeler, U.S. Marshal, to Alex. C. Botkin, U.S. Marshal, at Deer Lodge Penitentiary, April 12, 1878," ibid.

32. "An Act to Regulate and Govern the Montana Penitentiary," 7; "Physicians Report, Montana Penitentiary, November 15, 1873," Montana Territorial Prison Records, MHS; "Report of Prisoners Confined in the Penitentiary to the Commissioners of Said Penitentiary," n.d., Records of Montana Territory Executive Office, MHS.

33. "Descriptive List of Prisoners."

34. Ibid.

35. Ibid., and "Montana Prison Convict Register, March 1879 through November 1910," Montana Prison Records. For the best overview of women prisoners in the late nineteenth-century American West, see Butler, *Gendered Justice*. For general studies of incarcerated women in other regions, consult Nicole Hahn Rafter, *Partial Justice: Women in State Prisons, 1800–1935* (Boston: Northeastern University Press, 1985), and Estelle B. Freedman, *Their Sisters' Keepers: Women's Prison Reform in America, 1830–1930* (Ann Arbor: University of Michigan Press, 1981).

36. "Montana Prison Convict Register."

37. Ibid.

38. For prisoner financial status upon imprisonment and upon release, see the miscellaneous ledgers in Montana State Board of Prison Commissioner Records, vol. 60, MHS.

39. "Rules and Regulations for the Government of the Montana Penitentiary," November 15, 1873, in "Report of the Board of Directors to Governor Potts," Montana Territorial Prison Records; suit of clothes stipulation, *Laws, Memorials and Resolutions of the Territory of Montana, Passed at the Seventh Session of the Legislative Assembly, at Virginia City, December 4, 1871 to January 12, 1872* (Deer Lodge: n.p., 1872), 566. After statehood, inmates were allowed to keep small fractions of their earnings and to purchase items while in prison.

40. For example, see Governor Potts to Warden C. B. Adriance, November 28, 1872, and Potts to William Wheeler, December 3, 1872, Montana Governor's Papers, MHS. For Colorado's attempts to defray its inmate costs, see McGinn, *At Hard Labor*, 53–96.

41. Governor Potts to C. B. Adriance, Warden, November 27, 1872, Montana Governors Papers, MHS. Original emphasis retained.

42. "Rules and Regulations," November 15, 1873, Montana Territorial Prison Records, MHS; *Congressional Globe,* 41st Cong., 3d sess., pt. 3: 330; C. B. Adriance to Potts, January 15, 1873, Montana Territorial Prison Records, MHS; "An Act to Regulate and Govern the Montana Penitentiary," 7; warden complaint, William F. Wheeler to H. H. Bancroft, October 23, 1877, Wheeler Papers, MHS.

43. "Descriptive List of Prisoners."

44. For turn-of-the-century populations, see *Annual Report of the Board of State Prison Commissioners, 1907–1911* (Helena: State Publishing Company, 1911).

45. "An Act to Regulate and Govern the Montana Penitentiary," 7–8. Foucault, however, believed that teaching useful skills or obtaining profit for the state off inmate labor was inconsequential. Penal labor is important, he contended, because it produces "the constitution of a power relation, an empty economic form, a schema of individual submission and of adjustment to a production apparatus," even a feckless one such as make-work prison labor. Furthermore, "what one is trying to restore in this technique of correction is . . . the obedient subject, the individual subject to habits, rules, orders, an authority that is exercised continually around him and upon him, which he must allow to function automatically in him." Foucault, *Discipline and Punish,* 243 and 128–29.

46. For representative scholarship, see Foucault, *Discipline and Punish,* 27, 170, and 189; Halttunen, "Humanitarianism and the Pornography of Pain;" Elizabeth Lunbeck, *The Psychiatric Persuasion: Knowledge, Gender, and Power in Modern America* (Princeton: Princeton University Press, 1994); Barron Lerner, *Contagion and Confinement: Controlling Tuberculosis along the Skid Road* (Baltimore: Johns Hopkins University Press, 1998); Gerald Grob, *Mental Illness and American Society, 1875–1940* (Princeton: Princeton University Press, 1983); Anne Digby, *Madness, Morality and Medicine: A Study of the York Retreat* (New York: Cambridge University Press, 1985); Andrew Scull, ed., *Madhouses, Mad-Doctors, and Madmen: The Social History of Psychiatry in the Victorian Era* (Philadelphia: University of Pennsylvania Press, 1981); and Mary Ann Jiminez, *Changing Faces of Madness: Early American Attitudes and Treatment of the Insane* (Hanover, N.H.: University Press of New England, 1985).

47. Foucault, *Discipline and Punish,* 27; also see 170 and 189.

48. Ibid., 139.

49. "Inventory, 1878," Montana Territorial Prison Records, MHS.

50. "Descriptive List of Prisoners" and "Montana Prison Convict Register."

51. See extensive pardon documentation in "Applications for Executive Pardons, 1870–72 and 1875–1889," Montana Executive Office Records, Territorial Records, MHS. For a survey of both the methodological strengths and weaknesses of using jail and prison registers to illuminate class, gender, and racial issues in relation to imprisonment patterns and crime rates, see Harvey Graff, "Crime and Punishment in the Nineteenth Century: A New Look at the Criminal," *Journal of Interdisciplinary History* 7 (Winter 1977): 477–91. Also see Clare McKanna, "Ethnics and San Quentin Prison Registers: A Comment on Methodology," *Journal of Social History* 18 (Fall 1985), 481.

52. Ibid., 480; Hietter, "A Surprising Amount of Justice"; Liping Zhu, *A Chinaman's Chance: The Chinese on the Rocky Mountain Mining Frontier* (Boulder: University of Colorado Press, 1997), 154.

53. After the mid-1880s, however, Wunder concludes that Montana courts "became anti-Chinese too," though again, the number of Chinese in the penitentiary do not reflect this sentiment within the criminal justice branch. John R. Wunder, "Law and Chinese in Frontier Montana," *Montana, the Magazine of Western History* 30 (Summer 1980): 18–31 (qtn., 18). In fact, as Robert Swartout notes, "between 1900–1918, only six Chinese residents were sent to the state penitentiary, four of them for the same crime." Robert Swartout, "Kwangtung to Big Sky: The Chinese in Montana, 1864–1900," in, *The Chinese on the American Frontier*, ed. Arif Dirlik (Lanham, Md.: Rowman and Littlefield, 2001): 376. Lucy Salyer, in "Captives of Law: Judicial Enforcement of the Chinese Exclusion Laws, 1891–1905," *Journal of American History* 76 (June 1989): 91–117, argues that in the late nineteenth century, at least in California, judges may have inherited legal traditions that constrained discriminatory actions against the Chinese. Also see Charles McClain, *The Chinese Struggle Against Discrimination in Nineteenth-Century America* (Berkeley: University of California Press, 1994), and John Wunder, "Chinese in Trouble: Criminal Law and Race on the Trans-Mississippi West Frontier," *Western Historical Quarterly* 27 (January 1986): 25–41.

54. For an overview of anti-Chinese sentiment in Montana, see Larry D. Quinn, "'Chink Chink Chinaman': The Beginning of Nativism in Montana," *Pacific Northwest Quarterly* 58 (April 1967): 82–89; Territory of Montana v. Ah Wah, Case #528, Criminal and Civil Files, Deer Lodge County (2d Judicial District); *New North-West* (Deer Lodge), May 26, 1871.

55. "Descriptive List of Prisoners."

56. Ibid. Between 1871 and 1885, 41 out of a total population of 382 (11 percent) were categorized as Chinese, Negro, Indian, or Mexican. The 1870 census reported 9.6 percent of the population as nonwhite; in 1880, 11.1 percent; in 1890, 11.8. *The Statistics of the Population of the United States . . . Compiled From the Original Returns of the Ninth Census* (Washington, D.C.: U.S. Government Printing Office, 1872); *Compendium of the Tenth Census* (Washington, D.C.: U.S. Government Printing Office, 1883), 360; *Report on the Population of the United States and the Eleventh Census, 1890,* Part I (Washington, D.C.: U.S. Government Printing Office, 1895).

57. *Compendium of the Tenth Census,* 1880, 518; "Descriptive List of Prisoners"; "Montana Prison Convict Register"; *Annual Report of the Board of Prison Commissioners, 1907–1911.*

58. For details on Sanchez, see *New North-West* (Deer Lodge), December 6, 1878, and Butler, *Gendered Justice,* 72. For Drouillard background, see Butler, *Gendered Justice,* 124–26.

59. Butler, "Still in Chains," 34 and passim; "Descriptive List of Prisoners"; "Montana Prison Convict Register."

60. "Descriptive List of Prisoners"; "Applications for Executive Pardons, 1870–72." Quote from "Bozeman petitioners to Governor Potts, July 9, 1872" (case of Moi Toi) in "Applications." The presence of a sixteen-year-old Native American in an institution that had housed no other whites of the same age in its history could be a fair indicator of discrimination in the local court. For an overview of the circumstances surrounding the incarceration of these four Northern Cheyenne, see Allen Chronister, "Elk Head and White Bear: Warrior Artists in the Early Reservation Period," *Montana, the Magazine of Western History* 48 (Summer 1998): 36–39.

61. C. F. Musigbrod to Governor Potts, September 5, 1874, Records of Montana Territory Executive Office, MHS.

62. "Descriptive List of Prisoners." Nonwhites accounted for a lowly 2 percent of all escapes; only one out of fifty-four attempted escapes during the period 1871–1885 can be attributed to a non-Anglo.

63. Given the dearth of firsthand accounts, there is little way of knowing with precision what types, if any, of racial, ethnic, and cultural alliances or antagonisms developed in the early years of the prison. Strong hierarchies, based on religious persuasion (non–Church of Latter-day Saints versus Church of Latter-day Saints), are documented in the both the Utah and Wyoming territorial penitentiaries during these years, and racial hierarchies were present in the Arizona territorial prison.

Again, only inference can be made on conditions within the Montana prison during the same period. See Rudger Clawson, *Prisoner for Polygamy: The Memoirs and Letters of Rudger Clawson at the Utah Territorial Penitentiary, 1884–87,* ed. Stan Larson (Urbana and Chicago: University of Illinois, 1993); Gordon Olsen, "'I Felt Like I Must Be Entering . . . Another World': The Anonymous Memoirs of an Early Inmate of the Wyoming Penitentiary," *Annals of Wyoming* 47 (Fall 1975): 152–90. The 1873 inmate petition was in support of Dr. O. B. Whitford. Records of Montana Territory Executive Office, MHS.

64. Nor do the shifting levels of incarceration in the territory appear to follow any distinct economic cycle or cycles affecting Montana society. The Marxist sociologist Christopher Adamson has determined that historically "the labor supply and the business cycle influence how populations are processed through the criminal justice system." Certainly this is true with regard to the use of inmate labor. But there is no evidence to suggest that those in economic power viewed territorial inmates as either economic threats prior to their incarceration—quasi-justification for their confinement—or as a readily exploitable labor resource, as Adamson concluded occurred in eastern and some midwestern American penitentiaries over the course of the nineteenth century. Christopher Adamson, "Toward a Marxian Penology: Captive Criminal Populations as Economic Threats and Resources," *Social Problems* 31 (April 1984): 437. For the role economics played in both rehabilitation and punishment in territorial Colorado, see McGinn, *At Hard Labor,* 53–74. Also see Rusche and Kirkenheimer, *Punishment and Social Structure,* and more recently, David F. Greenberg, *Crime and Capitalism: Readings in Marxist Criminology* (Philadelphia: Temple University Press, 1993).

65. In 1880 Idaho incarcerated 67 persons per 100,000 population; Wyoming, 91; Washington, 72; Utah, 37; and Colorado, 95. Montana, by contrast, incarcerated 135 persons per 100,000 in the population. In 1890, immediately after Montana achieved statehood, the figures went even higher: 157 per 100,000, while Idaho's rate was 115; Wyoming's, 16; Washington's, 72; Utah's, 85; and Colorado's, 127 per 100,000. Figures from Cahalan, *Historical Corrections Statistics,* 30. Also see De Lorme, "The Long Arm of the Law," 128–29.

66. Gerald Grob, a historian of mental illness and America's changing institutional responses to mental diseases, notes that "the mental hospital has always been more than simply an institution that offered care and treatment for the sick and disabled. Its structure and functions have usually been linked with a variety of exter-

nal economic, political, social, and intellectual forces, if only because the way in which a society handled problems of disease and dependency was partly governed by its social structure and values." Gerald Grob, *Mental Institutions in America: Social Policy to 1875* (New York: The Free Press, 1973), xi–xii.

67. The institution was to be located at Warm Springs, the site of a hotel and spa that Mitchell and Musigbrod had purchased two years earlier and named for the 160-degree, mineral-laden springs that bubbled to the surface there and that many believed to provide curative effects.

68. "State Board of Charities and Reform 1894 Report to Governor Rickards, 1894," Montana Governors Papers (Rickards), MHS.

69. This, and the patient information in the following paragraphs, is from Mitchell and Musigbrod report to Governor, January 1, 1881, in Montana Executive Office Records, MHS.

70. No detailed patient file for these individuals exists. Only statistical records maintained by the lessees and reported to the governor are available. Because the territory confined so few women, it is impossible to assess differing therapeutic approaches the staff used in relation to gender. For a general overview of women, mental illness, and psychiatry in the nineteenth and early twentieth centuries, see Denise Russel, *Women, Madness and Medicine* (London: Polity Press, 1995), and Lunbeck, *Psychiatric Persuasion,* passim.

71. A. H. Mitchell to Governor Potts, [1881], Montana Executive Office Records, MHS.

72. "Report of Dr. C. F. Musigbrod, 1891," ibid.

73. "Report of Inspection of Insane Hospital by C. K. Cole, M.D., January 27, 1885," ibid.

74. Pinel championed, as well, the type of nontherapeutic therapy utilized at Warm Springs by the original proprietors. See Philippe Pinel, *A Treatise on Insanity,* trans. D. D. Davis (1801; reprint, New York: Haffner, 1962).

75. A. H. Mitchell to Governor Potts, n.d. [1881], Montana Executive Office Records, MHS.

76. State law strictly precludes researchers from displaying or publishing any of the photos. As a postscript, after the turn of the century Montana was slow to share in any of the psychiatric and therapeutic revolutions that began to shake the foundations of the mental health industry elsewhere in America. In 1912 the asy-

lum officially became the Montana State Hospital and soon became home to more than 2,000 patients. The numbers steadily increased at the institution until the 1960s, when a nationwide deinstitutionalization movement began. The state of Montana continues to house many of its mentally ill at Warm Springs, but a large number of the older brick hospital buildings stand empty now, as does the equally silent Anaconda copper smelter that looms ten miles in the distance.

77. The rules and regulations promulgated by the initial state Board of Commissioners for the Insane emphasized that humanity, care, even respect for the patients were to be primary concerns. See "Rules and Regulations for the Government of the Insane Asylum," March 12, 1894, esp. rules 13–15, in Warm Springs State Hospital Records, MHS.

78. Ibid.

79. Richard Fox suggests that the same may have occurred in California. In his analysis of California's response to insanity between 1870 and 1930, Fox asserts that "to construct and encourage easy access to asylums might seem then to be a way of 'civilizing' the state. . . . Moreover, large expenditures for the insane might have seemed a means of increasing the state's prestige." Richard Fox, *So Far Disordered in Mind: Insanity in California, 1870–1930* (Berkeley: University of California Press, 1978), 23. For two Northwest studies, see Russell Hollander, "Life at the Washington Asylum for the Insane, 1871–1880," *The Historian* 44 (Spring, 1982): 229–41, and O. Larsell, "History of Care of Insane in the state of Oregon," *Oregon Historical Quarterly* 46 (December 1945): 295–326.

4 / NO WARDEN MORE EFFICIENT: FRANK CONLEY

Chapter epigraph: W. A. Clark, Jr., to Governor Joseph Dixon, May 4, 1921, Joseph M. Dixon Papers, Mansfield Library, University of Montana (UM), Missoula.

1. See oath of the "Law and Order Organization of Custer County," Small Collection, 1881, Montana Historical Society (MHS).

2. Figures from *Annual Report of the Board of State Prison Commissioners, 1891–1906* (Helena: State Publishing Company, 1906); *Annual Report of the Board of State Prison Commissioners, 1907–1911* (Helena: State Publishing Company, 1911); and *Annual Report of the Board of State Prison Commissioners, 1914–1932* (Helena: State Publishing Company, 1933) (copies available at MHS).

3. *Laws, Memorials and Resolutions of the State of Montana passed at the Second Regular Session of the Legislative Assembly, Helena, Montana, January 5, 1891–March 5, 1891* (Helena: Journal Publishing Company, 1891), 148. For a recent overview of the lease system and prison labor in other western states at this time, consult Butler, *Gendered Justice*, 175–82; for a case study on the nature of prison labor and the lease system in nearby Colorado, see McGinn, *At Hard Labor*, 53–151, passim. For a general overview of the evolution of the lease system in nineteenth-century America, consult Gildemeister, *Prison Labor and Convict Competition.*

4. "Message of Governor Joseph K. Toole to the Second Legislative Assembly of the State of Montana," *Laws, Memorials, and Resolutions of the State of Montana, Passed at the Second Legislative Session, 1891* (Helena: Journal Publishing Company, 1891).

5. *Third Annual Report of the Board of State Prison Commissioners of the State of Montana, December 1, 1893* (Butte: Inter Mountain Publishing Company, 1895).

6. For an overview of the road-building program, see Jon Axline, "Convict Labor," *Independent Record* (Helena), January 16, 1997.

7. See Adamson, "Toward a Marxian Penology," 437. For the role economics played in both rehabilitation and punishment in Colorado, see McGinn, *At Hard Labor*, 53–74; for a general overview, consult Egardo Rotman, "The Failure of Reform: United States, 1865–1965," in Morris and Rothman, *The Oxford History of the Prison*, 151–77.

8. "Rules and Regulations for the Government of the Montana State Prison, Adopted by the Board of State Prison Commissioners, September 3, 1891," Montana State Prison Records, MHS. Emphasis added.

9. *Annual Report of the State Board of Prison Commissioners* (Helena: The Independent Publishing Company, 1892).

10. *Annual Report of the Board of Prison Commissioners*, 1914 (Helena: State Publishing Company, 1915), 7.

11. *Third Annual Report of the Board of State Prison Commissioners of the State of Montana, December 1, 1893* (Butte: Inter Mountain Publishing Company, 1895), 7.

12. "Special Joint Investigating Committee of the Ninth Legislative Assembly," Ninth Legislative Assembly Records, MHS.

13. See *Silver State* (Deer Lodge), May 20, 1908.

14. For a detailed examination of the building program and the architectural

history at the prison in the decades framing the turn of the nineteenth century, see James McDonald, *Historic Structures Report: Montana State Prison* (Deer Lodge: Powell County Museum and Arts Foundation, 1981). The cellblock stood until 1959, when an earthquake in Yellowstone National Park irreparably damaged the foundation. The wall still stands on the periphery of downtown Deer Lodge.

15. Malone et al., *Montana,* 207. For free labor versus prison labor tension elsewhere in the United States circa 1890, see Gildemeister, *Prison Labor and Convict Competition,* passim.

16. *Silver State* (Deer Lodge) April 18, 1900.

17. The Billings scheme is outlined in *Laws, Memorials and Resolutions of the State of Montana, Passed at the Third Regular Session of the Legislative Assembly, Helena, Montana, January 2, 1893 to March 2, 1893* (Butte: Inter Mountain Publishing, 1893), 194–97. Consult Michael P. Malone, "Midas of the West: The Incredible Career of William Andrews Clark," *Montana, the Magazine of Western History* 33 (Autumn 1983): 10, for the political machinations forming the backdrop to the Helena to Anaconda capital fight and the dangling of institutions before various Montana communities in return for support in the heated 1894 election.

18. Larabie Bros & Co. et al., *Location of Montana State Prison,* January 20, 1893 (Helena: n.p., 1893).

19. Land holdings, Conley to H. B. Hurley, Butte, July 6, 1909, and Conley to C. H. Martin, Des Moines, Iowa, July 30, 1909, in Montana Prison Records, MHS.

20. Just down the road from the prison the business of insanity was also paying handsome dividends for the two proprietors, Musigbrod and Mitchell, during this time. In 1912, when the state passed legislation to purchase the property and obtain direct control of the institution, the Warm Springs complex was valued at nearly $900,000. Mitchell and Musigbrod bought the original property for approximately $13,000 and acquired an additional 1,500 acres of adjoining land between 1877 and 1886. See A. H. Mitchell to Governor B. F. Potts, (1881?), in Montana Executive Records, MHS; *New North-West* (Deer Lodge), September 9, 1887; and *Silver State* (Deer Lodge), September 26, 1912.

21. I am indebted to Mary Kay Horstman, formerly of Heritage Research Associates, Missoula, for this information. Conley's voluminous correspondence is now in Montana Prison Records, MHS. See those files for details of his ranching, horse breeding, and business empire—all intermingled with his prison correspondence— symbolic of his life. Evidence of a chauffeur comes from Conley's own admission

in 1909, see Conley to Butte Novelty Works, August 28, 1909, Montana Prison Records, MHS; prizefight, *Silver State* (Deer Lodge), August 1, 1918; bungalow description, *Daily Independent* (Helena), September 30, 1921.

22. Karlin, *Joseph M. Dixon of Montana, Part 2*, p. 87.

23. George Scharschug to Senator Thomas H. Carter, June 14, 1910, in Thomas H. Carter Papers, National Archives, Washington, D.C.

24. "Minutes of the Board of Prison Commissioners," vol. 1, 1890/91, Montana State Prison Records, MHS.

25. Ibid., 7.

26. "Conduct Record," vol. 37, Montana State Prison Records, MHS.

27. *Anaconda Standard,* October 6, 1895.

28. Thomas O'Brien, *Infamy Immortal* (Butte: Schwan Publishing, 1904), passim.

29. "Special Joint Investigating Committee of the Ninth Legislative Assembly."

30. Ibid.

31. For the investigation and trial, see Karlin, *Joseph M. Dixon of Montana, Part 2*, 87–117, and below.

32. "Senate Committee Appointed to Examine the State Penitentiary at Deer Lodge (February 20, 1891)," Second Montana Legislative Assembly Records, MHS.

33. The State Board of Charities had a different opinion, however, about the care of the state's insane at Warm Springs under the similar lease arrangement. In 1894 it reported that

> the whole system of managing public institutions of this character (or the pauper and insane classes)—poor farms, prisons, or asylums—by *contract* is an unwise policy, which the state ought to discontinue at the earliest possible moment. For the state to make merchandise of the dependent, defective and criminal classes in this manner is neither wisdom nor economy. This policy has been abandoned in nearly all the states of the Union. . . . [I]t is an ignoble thing for a great state to put the care of its wards upon this commercial basis.

See "State Board of Charities to Governor J. E. Rickards, 1894," Montana Governors Papers (Rickards), MHS.

34. For general surveys of progressivism, consult Arthur S. Link and Richard

McCormick, *Progressivism* (Arlington Heights, Ill.: Harlan Davidson, 1983); and Wiebe, *The Search for Order.* For progressivism in Montana, see Richard B. Roeder's "Montana in the Early Years of the Progressive Period," Ph.D. diss., University of Pennsylvania, 1971; and K. Ross Toole, *Twentieth-Century Montana: A State of Extremes* (Norman: University of Oklahoma Press, 1972), 195–272. For progressive reforms in state and federal prisons, see McKelvey, *American Prisons,* 197–216, Rothman, *Conscience and Convenience,* Rotman, "The Failure of Reform," and Jonathan Simon, *Poor Discipline: Parole and the Social Control of the Underclass, 1890–1990* (Chicago: University of Chicago Press, 1993).

35. There is strong evidence that the reform movement did make inroads among local police forces in some of the smallest and most remote towns of Montana between 1890 and 1918. The towns of Miles City, Kalispell, Hamilton, Dillon, Bozeman, and Glasgow adopted laws that, according to Robert A. Harvie and Larry V. Bishop, "introduced the ideal of police professionalism" and sought concurrently to eradicate immorality and vice in their communities. See Robert A. Harvie and Larry V. Bishop, "Police Reform in Montana, 1890–1918," *Montana, the Magazine of Western History* 33 (Spring 1983): 46–59 (qtn., 47). Also see Harvie, *Keeping the Peace,* passim.

36. The fullest contemporary expression of Progressive ideas and attitudes toward crime and punishment is in the *Annuals of the American Academy of Political and Social Sciences* 46 (March 1913), which devoted an entire issue to new penological philosophy. The titles of many of the articles are suggestive: "Industrial Penology"; "Reform through Labor"; "The Problem of Prison Labor"; and Roosevelt's piece, "The New Penology." For juvenile justice in Montana during this period, see Julie Marie Greenheck, "The Impact of Progressivism on Montana: The Child Labor Law and the Establishment of Juvenile Courts," senior honors thesis, Carroll College, Helena, 1991.

37. See *Laws, Memorials, and Resolutions, of the Territory of Montana, Passed at the Seventh Session of the Legislative Assembly* (Deer Lodge: James H. Mills, 1872) for a listing of the various territorial criminal laws and punishments, many of which the state modified and adopted in 1889.

38. *Proceedings of the Annual Congress of the National Prison Association of the United States, 1900* (Pittsburgh: Shaw Brothers, 1900), 373.

39. "An Act Providing for Indeterminate Sentences of Persons Convicted of

Crime, and for the Parole of Such Persons, and Prescribing the Duties of Officials in Connection therewith," *Laws, Resolutions and Memorials of the State of Montana passed by the 14th Regular Session of the Legislative Assembly* (Helena: State Publishing Company, 1915), chap. 14.

40. For the linkage between progressive reform and education within the nation's prisons, see Terry Angle, "The Development of Educational Programs in American Adult Prisons and Juvenile Reformatories During the Nineteenth Century," *Journal of Correctional Education* 33 (September 1982): 4–6; Thomas Gehring and Will R. Muth, "The Correctional Education/Prison Reform Link: Part I, 1840–1900," *Journal of Correctional Education* 36 (December 1985): 140–46; Albert R. Roberts, *Source Book on Prison Education: Past, Present, Future* (Springfield, Ill.: Charles C. Thomas, 1971), passim; and Carl C. Gaither, "Education Behind Bars: An Overview," *Journal of Correctional Education* 33 (June 1982): 19–22.

41. *Proceedings and Debates of Constitution Convention* (Helena: State Publishing Company, 1921), 425–26.

42. Ibid.

43. Quoted in Kent, *Montana State Prison History,* 50.

44. Conley and Thomas McTague to the Montana State Board of Prison Commissioners, November 30, 1902, Montana Governors Papers (Toole), MHS.

45. Quoted in Kent, *Montana State Prison History,* 51.

46. Ibid.

47. "Rules and Regulations, 1891."

48. Roundup *Tribune,* June 3, 1920.

49. Great Falls *Tribune,* January 2, 1918.

50. Untitled reminiscence of Charles Diggs Greenfield, Charles Diggs Greenfield, Jr., Family Papers, MHS. The assailant, who was later hanged in the prison yard in full view of the inmate population, stabbed Conley several times before the warden shot him. Conley's neck wounds required forty stitches and a lengthy hospital stay. For details of the incident, see *Silver State* (Deer Lodge), March 11, 1908.

51. Great Falls *Tribune,* January 2, 1918.

52. Quoted in Kent, *Montana State Prison History,* 35.

53. There is substantial scholarship treating the hostility and occasional violence organized labor faced in Montana between 1900 and 1920. The laws passed by the Montana legislature at the height of World War I were clearly repressive and just as clearly abridged the First Amendment. See Arnon Gutfield, *Montana's Agony:*

Years of War and Hysteria (Gainesville: University of Florida Press, 1979), and Jerry Calvert, *The Gibraltar: Socialism and Labor in Butte, Montana, 1895–1920* (Helena: Montana Historical Society Press, 1988).

54. Conley to Sharpless Walker, December 24, 1919, Montana State Prison Records, MHS.

55. Conley to Governor S. V. Stewart, February 20, 1920, ibid.

56. Conley to Charles K. Andrews, January 22, 1920, ibid.

57. Conley to E. A. Fisher, June 3, 1909, ibid.

58. In one of the more notorious cases, E. V. Starr had been sentenced to not less than ten years hard labor and fined $500 for refusing to kiss the American flag. The case was overturned on appeal. See Arnon Gutfield, "George Bourquin: A Montana Judge's Stand Against Despotism," *Western Legal History* 6 (Spring 1993): 51–68.

59. *Annual Report of the Board of State Prison Commissioners, 1918* (Butte: Inter Mountain Printing Company, 1919).

60. Consult Robert E. Evans, "Montana's Role in the Enactment of Legislation Designed to Suppress the Industrial Workers of the World," M.A. thesis, University of Montana, 1964; and Gutfield, *Montana's Agony,* 23–80.

61. Quoted in Kent, *Montana State Prison History,* 30.

62. Quoted in ibid., 45.

63. Ibid., 46.

64. Conley to Charles Andrews, Inspector in Charge, U.S. Department of Labor Immigration Services, Helena, November 11, 1919, Montana State Prison Records, MHS.

65. Conley to John H. McIntosh, October 18, 1919, ibid.

66. Conley to Governor S. V. Stewart, November 21, 1919, ibid.

67. Conley to Chief of Police, Calgary, Alberta, Canada, February 25, 1921, ibid.

68. Conley to Annie Leavenworth, January 10, 1920, ibid.

69. Quoted in Kent, *Montana State Prison History,* 47.

70. Quoted in Rothman, *Conscience and Convenience,* 184; "punks," Conley to J. W. Ryan, June 8, 1909, Montana State Prison Records, MHS.

71. "Minutes of the Board of Prison Commissioners," vol. 60, Montana State Prison Records, MHS. Daly's involvement, along with that of William Andrews Clark and, earlier in the century, that of Samuel T. Hauser, reflected the fact that three out of four of Montana's wealthiest habitants (Helena financier C. A. Broad-

water was the other) were directly involved with the prison at various points during the institution's early history.

72. See *Butte Miner,* August 19, 1920.

73. See ibid. and *Silver State* (Deer Lodge), May 13, 1903, October 11, 1917, and April 1, 1918.

74. This is the most exhaustively covered phase of Montana's political and economic history. For the best overview, see Michael Malone, *The Battle for Butte: Mining and Politics on the Northern Frontier, 1864–1906* (Seattle: University of Washington Press, 1981).

75. For Clark's early career in Deer Lodge, see Malone, "Midas of the West," 6.

76. There are many sources that discuss the involvement of the Anaconda Copper Mining Company in Montana affairs. See K. Ross Toole, "A History of the Anaconda Copper Mining Company: A Study in the Relationships Between a State and Its People and a Corporation, 1880–1950," Ph.D. diss., University of California at Los Angeles, 1954; Michael P. Malone, "Montana as a Corporate Bailiwick: An Image in History," in *Montana Past and Present* (Los Angeles: William Andrews Clark Library, 1976): 57–76; and David Emmons, "The Price of 'Freedom': Montana in the Late and Post-Anaconda Era," in *Politics in the Postwar American West,* ed. Richard Lowitt (Norman: University of Oklahoma Press, 1995), 120–34.

77. Charles Diggs Greenfield, untitled typescript reminiscences, Charles Diggs Greenfield, Jr., Family Papers, MHS. For admission of friendship with the Anaconda Company, see Conley to W. H. Trippett, April 15, 1921; Conley to C. H. Adams, April 15, 1921; Conley to John Hogan, April 15, 1921; Conley to Mr. Hutchens, April 15, 1921; and Conley to Dick Kilroy, April 15, 1921, all in Montana State Prison Records, MHS.

78. See the various receipts and letters between Conley and the business between 1914–1921 in Montana State Prison Records, MHS.

79. *Silver State* (Deer Lodge), September 3, 1914.

80. *Montana Nonpartisan* (Great Falls), November 22, 1919.

81. See Michael Malone and Diane Dougherty, "Montana's Political Culture: A Century of Evolution," in *The Montana Heritage: An Anthology of Historical Essays,* ed. Harry Fritz and Robert Swartout (Helena: Montana Historical Society Press, 1993), 180. In 1915 the Amalgamated liquidated and reorganized as the Anaconda

Copper Mining Company. After 1915 it had no further affiliation with the Standard Oil group. Malone, *Montana*, 230.

82. All discussions of Dixon and his policies are mere footnotes to Jules Karlin's comprehensive two-volume biography: *Joseph M. Dixon of Montana, Part 1: Senator and Bull Moose Manager, 1867–1917* (Missoula: University of Montana Press, 1974), and *Joseph M. Dixon of Montana, Part 2: Governor Versus the Anaconda, 1917–1934.*

83. "The Big Outfit," Jerome Locke to Dixon, January 18, 1921, quoted in ibid.; "invisible government," Dixon to John F. McKay, April 26, 1921, Dixon Papers, University of Montana (UM), Missoula.

84. Governor Joseph Dixon to Frank Conley, April 13, 1921, Dixon Papers, UM.

85. W. A. Clark, Jr., to Dixon, May 4, 1921, and April 16, 1921, ibid.

86. Dixon to W. A. Clark, Jr., April 25, 1921, ibid.

87. See Shirley DeForth, "The Montana Press and Governor Joseph M. Dixon, 1920–1922," M.A. thesis, University of Montana, 1959, pp. 102–106.

88. Figures in Toole, *Twentieth-Century Montana*, 266.

89. *Montana Board of Prison Commissioners, Twenty-Third Annual Report* (Helena: State Publishing Company, 1923), 25.

90. T. H. MacDonald, "Report of Investigation of Prison, 1921," Montana Governors Papers (Dixon), MHS.

91. After Conley's dismissal expenses declined to $400 a month.

92. For a full description of all the charges, see Helena *Record-Herald*, November 29, 1921; Helena *Independent*, November 30, 1921; and Deforth, "The Montana Press," 116 and note 61.

93. Dixon to C. T. Stewart and Wellington Rankin, November 21, 1921, Records of the Montana Attorney General, MHS.

94. Helena *Record-Herald*, April 6, 1922.

95. Ibid., December 24, 1921.

96. Anaconda *Standard*, April 14, 1921.

97. The three-month trial, with supporting documentation, produced a 10,000-page stenographic record. Montana State Prison Records, MHS. For selected key testimony, consult Helena *Independent*, June 15, 16, 18, 1922; Helena *Record-Herald*, July 7, 1922; and Karlin, *Joseph M. Dixon, Part 2*, 105–17.

98. Helena *Independent*, June 2, 1922.

99. *Silver State* (Deer Lodge), May 20, 1908.

100. Helena *Record-Herald,* November 28, 1922.

101. Because of the larger political questions embodied in this case, it has received fairly extensive scholarly attention. See DeForth, "The Montana Press," 102–48; and Karlin, *Joseph M. Dixon of Montana, Part 2,* 105–17, passim. Quote is from Karlin, 116.

5 / GETTING TOUGH ON CRIME

1. Inmate census material gleaned from Montana State Board of Prison Commissioners Annual Reports, vols. 23–28, and Board of Prison Commissioners Records, vol. 16, Montana Historical Society (MHS).

2. "Nobody Cares," *Montana Opinion* 1 (June 1957): 1–14.

3. "Board of Prison Commissioners, Transcript of Hearing, August 7, 1957," Montana Attorney General Records, MHS; "Report of Special Joint Committee of the Twenty-Second Legislative Assembly of the State of Montana on State Institutions at Deer Lodge, Galen, and Warm Springs, 1931," Montana Governors Papers (Aronson), MHS.

4. Dixon to Conley, April 12, 1921, Dixon Papers, University of Montana, Missoula.

5. From 1921 to 1958 the wardens, in order, were M. L. Potter, J. W. Cole, Austin B. Middleton, Theodore Bergstrom, Dudley Jones, John E. Henry, Lou Boedecker, F. O. Burrell, and William Benson.

6. "Transcript of Hearing, Board of Prison Commissioners, September 25, 1957," Montana State Prison Records, MHS. Between 1953 and 1955 Burrell allowed at least $18,529.41 to revert. Ibid., 58. Burrell's ineptitude is well documented in "Minute Book, 1952–58," Board of Prison Commissioner Records; "Minute Book 63," Montana State Board of Examiners Records; "Evaluation Report Montana State Prison by R. L. Wham," Montana State Board of Examiners Records; and the various papers and correspondence of then attorney general Forest Anderson, Montana Attorney General Records, all at MHS; and corroborated in my interview with William F. Crowley (an assistant attorney general for the state during the time), November 2, 1988, Missoula, Montana. Except for 1956, when the population averaged 566, between 1952 and 1958 the yearly prison population averaged more than 600, well above the 543 yearly average of the previous three decades. "Average

Inmate Population from 1927–1957," Montana Legislative Council Records, MHS. See Chart 5.

7. "Evaluation Report Montana State Prison by R. L. Wham," 18, Montana Attorney General Records (Anderson), MHS.

8. For wages, see the "Correction Benevolent Association Inc. of the City of New York Report," n.d., Montana Governors Papers (Ford), MHS. Pay increased by the 1950s to $200 per month, still far below the inflationary rate. For percentage of retirees, see "A Report by Kenyon J. Scudder, Director of Field Services, Osborne Assoc., Inc., September 15, 1957," 2, Montana Legislative Council Records, MHS; also see "Report of Eugene Tidball, February 3, 1958," ibid.

9. Dudley Jones to Governor Sam Ford, April 24, 1941, in Montana Governors Papers (Ford), MHS.

10. "Montana State Prison: A Report to the 36th Legislative Assembly by the Montana Legislative Council, December 1958," 36th Legislative Assembly Records, MHS.

11. Ibid.

12. "Nobody Cares," 13, and "Report and Recommendations of the Montana State Penal Institutions Survey Committee," Montana State Prison Records, MHS; rules quoted in Kent, *Montana State Prison History*, 61.

13. For prison life generally in the 1950s, I have drawn extensively on personal interviews with Carl Frodsham, Montana State Prison, Deer Lodge, Montana, August 29, 1988, and William Rose, Montana State Prison, Deer Lodge, Montana, November 6, 1988, in addition to the two inmate interviews in "Nobody Cares" and a lengthy and unpublished description of the conditions inside the prison written by an inmate in 1957, entitled "The True Facts Leading up to the Recent Uprising at the State Prison at Deer Lodge, Montana, July 30, 1957 as seen by an Observer and written by him," dated September 1957, Montana Legislative Council Records: Prison Subcommittee, MHS.

14. For an overview of some of these uprisings, see Sullivan, *Forlorn Hope*, 44–60.

15. "Prisoner Demands for July 30, 1957, Montana State Prison," Montana State Board of Examiners Records, MHS.

16. "Round One for the Convicts," *Silver State Post* (Deer Lodge), August 2, 1957; "Must We Make Country Club of Montana State Prison," ibid., August 16, 1957; *Daily Interlake* (Kalispell), February 2, 1958; Elaine Warner to Attorney General Anderson, October 29, 1957; Gladys Swindland to Anderson, September 26, 1957,

and "O. L. Timer" to Anderson, November 2, 1957, in Records of the Montana Attorney General, MHS.

17. The reform of the prison became a heated political issue between the Republican governor, Aronson, and the Democratic attorney general, Anderson; see "Statement of Attorney General Forrest H. Anderson before the Board of Examiners, November 3, 1958," and Anderson to Governor Aronson, November 1, 1957 and January 23, 1958, in Records of the Montana Attorney General, MHS.

18. William Rose, interview with author, Montana State Prison, Deer Lodge, November 8, 1988.

19. See Keith Edgerton, "A Tough Place to Live: The 1959 Montana State Prison Riot," *Montana, the Magazine of Western History* 42 (Winter 1992): 56–69.

20. See Mansfield's October 30, 1959, telegram to the Montana State Board of Prison Commissioners in Montana State Board of Examiners Records, MHS.

21. The AFL–CIO, the Montana Farmer's Union, and the Montana Council on Corrections were the only groups that publicly supported the bond issue. *The People's Voice* (Helena), November 4, 1960. On election results, see Ellis Waldron and Paul B. Wilson, *Atlas of Montana Elections 1889–1976*, (Missoula: University of Montana Press, 1978), 221.

22. Hugo Aronson and L. O. Brockman, *The Galloping Swede* (Missoula: Falcon Press, 1970), 122.

23. *Daily Interlake* (Kalispell), October 30, 1960; *Daily Missoulian*, November 1, 1960; *Silver State Post* (Deer Lodge), October 28, 1960.

24. Interview with William Crowley.

25. Total cost of the completed facility came to $5.7 million. Montana Department of Corrections, "Corrections History Overview—Montana," 12, http://www.cor.state.mt.us (accessed April 15, 2002).

26. See Kent, "Historic Structures Report," and Kent, *Montana Prison History*, for the efforts to save the institution.

27. U.S. Department of Justice, "Riot at Max: An Administrative Inquiry into the Circumstances Surrounding the Montana State Prison Riot of September 22, 1991" (Washington, D.C.: U.S. Government Printing Office, 1991).

28. *An Act Appropriating Money to Various State Agencies for the Biennium Ending June 30, 1995*, chap. 623, Laws of Montana, 53d Legislature, 1993; *An Act Generally Revising Corrections and Human Services Laws to Implement Budget Reductions*, chap. 578, ibid. I am indebted to Professor Ruey-Lin Lin, Montana State

University–Billings, for sharing with me his unpublished paper on the subject, "The Study of House Bill 685 (1993) Prison Inmate Population Cap/Limit on the Criminal Justice System: First of a Three Year Study—Montana State Prison," copy in author's possession.

29. Paxinos quoted in "Montana's plan to cut prison population blasted," Billings *Gazette,* December 10, 1993.

30. Lin, "The Study of House Bill 685," 7.

31. Another woman, Gamble's friend Fran Doran, also attended the dinner. Billings *Gazette,* November 4, 1994. The story was even further sensationalized and titillating because of Richards's youthful attractiveness.

32. Van Walkenburg quoted in *Missoulian,* November 2, 1994; James Gamble to Rick Day, Director, Department of Corrections and Human Services, November 3, 1994, in Montana Governors Papers (Racicot), MHS.

33. Great Falls *Tribune,* December 12, 2000.

34. The movement of Montana's prisoners out of state during this transition period caused considerable controversy, particularly after one inmate, Neal Hage, was beaten to death in 1997 in a private Texas facility during a brawl in the prison yard. For details of the incident, see Lubbock (Texas) *Avalanche-Journal,* May 17, 1997.

35. Great Falls *Tribune,* December 12, 2000.

36. "Debt to Society: Mother Jones.com Special Report: Rankings," http://www .motherjones.com/prisons/atlas (accessed May 9, 2002). Information on the website comes from the Bureau of Justice Statistics, the National Center for Education Statistics, the National Association of State Budget Officers, and the U.S. Census Bureau.

37. Bureau of Justice Statistics, "Prisoners under the jurisdiction of State or Federal correctional authorities, June 30 and December 31, 2001, and June 30, 2002" (Table 2), "Bureau of Justice Statistics Bulletin: Prison and Jail Inmates at Midyear, 2002," http://www.ojp.usdoj.gov/bjs/abstract/pjim02.htm (accessed April 2003).

38. "Debt to Society: Montana, Racial Inequality," http://www.motherjones .com/prisons/atlas (accessed May 9, 2002).

39. "Prison's racial disparity: Native Americans Make Up Disproportionate Percentage of Inmates," Billings *Gazette,* January 14, 2002. It is unclear if currently incarcerated Native Americans are spending greater periods in prison than their white counterparts; during the territorial period of the nineteenth century, there

existed no disparity between sentencing and time served among minority and non-minority populations.

40. State per capita income figures from Bureau of Economic Analysis, Table SA1-3, "Per capita personal income," http://www.bea.doc.gov/bea/regional/spi (accessed April 2003); state prison expenditures, Bureau of Justice Statistics, *State Prison Expenditures, 1996,* "Table 1. State prisons: Total operating, and capital expenditures, and operating expenditures per inmate, fiscal year 1996," http://www.ojp .usdoj.gov/bjs/pub/pdf/spe96.pdf (accessed August 1999); incarceration rate increase, "Debt to Society: Increase in Incarceration Rate," http://www.mother-jones.com/prisons/atlas (accessed May 9, 2002).

41. "Spending Shifts from Pupils to Prisons," Billings *Gazette,* February 12, 2001. State spending on prisons increased from 4.3 percent of the general fund budget to 9 percent. All figures for higher education and prison spending are adjusted for inflation and expressed in 1999 dollars; see "Debt to Society: Montana, Prisons vs. Education, Spending per resident from this state's general tax revenues on prisons and on higher education," http://www.motherjones.com/prisons/atlas (accessed May 9, 2002); education and incarceration comparisons, Bureau of Justice Statistics Special Report, "Education and Corrections Populations," http://www.ojp.usdoj .gov/bjs/pub/pdf/ecp.pdf (accessed January 2003).

Bibliography

PRIMARY AND MANUSCRIPT SOURCES

United States Documents

An Act Concerning the Disposition of Convicts. U.S. Statutes at Large 13 (1864).

An Act Setting Aside Certain Proceeds from Internal Revenue for the Erection of Penitentiaries in the Territories of Nebraska, Washington, Colorado, Montana, Arizona, and Dakota. U.S. Statutes at Large 14 (1867).

An Act Transferring Control of Certain Territorial Penitentiaries to the Several Territories in which the Same are Located. U.S. Statutes at Large 17 (1873).

An Act to Amend the Act Entitled An Act Transferring the Control of Certain Territorial Penitentiaries to the Several Territories in which the Same are Located. U.S. Statutes at Large 18 (1874).

Appropriations for Sundry Civil Expenses for Year Ending June 30, 1886. U.S. Statutes at Large 23 (1885).

Bureau of Economic Analysis. "Per capita personal income." Table SA1–3. http://www.bea.doc.gov/bea/regional/spi (accessed April 2003).

Bureau of Justice. Statistics On-Line. "Rate (per 100,0000 resident population) of sentenced prisoners under jurisdiction of State and Federal correctional authorities on December 31." Table 6.28. *Sourcebook of Criminal Justice Statistics 2000.* http://www.albany.edu/sourcebook (accessed May 5, 2002).

Bureau of Justice. Statistics. "Prisoners under the jurisdiction of State or Federal correctional authorities, June 30 and December 31, 2001, and June 30, 2002." Table 2. *Bureau of Justice Statistics Bulletin: Prison and Jail Inmates at Mid-*

year, 2002. http://www.ojp.usdoj.gov/bjs/pub/pdf/pjim02.pdf (accessed April 2003).

————. "Bureau of Justice Statistics Special Report, Education and Corrections Populations." http://www.ojp.usdoj.gov/bjs/pub/pdf/ecp.pdf (accessed January 2003).

————. "Prison Statistics, Summary Findings." http://www.ojp.usdoj.gov/bjs/prisons.htm (accessed May 7, 2003).

————. "State prisons: Total operating, and capital expenditures, and operating expenditures per inmate, fiscal year 1996." Table 1. State Prison Expenditures, 1996. http://www.ojp.usdoj.gov/bjs/pub/pdf/spe96.pdf (accessed August 1999).

U.S. Census Bureau. *Census 2000 Redistricting Data* (P.L. 94–171), Summary File, Tables PL1 and PL2, U.S. Census Bureau, American Fact Finder, Detailed Tables, Montana, PCT16, "Group Quarters Population by Group Quarters Type," and PCT17C, "Group Quarters Population by Sex, by Age, by Group Quarters Type (American Indian and Alaska Native Alone). http://factfinder.census.gov (accessed February 26, 2002).

U.S. Congress. House. *Congressional Globe,* 39th Cong., 2d sess., 1867.

U.S. Congress. House. *Congressional Globe,* 39th Cong., 3d sess., 1867.

U.S. Congress. House. *Congressional Globe,* 41st Cong., 3d sess., 1871, Appendix XII.

U.S. Congress. House. *Congressional Globe,* 42d Cong., 3d sess., 1874.

U.S. Department of Commerce. *1990 Census of Population: General Population Characteristics, Montana.* Washington, D.C.: Government Printing Office, 1992.

U.S. Department of the Interior. *The Statistics of the Population of the United States . . . Compiled From the Original Returns of the Ninth Census.* Washington, D.C.: Government Printing Office, 1872.

U.S. Department of the Interior. *Compendium of the Tenth Census.* Washington, D.C.: Government Printing Office, 1883.

U.S. Department of the Interior. *Report on the Population of the United States and the Eleventh Census.* Part 1. Washington, D.C.: Government Printing Office, 1895.

U.S. Department of Interior. Territorial Papers, Montana, Letters Received, February 5, 1867–November 25, 1889. Record Group 48. National Archives. Washington, D.C.

U.S. Department of Justice. Letters Sent by the Department of Justice. Record Group 60. National Archives. Washington, D.C.

U.S. Department of Justice. Instructions to U.S. Attorneys and Marshals, 1867–1904. Record Group 60. National Archives. College Park, Md.

U.S. Department of Justice. Letters Sent, General and Miscellaneous (1818–1904). Record Group 60. National Archives. College Park, Md.

U.S. Department of Justice. Records of the Attorney Generals, Letters Received, 1809–1870, Record Group 60, Montana, 1864–1870. National Archives. College Park, Md.

U.S. Department of Justice. Records of the Attorney Generals, Letters Received, Source Chronological Files, 1871–1884. Record Group 60, Montana, January 1871–June 1872. National Archives, College Park, Md.

U.S. Department of Justice. Source Chronological Files, Montana. Record Group 60. National Archives. Washington, D.C.

U.S. Department of Justice. *Source Book on Criminal Justice Statistics—1990.* Washington, D.C.: Government Printing Office, 1991.

U.S. Department of Justice. *Riot at Max: An Administrative Inquiry Into the Circumstances Surrounding the Montana State Prison Riot of September 22, 1991.* Washington, D.C.: Government Printing Office, 1991.

U.S. Department of State. Territorial Papers, Montana. Record Group 59, National Archives. Washington, D.C.

U.S. House of Representatives. *Report of Charles Bulfinch on the Subject of Penitentiaries.* 19th Cong., 2d sess., 1828, H. Rep. 98.

U.S. House of Representatives. *Wisconsin Penitentiary.* 25th Cong., 2d sess., 1837–38, H. Doc. 332.

U.S. House of Representatives. *Penitentiary, Iowa.* 26th Cong., 1st sess., 1839, H. Rep. 297.

U.S. House of Representatives. *Annual Report of the Secretary of the Interior.* 40th Cong., 2d sess., 1867–68, H. Ex. Doc. 1.

U.S. House of Representatives. *Letter from the Attorney General.* 41st Cong., 2d sess., 1870–71, H. Ex. Doc. 286.

U.S. House of Representatives. *Report of the Secretary of the Interior.* 42d Cong., 2d sess., 1871, H. Ex. Doc. 1.

U.S. House of Representatives. *Annual Report of the United States Attorney General.* 43d Cong., 2d sess., 1874–75, H. Ex. Doc. 1.

U.S. House of Representatives. *Report on the Defective, Dependent, and Delinquent Classes of the Population of the United States.* 47th Cong., 2d sess., 1881, H. Misc. Doc. 42, Part 21.

U.S. House of Representatives. *Report of the Governor of Montana, 1883.* 48th Cong., 1st sess., 1883–84, H. Ex. Doc. 1.

U.S. House of Representatives. *Annual Report of the Secretary of the Interior.* 48th Cong., 1st sess., 1883–84, H. Ex. Doc. 1.

U.S. House of Representatives. *Annual Report of the Secretary of Interior, 1884.* 48th Cong., 2d sess., 1884–85, H. Ex. Doc. 1.

U.S. Senate. *Letter of the Secretary of the Interior.* 40th Cong., 3d sess. 1868–69, Sen. Ex. Doc. 35.

Montana Territorial and State Documents

An Act Appropriating Money to Various State Agencies for the Biennium Ending June 30, 1995. Chap. 623. Laws of Montana, 53rd Legislature, 1993.

An Act Generally Revising Corrections and Human Services Laws to Implement Budget Reductions. Chap. 578. Laws of Montana, 53rd Legislature, 1993.

An Act Providing for Indeterminate Sentences of Persons Convicted of Crime, and for the Parole of Such Persons, and Prescribing the Duties of Officials in Connection therewith. Chap. 14. Laws of Montana, 14th Legislature, 1915.

Annual Report of the Board of State Prison Commissioners, 1907–1911. Helena: State Publishing Company. 1911.

Annual Report of the Board of State Prison Commissioners, 1914–1932. Butte: State Publishing Company. 1933.

Laws, Memorials and Resolutions of the State of Montana passed at the Second Regular Session of the Legislative Assembly, Helena, Montana, January 5, 1891– March 5, 1891. Helena: Journal Publishing Company. 1891.

Laws, Memorials and Resolutions of the State of Montana, Passed at the Third Regular Session of the Legislative Assembly, Helena, Montana, January 2, 1893 to March 2, 1893. Butte: Inter Mountain Publishing. 1893.

Laws, Memorials and Resolutions of the Territory of Montana, Passed at First Extraordinary Session of the Legislative Assembly, Convened by Proclamation

of Governor of Said Territory at Virginia City, April 14, 1873, to May 1873.
  Helena: n.p. 1874.

*Laws, Memorials and Resolutions of the Territory of Montana, Passed at the
  Seventh Session of the Legislative Assembly, at Virginia City, December 4,
  1871, to January 12, 1872.* Deer Lodge: n.p. 1872.

Second Annual Report of the State Board of Prison Commissioners. Helena:
  The Independent Publishing Company. 1892.

*Third Annual Report of the Board of State Prison Commissioners of the State
  of Montana, December 1, 1893.* Butte: Inter Mountain Publishing Company.
  1895.

Montana Territorial and State Records

Board of Prison Commissioner Records. Montana Historical Society, Helena
  (hereafter cited as MHS).

Fifteenth Montana Territorial Legislative Assembly Records. Record Series 250.
  MHS.

Law and Order Organization of Custer County. Small Collection 1881. MHS.

Montana Department of Corrections. "Corrections History Overview—
  Montana." http://www.cor.state.mt.us (accessed April 15, 2002).

Montana Governors' Papers. (Aronson, Cooney, Dixon, Ford, Potts, Racicot,
  Stewart, Toole) MHS.

Montana Legislative Council Records. MHS.

Montana Legislative Council Records: Prison Subcommittee. MHS.

Montana State Board of Examiners Records. MHS.

Montana State Hospital Records. MHS.

Montana Territorial Prison Records. Small Collection 909. MHS.

Ninth Montana Legislative Assembly Records. Record Series 365. MHS.

Records of Montana Territory Executive Office. Record Series 40. MHS.

Records of the Montana Attorney General. MHS.

Second Montana Legislative Assembly Records. Record Series 153. MHS.

Territory of Montana v. Ah Wah. Case Number 528. Criminal and Civil Files.
  Deer Lodge County (2d Judicial District), Anaconda, Montana.

Thirty-sixth Montana Legislative Assembly Records. MHS.

Warm Springs State Hospital Records, 1877–1973. MHS.

Published and Unpublished Papers

Carter, Thomas H. Papers. National Archives. Washington, D.C.

Dixon, Joseph M. Papers. Maureen and Mike Mansfield Library, Missoula, Montana.

Garfield, James A. Papers. Library of Congress. Washington, D.C.

Greenfield, Charles Diggs, Jr. Family Papers. MHS.

Lin, Ruey-Lin. "The Study of House Bill 685 (1993) Prison Inmate Population Cap/Limit on the Criminal Justice System: First of a Three Year Study— Montana State Prison." Manuscript in author's possession.

Maginnis, Martin. Papers. Manuscript Collection 50. MHS.

Potts, Benjamin. Letters. Manuscript Series 35. MHS.

Wheeler, William F. Papers. Manuscript Collection 65. MHS.

Newspapers

Anaconda *Standard*

Billings *Gazette*

Butte *Miner*

Daily Herald (Helena)

Daily Independent (Helena)

Daily Inter Mountain (Butte)

Daily Interlake (Kalispell)

Daily Missoulian (Missoula)

Fallon County Times (Baker)

Great Falls *Tribune*

Independent Record (Helena)

Lubbock (Texas) *Avalanche-Journal*

Montana Nonpartisan (Great Falls)

Montana Post (Virginia City)

New North-West (Deer Lodge City)

Rocky Mountain Gazette (Helena)

Roundup *Tribune*

Silver State (Deer Lodge City)

Silver State Post (Deer Lodge)

People's Voice (Helena)

Weekly Independent (Deer Lodge City)

SECONDARY SOURCES

Books

Alexander, Thomas G. *A Clash of Interests: Interior Department and Mountain West, 1863-96.* Provo: Brigham Young University Press, 1977.

Annals of the American Academy of Political and Social Sciences 46 (March 1913).

Aronson, Hugo, and L. O. Brockman. *The Galloping Swede.* Missoula: Falcon Press, 1970.

Ayers, Edward. *Vengenance and Justice: Crime and Punishment in the Nineteenth-Century American South.* New York: Oxford University Press, 1984.

Bakken, Gordon. *The Development of Law on the Rocky Mountain Frontier: Civil Law and Society, 1850–1912.* Westport, Conn.: Greenwood Press, 1983.

———. *Practicing Law in Frontier California.* Lincoln: University of Nebraska Press, 1991.

———, ed. *Law in the Western United States.* Norman: University of Oklahoma Press, 2000.

Bancroft, Hubert Howe. *The History of Washington, Idaho and Montana, 1846–1889.* San Francisco: The History Company, 1890.

Barnes, Elmer. *The Evolution of Penology in Pennsylvania: A Study in American Social History.* Indianapolis: Bobbs-Merrill, 1927; reprint, Montclair, N.J.: Patterson Smith, 1968.

Bender, Thomas. *Toward an Urban Vision: Ideas and Institutions in Nineteenth-Century America.* University of Kentucky Press: Lexington, 1975.

Bentham, Jeremy. *The Works of Jeremy Bentham.* Vol. 4. *Panopticon, or the Inspection House.* New York: Russell and Russell, 1962.

Bensel, Richard. *Yankee Leviathan: The Origins of Central State Authority in America, 1859–1877.* New York: Cambridge University Press, 1990.

Bookspan, Shelley. *A Germ of Goodness: The California State Prison System, 1851–1944.* Lincoln: University of Nebraska Press, 1990.

Boyer, Paul. *Urban Masses and Moral Order in America, 1820–1920.* Cambridge, Mass.: Harvard University Press, 1978.

Brace, Charles Loring. *The Dangerous Classes of New York, and Twenty Years'*
Work Among Them. New York: Wynkoop and Hallenbeck, 1872.

Brown, Richard Maxwell. *Strain of Violence: Historical Studies of American Vio-*
lence and Vigilantism. New York: Oxford University Press, 1975.

————. *No Duty to Retreat: Violence and Values in American History and Society.*
New York: Oxford University Press, 1991.

Bureau of Justice Statistics. *Historical Corrections Statistics in the United States,*
1850–1984, by Margaret Cahalan. Rockville, Md.: Westat, Inc., 1986.

Butler, Anne. *Daughters of Joy, Sisters of Misery: Prostitutes in the American West,*
1865–1890. Urbana: University of Illinois Press, 1985.

————. *Gendered Justice in the American West: Women Prisoners in Men's*
Penitentiaries. Urbana: University of Illinois Press, 1997.

Callaway, Lew L. *Montana's Righteous Hangmen: The Vigilantes in Action.*
Norman: University of Oklahoma Press, 1982.

Carleton, Mark. *Politics and Punishment: The History of the Louisiana State Penal*
System. Baton Rouge: Louisiana State University Press, 1971.

Caughey, John W., ed. *Their Majesties the Mob.* Chicago: University of Chicago
Press, 1960.

Clawson, Rudger. *Prisoner for Polygamy: The Memoirs and Letters of Rudger*
Clawson at the Utah Territorial Penitentiary, 1884–87. Edited by Stan Larson.
University of Illinois: Urbana and Chicago, 1993.

Colvin, Mark. *Penitentiaries, Reformatories, and Chain Gangs: Social Theory and*
the History of Punishment in Nineteenth-Century America. New York: St. Martin's Press, 1997.

Crawford, William. *Report on the Penitentiaries of the United States.* London:
House of Commons, 1834.

Culberson, William C. *Vigilantism: Political History of Private Power in America.*
New York: Greenwood Press, 1990.

Cummings, Homer, and Carl McFarland. *Federal Justice: Chapters in the History*
of Justice and the Federal Executive. New York: Macmillan, 1937.

Curtin, Mary Ellen. *Black Prisoners and Their World, Alabama, 1865–1900.*
Charlottesville: University Press of Virginia, 2000.

Dalsheim, Stephen. *The United States Penitentiary for the District of Columbia,*
1826–1862. Vols. 1953–56. Washington, D.C.: Records of Columbia History
Society, 1945.

de Beaumont, Gustave, and Alexis de Tocqueville. *On the Penitentiary System in the United States and Its Application in France.* Philadelphia: Carey, Lea & Blanchard, 1833.

Digby, Anne. *Madness, Morality and Medicine: A Study of the York Retreat.* New York: Cambridge University Press, 1985.

Dimsdale, Thomas. *The Vigilantes of Montana.* Virginia City, Mont.: 1865, reprint, Norman: University of Oklahoma Press, 1953.

Donziger, Steven R., ed. *The Real War on Crime.* New York: HarperCollins, 1996.

Dumm, Thomas. *Democracy and Punishment: Disciplinary Origins of the United States.* Madison: University of Wisconsin Press, 1987.

Dyer, Joel. *The Perpetual Prisoner Machine: How America Profits from Crime.* Boulder: Westview Press, 2000.

Emmons, David. *The Butte Irish: Class and Ethnicity in an American Mining Town, 1880–1920.* Urbana: University of Illinois Press, 1989.

Foucault, Michel. *Discipline and Punish: The Birth of the Prison.* Translated by Alan Sheridan. New York: Vintage Books, 1977.

Fox, Richard. *So Far Disordered in Mind: Insanity in California, 1870–1930.* Berkeley: University of California Press, 1978.

France, George W. *The Struggles for Life and Home in the North-West by a Pioneer Homebuilder: Life, 1865–89.* New York: I. Goldman, 1890.

Freedman, Estelle. *Their Sisters' Keepers: Women's Prison Reform in America, 1830–1930.* Ann Arbor: University of Michigan Press, 1981.

Friedman, Lawrence, and Robert Percival. *The Roots of Justice: Crime and Punishment in Alameda County, California, 1870–1910.* Chapel Hill: University of North Carolina Press, 1981.

Garland, David. *Punishment and Modern Society: A Study in Social Theory.* New York: Oxford University Press, 1990.

Gildemeister, Glen. *Prison Labor and Convict Competition with Free Workers in Industrializing America, 1840–1890.* New York: Garland, 1987.

Greenberg, David F. *Crime and Capitalism: Readings in Marxist Criminology.* Philadelphia: Temple University Press, 1993.

Grob, Gerald. *Mental Institutions in America: Social Policy to 1875.* New York: The Free Press, 1973

———. *Mental Illness and American Society, 1875–1940.* Princeton: Princeton University Press, 1983.

Guice, John D. *The Rocky Mountain Bench: The Territorial Supreme Courts of Colorado, Montana, and Wyoming, 1864–1912.* New Haven: Yale University Press, 1972.

Gutfield, Arnon. *Montana's Agony: Years of War and Hysteria.* Gainesville: University of Florida Press, 1979.

Hawthorne, Nathaniel. *The Scarlet Letter.* New York: Harper Row, 1967.

Harrison, Fred. *Hell Holes and Hangings.* Clarendon, Tex.: Clarendon Press, 1968.

Harvie, Robert. *Keeping the Peace: Police Reform in Montana, 1889–1918.* Helena: Montana Historical Society Press, 1994.

Hindus, Michael. *Prison and Plantation: Crime, Justice, and Authority in Massachusetts and South Carolina.* Chapel Hill: University of North Carolina Press, 1980.

Hine, Robert V., and John Mack Faragher. *The American West: A New Interpretive History.* New Haven: Yale University Press, 2000.

Hirsch, Adam. *The Rise of the Penitentiary: Prisons and Punishment in Early America.* New Haven: Yale University Press, 1992.

Howard, Joseph Kinsey. *Montana: High, Wide, and Handsome.* Lincoln: University of Nebraska Press, 1943.

Jiminez, Mary Ann. *Changing Faces of Madness: Early American Attitudes and Treatment of the Insane.* Hanover, N.H.: University Press of New England, 1985.

Johnson, Andrew. *The Papers of Andrew Johnson.* Edited by Paul Bergeron. Vol. 9. Knoxville: University of Tennessee Press, 1991.

Johnson, David Alan. *Founding the Far West: California, Oregon, and Nevada, 1840–1890.* Berkeley: University of California Press, 1992.

Jordan, Phillip. *Frontier Law and Order.* Lincoln: University of Nebraska Press, 1970.

Kaczorowski, Robert J. *The Politics of Judicial Interpretation: The Federal Courts, Department of Justice and Civil Rights, 1866–1876.* Dobbs Ferry, N.Y.: Oceana Publications, 1985.

Karlin, Jules. *Joseph M. Dixon of Montana, Part 1: Senator and Bull Moose Manager, 1867–1917.* Missoula: University of Montana Press, 1974.

———. *Joseph M. Dixon of Montana, Part 2: Governor versus the Anaconda, 1817–1934.* Missoula: University of Montana Press, 1974.

Kent, Phillip. *Montana State Prison History.* Deer Lodge: Powell County Museum and Arts Foundation, 1979.

Keve, Paul. *The History of Corrections in Virginia.* Charlottesville: University
    Press of Virginia, 1986.

————. *Prisons and the American Conscience: A History of Federal Corrections.*
    Carbondale: Southern Illinois University Press, 1991.

Langford, Nanthaniel Pitt. *Vigilante Days and Ways.* 1890; reprint, Missoula:
    University of Montana Press, 1957.

Larabie Bros & Co., et al. *Location of Montana State Prison.* Helena: n.p., 1893.

Lasch, Christopher. *The World of Nations: Reflections on American History, Poli-
    tics, and Culture.* New York: Alfred Knopf, 1973.

Lerner, Barron. *Contagion and Confinement: Controlling Tuberculosis along the
    Skid Road.* Baltimore: Johns Hopkins University Press, 1998.

Lewis, David. *From Newgate to Dannemora: The Rise of the Penitentiary in New
    York, 1796–1845.* Ithaca: Cornell University Press, 1965.

Lewis, Orlando. *The Development of American Prisons and Prison Customs, 1776–
    1845.* New York: Patterson Smith, 1967.

Limbaugh, Ronald. *Rocky Mountain Carpetbaggers: Idaho's Territorial Governors,
    1863–1890.* Moscow: University of Idaho Press, 1982.

Limerick, Patricia Nelson, Clyde A. Milner II, and Charles Rankin, eds. *Trails
    Toward a New Western History.* Lawrence: University Press of Kansas,
    1991.

Link, Arthur S., and Richard McCormick. *Progressivism.* Arlington Heights, Ill.:
    Harlan Davidson, 1983.

Lunbeck, Elizabeth. *The Psychiatric Persuasion: Knowledge, Gender, and Power
    in Modern America.* Princeton: Princeton University Press, 1994.

Malone, Michael. *The Battle for Butte: Mining and Politics on the Northern Fron-
    tier, 1864–1906.* Seattle: University of Washington Press, 1981.

————, Richard Roeder, and William Lang. *Montana: A History of Two Centuries.*
    Rev. ed. Seattle: University of Washington Press, 1991.

Mancini, Matthew. *One Dies, Get Another: Convict Leasing in the American
    South, 1866–1928.* Columbia: University of South Carolina Press, 1996.

Masur, Louis P. *Rites of Execution: Capital Punishment and the Transformation
    of American Culture, 1776–1865.* New York: Oxford University Press, 1989.

Mauer, Marc. *Race to Incarcerate.* New York: The New Press, 1999.

McClain, Charles. *The Chinese Struggle Against Discrimination in Nineteenth-
    Century America.* Berkeley: University of California Press, 1994.

McDonald, James. *Historic Structures Report, Montana State Prison.* Deer Lodge: Powell County Museum and Arts Foundation, 1981.

McGinn, Elinor. *At Hard Labor: Inmate Labor at the Colorado State Penitentiary, 1871–1940.* New York: Peter Lang, 1993.

McGrath, Roger. *Gunfighters, Highwaymen, and Vigilantes: Violence on the Frontier.* Berkeley: University of California Press, 1984.

McKanna, Clare V., Jr. *Homicide, Race, and Justice in the American West, 1880–1920.* Tucson: University of Arizona Press, 1997.

McKelvey, Blake. *American Prisons: A History of Good Intentions.* Montclair, N.J.: Patterson Smith, 1977.

Melossi, Dario. *The State of Social Control: A Sociological Study of Concepts of State and Social Control in the Making of Democracy.* New York: St. Martin's Press, 1990.

Monkkonen, Eric. *The Dangerous Class: Crime and Poverty in Columbus, Ohio, 1860–1885.* Cambridge: Harvard University Press, 1975.

———. *Police in Urban America, 1860–1920.* New York: Cambridge University Press, 1981.

Montana Almanac. Missoula: Montana State University Press, 1957.

Munson, Lyman E. "Pioneer Life in Montana." *Contributions to the Historical Society of Montana.* Vol. 5. Helena: State Publishing Company, 1904.

O'Brien, Thomas. *Infamy Immortal.* Butte: Schwan Publishing, 1904.

Oshinsky, David M. *Worse than Slavery: Parchman Farm and the Ordeal of Jim Crow Justice.* New York: The Free Press, 1996.

Percival, Robert. *The Roots of Justice: Crime and Punishment in Alameda County, California, 1870–1910.* Chapel Hill: University of North Carolina Press, 1981.

Pinel, Philippe. *A Treatise on Insanity.* Translated by D. D. Davis. New York: Haffner, 1962.

Piscotta, Alexander. *Benevolent Repression: Social Control and the American Reformatory-Prison Movement.* New York: New York University Press, 1994.

Pomeroy, Earl. *The Territories and the United States, 1861–1890: Studies in Colonial Administration.* Philadelphia: University of Pennsylvania Press, 1947.

Proceedings of the Annual Congress of the National Prison Association of the United States, 1900. Pittsburgh: Shaw Brothers, 1900.

Rafter, Nicole Hahn. *Partial Justice: Women in State Prisons, 1800–1935.* Boston: Northwestern University Press, 1985.

Reid, John Phillip. *Law for the Elephant: Property and Social Behavior on the Overland Trail.* San Marino, Calif.: Huntington Library Press, 1980.

Robbins, William G. *Colony and Empire: The Capitalist Transformation of the American West.* Lawrence: University Press of Kansas, 1994.

Roberts, Albert R. *Source Book on Prison Education: Past, Present, Future.* Springfield, Ill.: Charles C. Thomas, 1971.

Rothman, David. *The Discovery of the Asylum: Social Order and Disorder in the New Republic.* Boston: Little Brown, 1971.

―――. *Conscience and Convenience: The Asylum and Its Alternatives in Progressive America.* Boston: Little Brown, 1980.

Rusche, Georg, and Otto Kirchheimer. *Punishment and Social Structure.* New York: Columbia University Press, 1939.

Russell, Denise. *Women, Madness, and Medicine.* London: Polity Press, 1995.

Schmeckebier, Laurence F. *The District of Columbia: Its Government and Administration.* Baltimore: Johns Hopkins University Press, 1928.

Scull, Andrew, ed. *Madhouses, Mad-Doctors, and Madmen: The Social History of Psychiatry in the Victorian Era.* Philadelphia: University of Pennsylvania Press, 1981.

Simon, Jonathan. *Poor Discipline: Parole and the Social Control of the Underclass, 1890–1990.* Chicago: University of Chicago Press, 1993.

Slotkin, Richard. *Gunfighter Nation.* New York: Atheneum, 1992.

Smith, Henry Nash. *Virgin Land: The American West as Symbol and Myth.* Cambridge: Harvard University Press, 1950.

Spence, Clark. *Territorial Politics and Government in Montana, 1864–89.* Urbana: University of Illinois Press, 1975.

Spierenburg, Pieter. *The Spectacle of Suffering: Executions and the Evolution of Repression: From a Preindustrial Metropolis to the European Experience.* New York: Cambridge University Press, 1984.

Stegner, Wallace. *Wolf Willow: A History, a Story, and a Memory of the Last Plains Frontier.* New York: Penguin Books, 1990.

Sullivan, Larry. *The Prison Reform Movement: Forlorn Hope.* Twayne's Social Movement Series. Boston: Twayne Publishers, 1990.

Teeters, Negley, and John D. Shearer. *The Prison at Philadelphia: Cherry Hill.* New York: Columbia University Press, 1957.

Toole, K. Ross. *Montana: An Uncommon Land.* Norman: University of Oklahoma Press, 1959.

———. *Twentieth-Century Montana: A State of Extremes.* Norman: University of Oklahoma Press, 1972.

Trachtenberg, Alan. *The Incorporation of America: Culture and Society in the Gilded Age.* New York: Hill and Wang, 1982.

Trattner, Walter I., ed. *Social Welfare or Social Control? Some Historical Reflections on Regulating the Poor.* Knoxville: University of Tennessee Press, 1983.

Waldron, Ellis, and Paul B. Wilson. *Atlas of Montana Elections, 1889–1976.* Missoula: University of Montana Press, 1978.

Walker, Donald. *Penology for Profit: A History of the Texas Prison System.* Austin: Texas A&M Press, 1988.

Walker, Samuel. *Popular Justice: A History of American Criminal Justice.* 2d ed. New York: Oxford University Press, 1998.

Walton, John. *Western Times and Water Wars: State, Culture, and Rebellion in California.* Berkeley: University of California Press, 1992.

White, Richard. *"It's Your Misfortune and None of My Own": A New History of the American West.* Norman: University of Oklahoma Press, 1991.

Wiebe, Robert. *The Search for Order, 1877–1920.* New York: Hill & Wang, 1967.

Wines, Enoch. *The State of Prisons and Child Saving Institutions in the Civilized World.* 1880; reprint, Montclair, N.J.: Patterson Smith, 1986.

Wunder, John. *Inferior Courts, Superior Justice: A History of the Justices of the Peace on the Northwest Frontier, 1853–1889.* Westport: Greenwood Press, 1979.

Zhu, Liping. *A Chinaman's Chance: The Chinese on the Rocky Mountain Mining Frontier.* Boulder: University of Colorado Press, 1997.

Articles, Essays, and Reviews

Adamson, Christopher. "Toward a Marxian Penology: Captive Criminal Populations as Economic Threats and Resources." *Social Problems* 31 (April 1984): 435–58.

Angle, Terry. "The Development of Educational Programs in American Adult Prisons and Juvenile Reformatories during the Nineteenth Century." *Journal of Correctional Education* 33 (September 1982): 4–6.

Bishop, Larry V., and Robert A. Harvie. "Law and Order in Beaverhead County, Montana, 1895–1916." *Journal of Police Science and Administration* 8 (Spring 1980): 173–82.

———. "Law Enforcement in Custer County, Montana, 1893–1918." *Police Studies* 3 (Summer 1980): 3–11.

———. "Law Order and Reform in the Gallatin, 1893–1918." *Montana, the Magazine of Western History* 30 (Spring 1980): 16–25.

———. "Police Reform in Montana, 1890–1918." *Montana, the Magazine of Western History* 33 (Spring 1983): 46–59.

Brown, Kate. "Gridded Lives: Why Kazakhstan and Montana Are Nearly the Same Place." *American Historical Review* 106 (February 2001): 17–48.

Brown, Richard Maxwell. "The History of Vigilantism in America." In *Vigilante Politics*, ed. H. Jon Rosenbaum and Peter C. Sederberg, 79–109. Philadelphia: University of Pennsylvania Press, 1976.

———. "Law and Order on the American Frontier: The Western Civil War of Incorporation." In *Law for the Elephant, Law for the Beaver: Essays in the Legal History of the North American West*, ed. John McLaren, Hamar Foster, and Chet Orloff, 74–89. Saline, Mich.: McNaughton and Gunn, 1992.

———. "Western Violence, Structure, Values, Myth." *Western Historical Quarterly* 24 (February 1993): 5–20.

———. "Violence." In *The Oxford History of the American West*, eds., Clyde A. Milner II, Carol O'Connor, and Martha A. Sandweiss, 393–426. New York: Oxford University Press, 1994.

Burlingame, Merrill G. "Montana's Righteous Hangmen: A Reconsideration." *Montana, the Magazine of Western History* 28 (October 1978): 36–49.

Butler, Anne. "Still in Chains: Black Women in Western Prisons, 1865–1910." *Western Historical Quarterly* 20 (February 1989): 20–35.

———. "Women's Work in Prisons of the American West, 1865–1920." *Western Legal History* 7 (Summer/Fall 1994): 201–22.

———. "Selling the Popular Myth." In *The Oxford History of the American West*, ed. Clyde A. Milner II, Carol O'Connor, and Martha A. Sandweiss, 771–802. New York: Oxford University Press, 1994.

Callaway, Lew. "Joseph Alfred Slade: Killer or Victim?" *Montana Magazine of History* 3 (January 1953): 5–34.

Chronister, Allen. "Elk Head and White Bear: Warrior Artists in the Early Reservation Period." *Montana, the Magazine of Western History* 48 (Summer 1998): 34–47.

Conley, John. "Prisons, Production and Profit: Reconsidering the Importance of Prison Industries." *Journal of Social History* 4 (Fall 1980): 257–75.

———. "Revising Conceptions about the Origin of Prisons: The Importance of Economic Considerations." *Social Science Quarterly* 62 (1981): 247–58.

———. "Economics and the Social Reality of Prisons." *Journal of Criminal Justice* 10 (1982): 25–35.

"Debt to Society." http://www.motherjones.com/news/special_reports/prisons/rankings2.html (accessed May 9, 2002).

De Lorme, Roland. "Crime and Punishment in the Pacific Northwest Territories: A Bibliographic Essay." *Pacific Northwest Quarterly* 76 (April 1985): 42–51.

———. "The Long Arm of the Law: Crime and Federal Law Enforcement in the Northern Tier Territories." In *Centennial West: Essays on the Northern Tier States,* ed. William Lang, 122–42. Seattle: University of Washington Press, 1991.

Deverell, William. "The Significance of the American West in the History of the United States." *Western Historical Quarterly* 25 (Summer 1994): 185–206.

DeVoto, Bernard. "The West: A Plundered Province." *Harper's Magazine* (August 1934): 355–64.

Edgerton, Keith. "'A Tough Place to Live': The 1959 Montana State Prison Riot." *Montana, the Magazine of Western History* 42 (Winter 1992): 56–69.

Emmons, David. "The Price of 'Freedom': Montana in the Late and Post-Anaconda Era." In *Politics in the Postwar American West,* ed. Richard Lowitt, 120–34. Norman: University of Oklahoma Press, 1995.

Gaither, Carl C. "Education Behind Bars: An Overview." *Journal of Correctional Education* 33 (June 1982): 19–22.

Gehring, Thomas, and Will R. Muth. "The Correctional Education/Prison Reform Link: Part I, 1840–1900." *Journal of Correctional Education* 36 (December 1985): 140–46.

Graff, Harvey. "Crime and Punishment in the Nineteenth Century: A New Look at the Criminal." *Journal of Interdisciplinary History* 7 (Winter 1977): 477–91.

Gutfield, Arnon. "George Bourquin: A Montana Judge's Stand Against Despotism." *Western Legal History* 6 (Spring 1993): 51–68.

Hauff, Jeffrey L. "Wyoming's First Penitentiary: Archaeology of a Victorian-Era Correctional Institution." *Wyoming Archaeologist* 31 (3–4): 59–65.

Hietter, Paul T. "A Surprising Amount of Justice: The Experience of Mexican and Racial Minority Defendants Charged with Serious Crimes in Arizona, 1865–1920." *Pacific Historical Review* 70 (May 2001): 183–220.

Hollander, Russell. "Life at the Washington Asylum for the Insane, 1871–1880." *The Historian* 44 (Spring 1982): 229–41.

Johnson, David. "Vigilance and the Law: The Moral Authority of Popular Justice in the Far West." *American Quarterly* 33 (1981): 558–86.

Kaminer, Wendy. "Federal Offense." *Atlantic Monthly* (June 1994): 102–109.

Larsell, O. "History of Care of Insane in the state of Oregon." *Oregon Historical Quarterly* 46 (December 1945): 295–326.

Lemisch, Jesse. "The American Revolution Seen from the Bottom Up." In *Towards A New Past: Dissenting Essays in American History*, ed. Barton J. Bernstein, 3–45. New York: Random House, 1968.

Limerick, Patricia Nelson. "What on Earth is the New Western History?" *Montana, the Magazine of Western History* 40 (Summer 1990): 61–64

Malone, Michael. "Montana as a Corporate Bailiwick: An Image in History." In *Montana Past and Present*, ed. Michael Malone and Richard Roeder, 57–76. Los Angeles: William Andrews Clark Library, 1976.

———. "Midas of the West: The Incredible Career of William Andrews Clark." *Montana, the Magazine of Western History* 33 (Autumn 1983): 2–17.

Malone, Michael, and Diane Dougherty. "Montana's Political Culture: A Century of Evolution." In *The Montana Heritage: An Anthology of Historical Essays*, ed. Harry Fritz and Robert Swartout. Helena: Montana Historical Society Press, 1993.

McAfee, Ward. "The Formation of Prison-Management Philosophy in Oregon, 1843–1915." *Oregon Historical Quarterly* 91 (Fall 1990): 259–84.

McKanna, Clare, Jr. "Ethnics and San Quentin Prison Registers: A Comment on Methodology." *Journal of Social History* 18 (Fall 1985): 477–82.

McKelvey, Blake. "Penology in the Westward Movement." *Pacific Historical Review* 2 (November 1933): 418–38.

Merrill, Karen. "In Search of the Federal Presence in the American West." *Western Historical Quarterly* 30 (Winter 1999): 449–73.

Moynahan, J. M. "They've Hanged the Sheriff! Montana's First Jail." *American Jails* (January/February 1994): 55–62.

Mueller, Oscar O. "The Central Montana Vigilante Raids of 1884." *Montana, the Magazine of Western History* 1 (January 1951): 23–35.

Myers, Rex C. "The Fateful Numbers 3–7–77: A Reexamination." *Montana, the Magazine of Western History* 24 (Autumn 1974): 67–70.

"Nobody Cares." *Montana Opinion* 1 (June 1957): 1–14.

Olsen, Gordon. "'I Felt Like I Must be Entering . . . Another World': The Anonymous Memoirs of an Early Inmate of the Wyoming Penitentiary." *Annals of Wyoming* 47 (Fall 1975): 152–90.

Piscotta, Alexander. "Corrections, Society, and Social Control in America: A Metahistorical Review of the Literature." *Criminal Justice History* 2 (1981): 109–30.

Quinn, Larry D. "'Chink Chink Chinaman': The Beginning of Nativism in Montana." *Pacific Northwest Quarterly* 58 (April 1967): 82–89.

Robbins, William G. "The 'Plundered Province' Thesis and the Recent Historiography of the American West." *Pacific Historical Review* 55 (November 1986): 577–97

Rothman, David. "Perfecting the Prison: United States, 1789–1865." In *The Oxford History of the Prison: The Practice of Punishment in Western Society*, ed. Norval Morris and David J. Rothman, 100–16. New York: Oxford University Press, 1995.

Rotman, Egardo. "The Failure of Reform: United States, 1865–1965." In *The Oxford History of the Prison: The Practice of Punishment in Western Society*, ed. Norval Morris and David Rothman, 151–77. New York: Oxford University Press, 1998.

Salyer, Lucy. "Captives of Law: Judicial Enforcement of the Chinese Exclusion Laws, 1891–1905." *Journal of American History* 76 (June 1989): 91–117.

Schwartz, Joel. "The Penitentiary and Perfectibility in Tocqueville." *Western Political Quarterly* 38 (March 1985): 7–26.

Silliman, Lee. "1870: To the Hangman's Tree." *Montana, the Magazine of Western History* 28 (Autumn 1978): 50–57.

Slotkin, Richard. "Apotheosis of the Lynching: The Political Uses of Symbolic Violence." *Western Legal History* 6 (Winter/Spring 1993): 1–16.

Smurr, John. "Afterthoughts on the Vigilantes." *Montana, the Magazine of Western History* 8 (Spring 1958): 8–20.

Spence, Clark. "The Territorial Bench in Montana: 1864–1889." *Montana, the Magazine of Western History* 13 (January 1963): 25–32.

———. "We Want a Judge: Montana Territorial Justice and Politics." *Journal of the West* 20 (January 1981): 7–13.

Swartout, Robert. "Kwangtung to Big Sky: The Chinese in Montana, 1864–1900." In *The Chinese on the American Frontier,* ed. Arif Dirlik. Lanham, Md.: Rowman and Littlefield, 2001.

Tracy, Charles A. "Race, Crime and Social Policy: The Chinese in Oregon, 1871–1885." *Crime and Social Justice* 11 (Winter 1980): 11–25.

Tydeman, William. "The Landscape of Incarceration: Idaho's Old Penitentiary." *Idaho Yesterdays* 38 (Summer 1994): 3–12.

Udall, Stewart, Robert Dykstra, Michael Bellesiles, Paula Mitchell Marks, and Gregory Nobles. "How the West Got Wild: American Media and Frontier Violence." *Western Historical Quarterly* 31 (Autumn 2000): 277–95.

Wilson, James. "Frontier in the Shadows: Prisons in the Far Southwest, 1850–1917." *Arizona and the West* 22 (Winter 1980): 323–42.

Wooster, Donald. "New West, True West: Interpreting the Region's History." *Western Historical Quarterly* 18 (April 1987): 157–76.

Wunder, John R. "Law and Chinese in Frontier Montana." *Montana, the Magazine of Western History* 30 (Summer 1980): 18–31.

———. "Chinese in Trouble: Criminal Law and Race on the Trans-Mississippi West Frontier." *Western Historical Quarterly* 27 (January 1986): 25–41.

———. "Persistence and Adaptation: The Emergence of a Legal Culture in the Northern Tier Territories, 1853–1890." In *Centennial West: Essays on the Northern Tier States,* ed. William Lang, 104–21. Seattle: University of Washington Press, 1991.

Theses and Dissertations

Adamson, Christopher X. "Hard Labor: The Form and Function of Prison Labor in Nineteenth-Century America." Ph.D. dissertation, Princeton University, 1982.

DeForth, Shirley. "The Montana Press and Governor Joseph M. Dixon, 1920–1922." M.A. thesis, University of Montana, 1959.

Ellis, Mark. "Law and Order in Buffalo Bill's Country: Crime and Criminal Justice in Lincoln County, Nebraska, 1868–1910." Ph.D. dissertation, University of Nebraska–Lincoln.

Evans, Robert. "Montana's Role in the Enactment of Legislation Designed to Suppress the Industrial Workers of the World." M.A. thesis, University of Montana, 1964.

Fornes, Norman O. "The Origins and Early History of the United States Department of the Interior." Ph.D. dissertation, Pennsylvania State University, 1964.

Greenheck, Julie Marie. "The Impact of Progressivism on Montana: The Child Labor Law and the Establishment of Juvenile Courts." Senior honors thesis, Carroll College, Helena, Montana, 1991.

Hakola, John. "Samuel T. Hauser and the Economic Development of Montana: A Case Study in Nineteenth-Century Frontier Capitalism." Ph.D. dissertation, Indiana University, 1961.

Johnson, Judy. "For Any Good At All: A Comparative Study of State Penitentiaries in Arizona, Nevada, New Mexico, and Utah from 1900 to 1980." Ph.D. dissertation, University of New Mexico, 1987.

Knepper, Paul. "Imprisonment and Society in Arizona Territory." Ph.D. dissertation, Arizona State University, 1990.

Laythe, Joseph. "Bandits and Badges: Crime and Punishment in Oregon, 1875–1915." Ph.D. dissertation, University of Oregon, 1996.

Limbaugh, Ronald. "Attitudes of the Population of Idaho Toward Law and Order, 1860–1870." M.A. thesis, University of Idaho, 1962.

McGinn, Elinor. "Inmate Labor at the Colorado State Prison, 1871–1940." Ph.D. dissertation, University of Colorado, 1990.

Raffety, Robert O. "The History and Theory of Capital Punishment." M.A. thesis, University of Montana, 1968.

Roeder, Richard. "Montana in the Early Years of the Progressive Period." Ph.D. dissertation, University of Pennsylvania, 1971.

Thomson, George. "The History of Penal Institutions in the Rocky Mountain West, 1846–1900." Ph.D. dissertation, University of Colorado, 1965.

Interviews

Crowley, William F. Interview by Keith Edgerton, November 2, 1988. Missoula, Montana.

Frodsham, Carl. Interview by Keith Edgerton, August 29, 1988. Deer Lodge, Montana.

Rose, William. Interview by Keith Edgerton, November 6, 1988. Deer Lodge, Montana.

Index

Adriance, C. B., 45, 54
Ah Tung, 62
Ah Wah, 59
Albo, Fred, 87
Amalgamated Copper Mining Company, 89
American Prison Association, 85
Anaconda Copper Mining Company, 13, 89; as the "Big Outfit," 91; smelter, 15
Anaconda *Standard*, 94
Anderson, Forrest, 105
Argenta, 27
Aronson, Hugo, 103, 105
Atlanta, Georgia: federal prison, 17
Attorney General (U.S.), 27, 42
Auburn-style prison: architecture described, 31–32, 36; discipline, 101, 128n52
Axe Handle, 11, 62

Bannack, 5, 27
Bensel, Richard, quoted, 120n36

Bentham, Jeremy, 32
Bickford, 82
Billy the Kid, 11
Bitterroot Mountains, 19
Botkin, Alexander, 42
Bozeman, 12, 49
Brace, Charles Loring, 16
Brown, Kate, 17–18
Brown, Richard Maxwell, 14
Bureau of the Census, 17
Burrell, Faye O., 99–100
Butler, Anne, 61
Butte, 49, 60
Butte Miners Union strike (1914), 90

California incarceration rate, 37
Carter, Thomas, 76
Cassidy, Butch, 11
Choate, Fred, 69
Christensen, Fred O., 85
Clancy, William F., 88

Clark, William A., 26, 75; prison philanthropy of, 83, 102; relationship with Frank Conley, 88–89. *See also* Conley, Frank; Hauser, Samuel T.

Clark, William A., Jr., 88, 92, 94

Colorado territorial penitentiary, 29, 31, 130n10

Congress (U.S.): initial territorial penitentiary appropriation, 29; subsequent appropriations, 39; territorial prison management, 41–42

Conley, Frank: arrival at prison, 69; attitudes toward prison reform, 84; death of, 96; and homosexual inmates, 87; and Industrial Workers of the World, 85–86; and inmate labor, 73, 76, 77; and inmate punishment, 77; marriage of, 75; and minority inmates, 87; personal power of, 70, 75–77, 81; prison construction under, 97; and ranch holdings, 73, 75; relationship with the Anaconda Company, 89; salary, 76; trial of, 94–96; and warden's court, 84, 144n50; and William A. Clark, 75. *See also* Dixon, Joseph M.; McTague, Thomas

Conley, James, 77

"Contract with America," 106

copper mines and mining, xvi, 12

Crosby, John, 42

Crowley, William, 105

Custer County, 69

Daly, Marcus, 88

Dance, W. B., 27

Day, Rick, 109

Deadwood Dick, 11

Deer Lodge City, 49; as county jail, 41; and inmate labor, 74; and local merchants, 74; newspaper, 30

Deer Lodge Valley: climate, 45; proximity to Anaconda smelter, 15, 16

Delano, Columbus, 37

De Lorme, Roland, 117n26

Department of Interior (U.S.), 27, 30, 36, 40, 42, 43

Department of Justice (U.S.), 17, 30, 32, 40, 43

Detroit, Federal House of Correction, 26, 27, 35

deviancy, 57

Dimsdale, Thomas, 4

Dixon, George, 3, 5, 9–10, 11, 18; coerced confession of, 6–7, 115n15; compared with J. A. Slade's punishment, 8; trial of, 7

Dixon, Joseph, 13, 69, 91–96. *See also* Conley, Frank

Doiron, Renee, 108

Dooley, William, 86

Doran, Fran, 151n31

Dostoevsky, 11

Drouillard, Mary (aka Angelina), 11, 61

Duane, Patrick, 59

Eastern Montana State Prison, Billings, 74

Evans, Deborah, 108

Federal government: administration of justice in territories, 22; designation of cultural and political boundaries, 18; establishment of Indian reservations, 17; and penitentiary at Deer Lodge City, 7; response to crime in the West, 14

Flathead Lake, 72

Foley, Michael, 44

Fort Leavenworth, Kansas, 17

Foucault, Michel, xv; quoted, 18, 57, 134n45

Fox, Richard, quoted, 139n79

Gallatin County, 44

Gamble, James "Mickey," 108

Grant, Ulysses, 23, 38

Great Depression, xvi

Grey, Zane, 11

Grob, Gerald, quoted, 137n66

Hage, Neal, 151n34

Hallenbeck, E. L., 69

Hanson, John, 6

Harney, Edward, 88

Hauser, Samuel T.: and cheap inmate labor, 26; relocation to Deer Lodge Valley, 27; and Hezekiah Hosmer, 26; and William A. Clark, 26

Hawthorne, Nathaniel, quoted, 19

Heinze, F. Augustus, 89

Helena, 49; jail, 7; lynchings, 20, 124n13

Henderson, F. A., 95

Hietter, Paul, 58

Higgins, C. P., 88

Higgins, Frank, 88

Horsky, A. J., 94–95

Horstman, Mary Kay, 141n21

Hosmer, Hezekiah, 24, 26

Howling Wolf, 62

Hughes, Samuel, 59

Idaho Territorial Penitentiary, 130n10

Idaho Territory, 19

incarceration: economics of, 137n64; long-term impact on state budgets, xiii; rate during territorial years, 12; rate during the 1950s, 148n6

indeterminate sentence, 81

inmates, territorial: African American women, 61; average life sentence, 43; Chinese, 62, 135n53; clothing, 52; discrimination against, 58; good time policy, 44; hierarchies, 62, 136n63; historical neglect of, 9; idleness of, 54; inaugural group, 7; labor, 49, 54–55, 56; lack of education, 11; lack of employment skills, 11; Native Americans, 61, 136n60; occupations of, 47; pardons of, 43–44, 58, 61–62; personal finances of, 49; petition to retain physician, 47; on prison register, 57; racial and ethnic composition, 59, 136n56; and racism, 60; recidivism, 55; sentence reductions of, 56; typical crimes of, 10, 47, 116n21; as "warts and pustules," 10; women, 47, 49, 61. *See also* Montana territorial prison

insane asylum, 43, 57. *See also* Montana territorial asylum
Iowa State Penitentiary, 27–28

James, Jesse, 11
Jessrang, George, 11
Johnson, Andrew, 22
Johnson, David, quoted, 20–22

Kelley, Cornelius, 88
Kelley, Robert, 41
Knowles, Hiram, 82
Kremer, J. Bruce, 88

L'Amour, Louis, 11
Lang, Fritz, 86
Larabie, S. E., 88
Lee, Lincoln, 69
Lee Yim, 11
Lewiston, Idaho, 19
Life Magazine, 104
Liping Zhu, 58
London Times, 104
lynchings, 22; end of, 33. *See also* vigilantism

Madison County, 44
Maginnis, Martin, 41, 43
Mansfield, Mike, 104
McAdoo, William, 88
McDonald, T. H., 92–94
McIntosh, John, 86
McKanna, Clare, 58
McNeil Island, Washington, 17
McTague, Thomas, 70; and Frank

Conley, 73, 75, 81; and inmate cooks, 77; and ranch holdings, 73, 75. *See also* Conley, Frank
Meagher, Thomas Francis, 22–23, 26
Merrill, Frank, 59
Missoula, 12, 49
Mitchell, A. H., 30, 64–65
Montgomery, Nellie, 5
Montana: bond issue (1960), 104, 150n21; community-based correctional programs, 106; cost of confinement in territorial period, 26; education versus prison spending, 110; improvised jails in, 20, 25; local juries, 19, 24, 38, 62; per capita incarceration rate, modern, 113n2; per capita incarceration rate, during territorial period, 37, 130n6; per capita income, rank, xii, 110; second and third territorial legislatures nullified, 22; territorial legislature (1874), 41
Montana Department of Corrections, 106
Montana Highway Patrol, xiv
Montana National Guard, xiv–xv, 104
Montana Nonpartisan, 90
Montana State Board of Charities, 64–65, 79; and care of insane, 142n33
Montana State Board of Prison Commissioners, 72–73, 79, 82, 86, 87, 95, 103
Montana State Legislature: anti-

sedition act (1917), 86, 145n58; legislative committee (1931), 98; special legislative investigative committee (1905), 73

Montana State Prison: average inmate population (1890–1917), 70; cell-block conditions, 98; cellblock expansion (1890s), 74; dungeon described, 77–78; earthquake damage (1959), 105; and federal government, xv; general conditions (1950s), 102; increase in inmate population (1990s), 109; initial budget, xii; inmate labor at, 83, 101–2, 105; invisibility in historical record, 12; lease arrangement, 70; minority inmates, 12; Native American incarceration rates, 13, 109–10, 119n32, 151n39; and organized labor, 74; personnel turnover at, xvi; and power, xi; political indifference about, xvii; political patronage at, 99; and progressive era reform, 80–81; public opinion about, xiii; road building projects, 72; staff (1950s), 100; transferred from federal government to state, 70. *See also* Prison riots

Montana territorial asylum: xv, xvii; lack of sanitation, 65; location of, 138n67; patient clothing, 66; patient demographics, 64; patient labor, 67; property value of, 141n20; renaming to Montana State Hos-

pital, 139n76; therapeutic procedures, 65–66. *See also* insane asylum

Montana territorial prison: board of directors, 54; building contractor, 30; commission board, 41; deterrence of crime, 64; disease in, 45; discipline procedures in, 45; initial inmates, 35; inventory (1878), 45; log structures at, 131n14; as "monument to folly," xiii, 32; official name, 31; physician, 47; and power, 33, 56, 64, 67; razing of structures, 99; success and failures, 63–64. *See also* inmates, territorial; United States Penitentiary at Deer Lodge City

Morony, John G., 88

Munson, Lyman, 24; and National Prison Association, 17

Murray, James A., 88

Musigbrod, C. F., 62, 64–65

National Prison Association, 17, 81

National Prison Congress, 80

"national prison" (Washington, D.C.), 28

nativism, 58

Nevada incarceration rate, 37

New Mexico territorial penitentiary, 28

New North-West, editor quoted, 30

"New Penology," 80

New York State Prison Reform Commission, 70

New York Times, 104
Nolan, C. B., 94
Norris, Edwin, 88
Northern Pacific Railroad, 17, 49

O'Brien, Thomas, 78
Osborne, Thomas Mott, 70

Panic of 1893, 74
panopticon, 32
Paxinos, Dennis, 107
Pierre, 62
Pinel, Philippe, 65
Plummer, Henry, 19
Potter, M. W., 92
Potts, Benjamin Franklin, 23, 35, 41, 45,
    52, 54, 62; correspondence to Presi-
    dent Grant, 38; and George Dixon,
    8; guard request, 33; initial tour of
    prison, 31; and territorial prison
    budget, 40; as U.S. Superintendent
    of Indian Affairs, 37
Powell County Museum and Arts
    Foundation, 106
Powell, Floyd, 103–4
Powers, Thomas, 77
Prickly Pear Gulch, 6
prison administrators, 10
Prison riots: of 1957, xvi, 13, 102–3;
    of 1959, xiv, xvi, 13, 104–6; of 1991,
    xiv, 106
prisons: assistance with capitalistic
    development, 15; as defining equal-
    ity, 18; as institutional conquest,
    16; Jackson-era discipline, 15–16;

and power, 13, 111; as socializing
    institution, 16
prostitution, 61

Racicot, Marc, 107–9
Rankin, Jeannette, 92
Rankin, Wellington, 92
Reber, 86
Red Lobster restaurant, Billings, 108
Regional correctional centers, xvi, 109
Richards, Becky, 108
Rockefeller, John D., 89
Rodewald, Fred, 85
Roosevelt, Franklin, 88
Roosevelt, Theodore, 80, 91
Rothe, Theodore, 103–4

Sanchez, Felicita, 60–61
San Pierre, 62
Seeley Lake, 108
Slade, J. A. (aka "Captain Slade"), 3;
    execution of, 4, 8, 20, 21
Smith, Green Clay, 5, 24–26
Smith, William, 11
Standard Oil, 89
Stand-to-One-Side, 62
Stegner, Wallace, quoted, 3
Stewart, Samuel V., 88
Swan River, 109
Symes, George Judge, 7

Territorial Bureau (U.S. Department
    of State), 28
Territorial Penitentiaries Act (1867),
    28

Time Magazine, 104

Tocqueville, Alexis de, 15

Trachtenberg, Alan, 14

Treasury Department (U.S.):
territorial penitentiary plans
for Colorado and Montana,
29, 43

Twain, Mark, 3

United States Penitentiary at Deer
Lodge City, 31; official completion,
43. *See also* Montana territorial
prison

Utah territorial penitentiary, 28

vigilantism: xv; impact in Montana, 5;
as public ritual, 21–22; as symbolic
code, 123n5; transformation of, 8–9

Virginia City: 3, 27, 49; maintenance
of prisoners in, 20; newspaper editor quoted, 25; vigilance committee
of, 4

Wade, Benjamin, 22

Walkenburg, Fred Van, 108

"War on Drugs," 106

Wells, George, 44

western prisons: disciplinary regimes,
12; historical neglect, 9; mythology
of, 11, 117n25; torture in, 12

Wheeler, Burton K., 91, 92

Wheeler, William, 23, 33, 40

White Bear, 62

Wines, Enoch, 17

Wisconsin territorial penitentiary, 31

Wister, Owen, 11

Women's prisons: Billings, xvi, 107;
Warm Springs, 107

Wunder, John, 58

Wyman, Jack, 95